Dedicated to the memory of the seamen and sailors of all nations who served on Arctic convoys, especially those who did not return.

*boreas domus, mare amicus*

# Unfortunate Occurrences and Knavish Tricks

**The last voyage of the SS Capira**

24th November 1941 to 31st August 1942

## John Chuter

UNIFORM

UNIFORM

First published by Uniform
an imprint of the Unicorn Publishing Group LLP, 2021
5 Newburgh Street
London W1F 7RG

www.unicornpublishing.org

10 9 8 7 6 5 4 3 2 1

ISBN 978-1-913491-38-3

Cover design Unicorn Publishing Group
Typeset by Vivian@Bookscribe

Printed by Gomer Press, Wales

# Contents

# Acknowledgements

I am indebted to many individuals and organisations for assisting me in bringing this account together. Among the latter, I am especially grateful to the staffs of the National Archives at Kew, the Guildhall Library London, the UK Maritime & Coastguard Agency, the UK Ministry of Defence (Naval Historical Branch), the US National Archives & Records Administration, the US Department of Transportation (Maritime Administration), the Embassy of the Russian Federation London, the Imperial War Museum and the National Maritime Museum. Special thanks must be given to the staff of the Caird Library at Greenwich for uncovering Tom Chilvers' unpublished diary containing an account of convoys PQ16 and QP13, plus an account of life in Murmansk during the period covered by this book. Tom Chilvers' son Stuart also provided much background on his father that proved invaluable to putting times and characters in context.

Among other individuals who have assisted and encouraged me, special thanks must go to my friend Austin Byrne. He provided many a vivid account of life as a DEMS gunner on the ill-fated SS *Induna* during its passage in convoy PQ13, and his subsequent experience surviving four days in an open boat before being picked up by a Russian destroyer and taken to Murmansk. A number of friends in Russia have also given me much information and encouragement. Among them, specific acknowledgement must go to the late Ekaterina (Katya) Ermolina, who provided a number of photographs and pointed me towards the unpublished account of wartime Murmansk by Vladimir Loktev. In Iceland Fridthor Eydal provided valuable information on the rescue of survivors from QP13. For information on the US Navy's Armed Guard, I am indebted to the late Matty Louchran and other unsung heroes of that wartime organisation who corresponded with me during this project including Richard M. Bryant, Reginald W. Curtis, Joseph E. Dulka, Russell L. Gillespie, Josh Jones, Stafford Ricks and Allen A. Stager. I would also wish to acknowledge the family of the late Lieutenant T.B. Johnston RNVR of HMS *Niger* for permitting publication of extracts from his letters and Jill Britton for allowing me access to her father, Tom Heley's, Service

Record and related papers which allowed me to put the technicalities of radar in a more human context.

Finally, I have been given much encouragement and advice from a wide circle of friends and colleagues who have given freely of their time to comment on the text. Their efforts have proved invaluable, but the conclusions and any remaining errors are entirely mine.

John Chuter
Braithwaite Village, West Yorkshire, July 2020

# Foreword

The Battle of the Atlantic was the longest campaign of the Second World War. It started on its first day 3 September 1939 with the sinking of the liner SS *Athenia* and ended 2,074 days later with the sinking of SS *Avondale Park* on the night of 7 May 1945, the evening before Germany surrendered. During that period 5,140 ships totalling 21,500,000 tons were sunk and some 30,000 merchant seamen died, most with the sea being their only grave. This loss represented 1 in 4 of the men involved a horrifying casualty rate for any force. We owe them so much.

Winston Churchill in his memoirs said of the Battle 'The only thing that ever really frightened me during the war was the U-boat peril... I was even more anxious about this battle than I had been about the glorious air fight called the Battle of Britain.' Most members of the British public are completely unaware of these facts. If we had lost the Atlantic battle we would have lost the war.

One part of the Battle, now recognised as a separate campaign by the award of the Arctic Star, were the Arctic convoys supplying crucial goods to North Russia between 1941 and 1945. Some 4,000,000 tons of goods were supplied by 1400 merchant ships. 85 of those and 16 RN cruisers, destroyers and escorts protecting them were lost. Apart from attacks by U-boats, dive bombers, torpedo bombers and surface ships, the weather was the cruellest enemy of all. Huge raging seas and incredible cold meant that men only survived for minutes once in the water. Winston Churchill called it the '... the worst journey in the world'.

The sheer scale of these events makes them hard to comprehend so it is useful to personalise things and see how they influenced one man and indeed one ship. Brigadier Chuter has achieved just that using the papers of his late father, a merchant mariner, to show the impact on one man and the ship in which he served over a period of nine months of his ten years at sea.

The American freighter, the SS *Capira* was nothing special but typical of so many ships undertaking these hazardous voyages. The period covered 24 November 1941 to 31 August 1942, the day she was torpedoed and sunk, was when the outcome of the Battle of the Atlantic lay in the balance. Russian convoys were coming under growing attack and the convoys PQ 15 and QP 13, in which the author's father and the SS *Capira* took part, are worthy of study. There is considerable debate about the use of intelligence: whether local commanders or commanders-in-chief ashore had the best overall picture of what was going on. Often commanders had very little information on which to base their life and death decisions.

The Soviet authorities always tried to downplay the importance and sacrifice of those taking part in the Arctic convoys but now Russia acknowledges how important they were to her survival. There is a close bond between Arctic convoy and Russian veterans with visits and events often focused aboard HMS *Belfast* (an Arctic veteran herself) moored above Tower Bridge.

I welcome this book which adds a human dimension to the great events engulfing the world at that time.

Admiral the Right Honourable Lord West of Spithead GCB DSC PC

# Preface

I am not, by any stretch of the imagination, an historian. Nevertheless, in writing this account I have endeavoured to take an historian's approach; relying on primary sources and eyewitness accounts wherever possible, tempered by later analysis in order to get as close as possible to the reality of what happened during the last voyage of the SS *Capira*. Whether or not I have been successful, I leave for the reader to judge. However, I hope that in some small way, this account demonstrates what the enthusiastic amateur historian can achieve with the resources now at his (or her) disposal. Deep in the dusty archives at Kew, the Caird Library at Greenwich, the Guildhall Library in the City of London, the Imperial War Museum, or further afield in North American depositories in Washington, New York and Nova Scotia, lay a treasure trove of primary documentation providing a tangible link with the past. A link that is more than palpable, especially when handling original cabinet papers initialled in red ink by the prime minister when one can, with a little imagination, detect the lingering aroma of a Cuban cigar. Copies of some of this material are also available through the internet, either free or for a modest sum. A careful trawl through the internet itself, provided one does so with a critical eye, will also pay dividends for the avid researcher. I have also been privileged to talk to some of those who were witness to these events, and to gain some idea of what it was like at the individual level, infused (and sometimes confused) with all those conflicting emotions that war intensifies. Sadly, this is a fast diminishing resource. The events recorded here will soon pass from living memory, and become mere syllables of recorded time for successive generations of historians to pore over, dissect and reinterpret within new and as yet unexplored contexts. However, their efforts will no longer benefit from the privilege of engaging first hand with that visceral narrative provided by those who were there.

This book chronicles the circumstances surrounding the last voyage of an aging American freighter, the SS *Capira,* sailing under a Panamanian flag during the Battle of the Atlantic. It spans the period between November 1941 and September 1942 and in particular her passage in convoys PQ15,

QP13 and SC97. During this period, a number of tragic events directly associated with these convoys occurred and went largely unreported at the time. These events were subsequently overshadowed by the destruction of convoy PQ17 that took place during *Capira*'s return passage from Russia, and they have received little detailed analysis since then. Although they have been separately documented to a greater or lesser extent elsewhere, I have brought them together in an attempt to render a comprehensive picture in the context of that phase of the war when victory was by no means certain and defeat still a possibility. I have also attempted to convey the formidable challenges faced by all those involved from high command to deck hand and, in spite of their best endeavours to meet the immediate situation with an appropriate response, the tragic consequences that often ensued.

*Capira*'s last voyage coincided with events elsewhere that had a profound significance for the Battle of the Atlantic and hence the survival of this country during the Second World War. The strategic backdrop included the attack on Pearl Harbor that brought the United States into the war and occurred just as *Capira* set out on her voyage along the east coast of the UK prior to joining an Atlantic convoy bound for New York. Less than six months later, whilst *Capira* was discharging her cargo in north Russia, the US Navy was scoring a strategic victory at Midway. Midway not only marked the apogee of Japanese conquest in the Pacific but also enabled American unfettered commitment to the Battle of the Atlantic knowing that its western seaboard was now secure from the onward march of Japanese forces. Off the eastern seaboard, however, German U-boats were celebrating their second 'Happy Time', causing havoc among the unprotected merchantmen who plied those waters from the Caribbean to Nova Scotia, before joining the Atlantic convoys that provided the lifeline to the United Kingdom. Even further east, continuing German successes on land against Russia provoked a major concern that Russia might sue for peace. As a consequence, a concerted diplomatic and logistic effort was initiated by the United States and the United Kingdom to keep her in the war. The security of the supply route from the USA via Iceland to the north Russian ports of Archangel and Murmansk therefore grew in strategic importance becoming a target for German naval and air forces. This was also a time when naval signals intelligence dried up due to changes made to the German naval version of the Enigma encryption machine. As a consequence for most of 1942 the Allies were unable to read Dönitz' intentions for his U-boats in the Atlantic. This reinforced the need for well-coordinated air surveillance and offensive measures if the U-boat menace was to be countered. However, arguments for the redeployment of aircraft from the bomber offensive against Germany to the protection of convoys were robustly resisted by the RAF, with inevitable consequences.

It was against this strategic backdrop that the polyglot crew of the *Capira* continued to make their living as merchant seamen. Oblivious no doubt of the bigger picture these men and thousands more like them struggled against the elements and the enemy to keep Britain and Russia fed and supplied for war. Although technically civilians, their pro-rata casualty rate was higher than for any of the armed forces. It should also be remembered that German U-boat crews also suffered high casualty rates, mirroring in number the 30,000 merchant seamen who have no grave but the sea.

In spite of the tactics employed by the allied navies and the best endeavours of individuals to protect them, it is a tragic irony that *Capira*'s last voyage should be marked by more casualties caused by unfortunate occurrences of our own making than any knavish tricks inflicted by the enemy. The casualties, both in human lives and shipping, that were self-inflicted during this passage far outweighed any damage wrought by German planes or U-boats.

This then is the account of the circumstances surrounding that particular wartime voyage from the UK to Murmansk, and back via Boston and New York, in Convoys PQ15, QP13 and SC97.

**Time Zones:** A number of different time zones were used by merchant ships, naval warships and U-boats in this account and I have endeavoured to point out the differences where they may confuse the narrative. In general, the Royal Navy used GMT and would indicate that by suffixing a 'Z' to timings in its signal traffic. Convoys plying the Atlantic routes were usually 2 hours behind GMT. German U-boats, on the other hand, used MESZ – *Mitteleuropäische Sommerzeit* at the time of year covered here. This was the same time as in the German capital city of Berlin and was known as German Central Time or Berlin Time and was 2 hours ahead of GMT.

**Spelling:** US English spelling has been retained when quoting from US documents.

THE NORTH ATLANTIC

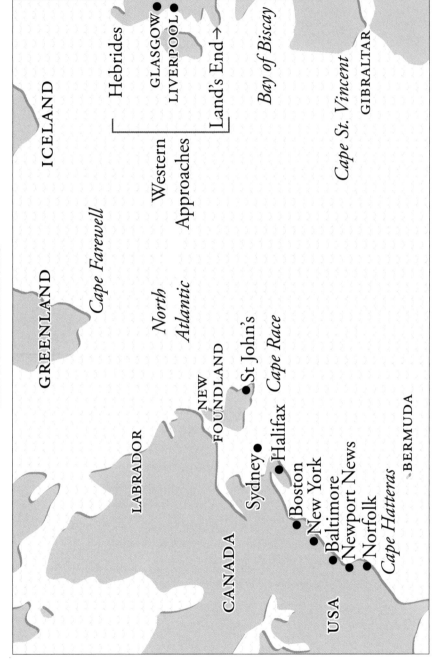

ICELAND

GREENLAND

Cape Farewell

Hebrides

GLASGOW ●
LIVERPOOL ●

Land's End →

Western
Approaches

Bay of Biscay

Cape St. Vincent

GIBRALTAR

North
Atlantic

St John's
Cape Race

NEW
FOUNDLAND

LABRADOR

Sydney ●
Halifax

Boston
New York
Baltimore
Newport News
Norfolk
Cape Hatteras

BERMUDA

CANADA

USA

# THE KOLA PENINSULA

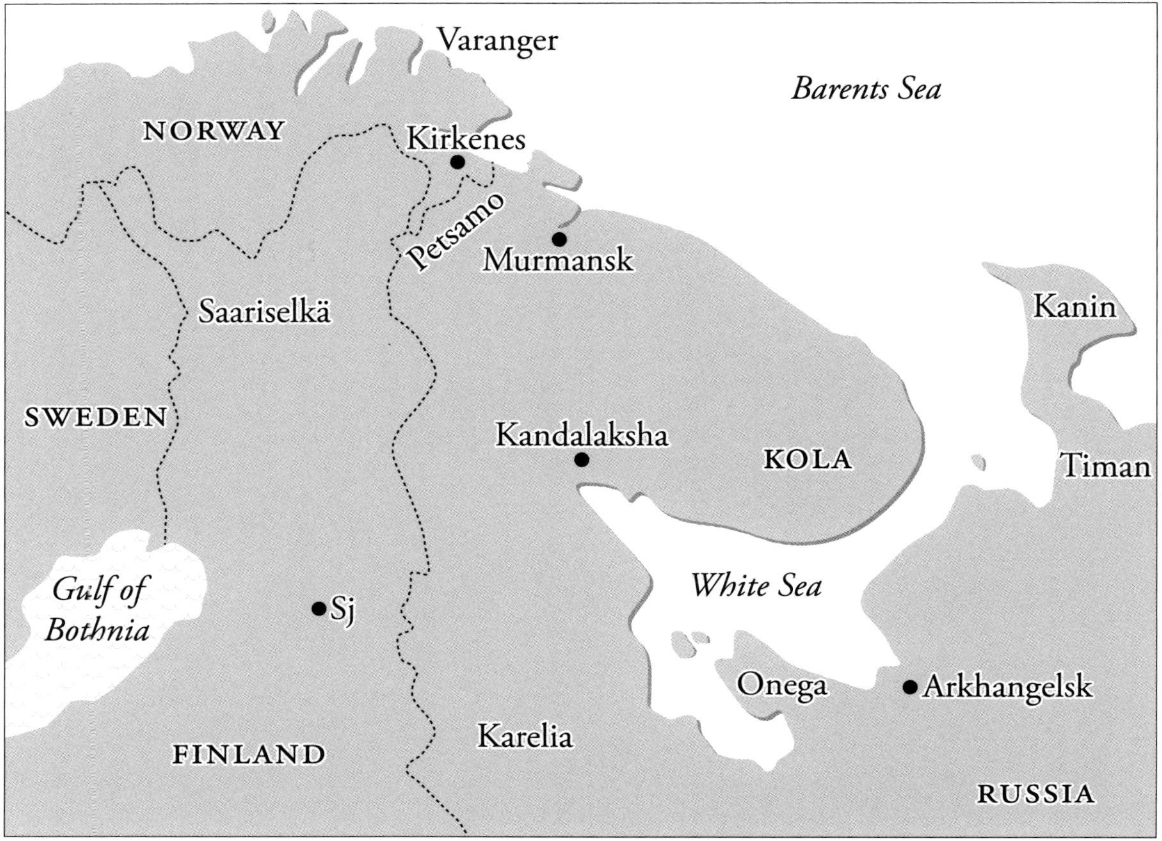

Barents Sea

Kanin

Timan

Arkhangelsk

RUSSIA

KOLA

White Sea

Onega

Varanger

Murmansk

Kirkenes

Petsamo

Kandalaksha

Karelia

NORWAY

Saariselkä

Sj

SWEDEN

FINLAND

Gulf of
Bothnia

# NORTH RUSSIAN CONVOY ROUTES

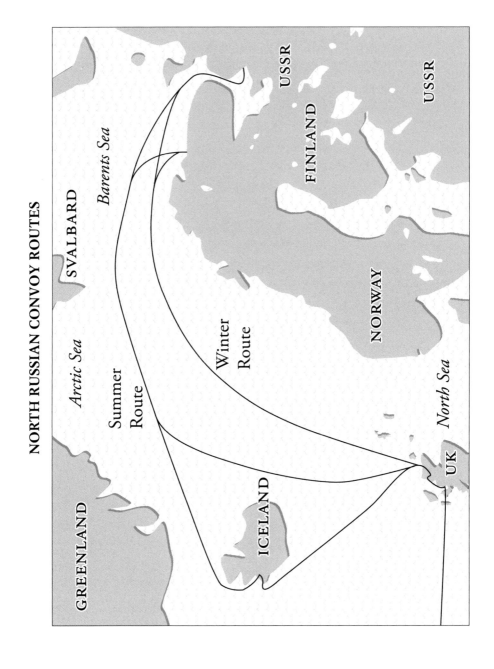

# List of Abbreviations

| | |
|---|---|
| **AB** | Able Bodied (Seaman) |
| **ACIC** | Admiral Commanding Iceland |
| **Aircraft:** | |
| **He 111** | Heinkel 111 (German twin engine bomber/torpedo bomber) |
| **Ju 88** | Junkers 88 (German twin engine multirole combat aircraft) |
| **Me 109** | Messerschmitt Bf 109 (German single engine fighter) |
| **Me 110** | Messerschmitt Bf 110 (German twin engine fighter-bomber) |
| **P 40** | Curtis, P 40 Warhawk (US single engine fighter) |
| **PBY 5A** | Consolidated PBY Catalina (US maritime patrol aircraft) |
| **A/S** | Anti-submarine |
| **ASDIC** | Anti-Submarine Detection & Identification Committee |
| **ASW** | Anti-submarine Warfare |
| **BEF** | British Expeditionary Force |
| **BdU** | Befehlshaber der Unterseeboote (German U-boat Command) |
| **CAM** | Catapult Armed Merchantman |
| **CEIO** | Convoy Equipment Inspection Officers |
| **CIGS** | Chief Imperial General Staff |
| **C-in-C** | Commander-in-Chief |
| **C-in-C HF** | Commander-in-Chief Home Fleet |
| **CNO** | Chief Naval Operations |
| **CO** | Commanding Officer |
| **Convoy Designations:** | |
| **HX** | Fast convoys from Halifax to the UK |
| **ON** | Outward to North America |
| **ONS** | Outward to North America Slow |
| **PQ** | Iceland to the Northern Russian Ports |
| **QP** | North Russian Ports to Iceland |
| **SC** | Slow convoys from Halifax or Sydney Nova Scotia to the UK |
| **CsOS** | Chiefs of Staff |
| **DAMS** | Defensively Armed Merchant Ship (WWI) |

**DDOD (M)** Deputy Director Operational Development (Mines)

**DEMS** Defensively Equipped Merchant Ship (WWII)

**D/F** Direction Finding

**DNC** Director Naval Communications

**DNI** Director Naval Intelligence

**DSC** Distinguished Service Cross

**DSO** Distinguished Service Order

**ETA** Estimated Time of Arrival

**FOC CS** Flag Officer Commanding Cruiser Squadron

**GMT** Greenwich Mean Time

**GPS** Global Positioning System

**GRT** Gross Registered Tonnage

**HF/DF** High Frequency/Direction Finding (Also known as 'Huff Duff')

**Hrs** Hours

**IBC** Iceland Base Command

**ICOMP** Iceland Ocean Meeting Point

**JIC** Joint Intelligence Committee

**KBE** Knight of the Order of the British Empire

**KTB** Kriegtagesbuch (German War Diary)

**Kts** Knots

**MG** Machine Gun

**MN** Merchant Navy

**MO** Medical Officer

**MOWT** Ministry Of War Transport

**MVO** Member of the Victorian Order

**OBE** Officer of the Order of the British Empire

**Radars:**

  **ASV1** Airborne surveillance radar

  **SW1C** Shipborne surveillance radar fitted mainly in RCN ships

  **SW2C** Shipborne surveillance radar fitted mainly in RCN ships

  **T 271** Shipborne surveillance radar (Centimetric radar)

  **T 279** Shipborne early warning & target acquisition radar

  **T 281** Shipborne early warning & target acquisition radar

**RAF** Royal Air Force

| | |
|---|---|
| **RCN** | Royal Canadian Navy |
| **RD** | Reserve Decoration |
| **RDF** | Range & Detection Finding (Radar) |
| **RN** | Royal Navy |
| **RNPS** | Royal Naval Patrol Service |
| **RNR** | Royal Naval Reserve |
| **RNVR** | Royal Naval Volunteer Reserve |
| **SBNO** | Senior British Naval Officer |
| **S/M** | Submarine |
| **SN** | Northern Mine Barrier |
| **T** | Temporary |
| **UZO** | *Unterwasser-zieloptik* (U-boat targeting device) |
| **USN** | United States Navy |

# 1 CAPIRA

## (24 NOVEMBER TO 5 DECEMBER 1941)

I must go down to the seas again, to the lonely sea and the sky,
And all I ask is a tall ship and a star to steer her by,
And the wheel's kick and the wind's song and the white sail's
   shaking,
And a grey mist on the sea's face, and a grey dawn breaking.

From *Sea Fever* by John Masefield

Anyone flying into London's City Airport today will no doubt spot the Millennium Dome situated like a large 'O' on a bend in the river Thames below. Either side of this prominent landmark sit two groups of docks. To the west is the Isle of Dogs with the West India and Millwall Docks, and to the east are the Royal Victoria, Royal Albert and King George V Docks, with the City Airport and its runways squeezed between them. Before the advent of container ships, these were London's major sea trade terminals, with all the associated paraphernalia of dockland. Dockers, stevedores, riggers, splicers, crane drivers, winch men, lighter men and tugboat men all have since gone. Little if any sea trade takes place there now, since the large container berths were built upriver at Tilbury in the 1960s. However, there is now trade of a different kind as these areas have been developed into the large business and conference complexes of Canary Wharf and the ExCel Centre. Modern dockland remains a vibrant place, but is now of a far different hue; with its pubs, cafés, shops and light railway conveying commuters daily to and from their high-rise places of work. Practically all vestiges of its previous role as one of the country's major seaports has been erased; but if one could be transported back in time to the dark days of the Second World War, a very different picture and purpose would emerge.

On Monday 24 November 1941, a young seaman walked into the Merchant Marine office at London's Victoria Dock. His apparent youth belied over four years' experience at sea, roughly half of which had been at war. Barely a month before, he had crossed the Atlantic from Sydney, Nova Scotia in convoy SC48, that had unexpectedly run into a number of German U-boats hunting as a 'wolf pack'. In the ensuing battle, that had lasted several days, nine merchant ships and two naval escorts went to the bottom, in addition to leaving one of the escorting destroyers badly damaged. Fortunately, his ship had survived the onslaught, arriving safely in the Thames the month before. And now he was about to sign on a ship ultimately bound for one of the north Russian ports via the United States, thereby facing the prospect of running the Atlantic gauntlet twice over again before sailing onwards into the even more hostile waters of the Barents Sea.

The ship was the SS *Capira*, an ageing freighter originally laid down in 1920 in Seattle as the SS *West Campgaw*. She was sailing under a Panamanian flag, and was showing her age following the battering she had received during her last voyage as part of convoy PQ1 to the Russian port of Archangel; the destination she was ultimately scheduled for at the end of this voyage. *Capira* was typical of many a freighter that plied the world's oceans between the wars. Displacing 5,050 tonnes and, on a good day, capable of around 10kts [18.5km/hr] she measured 133m from bow to stern and was 17m in the beam. Later wartime service necessitated protective additions to her superstructure, but her pre-war profile revealed a conventional layout. A single funnel abaft of a prominent bridge situated roughly amidships, masts both fore and aft, with derricks conveniently placed to load cargo into the holds. During the war, use was also made of her upper deck space to carry cargo that would not go into the holds, such as vehicles and crated materiel. Radio antennae were mounted on and between the ship's masts and the foremast had a crow's nest for observation. Since radar was still in its infancy and the associated technologies a closely-guarded secret, merchant ships would continue to rely on human observation for station keeping in convoys throughout the war and *Capira* was no exception to this. Moreover, ship-to-ship communication relied on visual signals during periods of radio silence, thus emphasising the need for a sharp lookout being maintained at all times.

*Capira's* crew of 39 were a hardworking and hard-worked body of men. Crew numbers were not lavish, quite the contrary; owners would not pay for more on-board effort than was absolutely necessary. The master, his three officers, the chief engineer and the boatswain ran the ship. These six key appointments, that on the *Capira* were filled by highly-skilled men hailing from five different countries, amounted to a combined experience of over a hundred years at sea. Under them were around ten seamen on general duties, a further dozen or so tending the engines, and around ten cooks and stewards, not forgetting a carpenter and the radio operator. Crews varied from voyage to voyage, as merchant seamen opted to change ships or shipping lines as economic and other factors dictated. For example, when *Capira* docked at New York in July 1942, at the end of her last voyage to Russia, only 13 of the crew of 39 had been aboard when she last docked in the United States in early January. At the conclusion of the July passage, the ship's master and the chief steward were the only two of the crew not to be discharged[1]. Even specialist appointments crucial to the operation of the ship, such as that of the chief engineer, were not carried over to the next voyage; individuals had to re-engage with the owners. Although many signed on again for the next passage, continual employment with a single shipping line, or in a particular ship, was not the right of the ordinary merchant seaman. Indeed, for a man independent in mind and character this may have suited him well. If he wanted a spell ashore he could have it, albeit without pay. Alternatively, if he wanted to sign on again and see a different part of the world on a different ship, nothing stood in his way. Provided he could find the right ship and shipmates to suit his temperament, any port of call was within his reach. In these and many other respects, merchant crews were very different from their navy counterparts. Such differences became even more apparent during wartime, when naval ships' companies were diluted with conscripted men who had little or no previous experience of life at sea. Training these individuals in the skills required to operate a warship, not to mention the need to subordinate individuality in the interests of the team, necessitated a strict disciplinary regime. In certain respects, this was also true of merchant ships. However, some of the more traditional methods of discipline required to run a warship were of little relevance to a merchant seaman. For example, spit and polish, apart from that required in large passenger liners, seldom (if ever) entered into his routine. That is not to suggest, however, that routine on board was not ordered, or that merchant ships were in any way less than 'shipshape'; making allowances of course for their age and the parsimony of their owners in matters of non-essential maintenance. When on board as when on shore, the merchant seaman wore what was most appropriately functional and was usually purchased by himself. Apart from the officers and the crew of large liners, it was not usual for uniforms to be issued by the owners. Whether his boots were polished, his face shaved, his trousers pressed or his shirt starched was of little consequence. Although technically a civilian, wartime service did on occasion invite him to acquire some military skills in addition to his seafaring ones. In the case of *Capira*'s crew, this extended to training in servicing and operating the guns fitted to the ship after she was requisitioned by the US authorities on her return to the United States the following March. However, it must be remembered that the overarching consideration in engaging these civilian-cum-combatant seamen lay in the knowledge and skills they possessed. These were not only essential for the profitability of the shipping lines and their owners, but also proved critical for the survival of the country.

The ship's master was Enjar Jensen, a Dane. In his mid-thirties, with just over twenty years at sea, he held the sole responsibility for his ship and its crew. He was accountable to the ship's owner who, from April 1942 when *Capira* was requisitioned for war service, was in effect the United States Government. Through the government, he also had a responsibility whilst at sea to a convoy commodore for the deployment and handling of his ship. This brought with it considerable restrictions; something of an unwelcome imposition for a man who had laboured hard for the relative independence synonymous with command that he had now achieved. Although he was the master, Jensen was by no means the oldest crew member. His British chief engineer Thomas Kinnear and a Chinese mess man, Heng Leon, were 55. The latter also had a total of 40 years seagoing service; more than anyone else on board. Born around 1887, and going to sea at the very beginning of the twentieth century aged 15, Heng Leon would have been more than familiar with the age of sail and may have even served in sailing ships. By contrast, there were two eighteen-year-olds in the crew. One of them, Vernon Jones, a British able seaman, declared that he had already served 4½ years at sea; therefore he would have begun his merchant service at the tender age of 13 or 14. If this was indeed the case, he had more than proved his mettle as a fast learner and competent able-bodied seaman. The other was Edward Nix, a British Canadian who worked in the engine room as a wiper. A wiper was the most junior crewmember in the engine room, responsible for cleaning the engine spaces and machinery, invariably a dirty task and not one to be envied.

Also numbered among the crew was a radio operator who, before the onset of hostilities, would have spent much of his time communicating, mostly in Morse code, with passing ships, land-based stations and other communication centres within radio range. Progress during the ship's passage would have been broadcast, monitored and reported to its owners and other interested parties such as Lloyds, the shipping insurers. On the outbreak of war, this changed. Radio communications monitored by the enemy could not only provide vital intelligence but also be used to triangulate and target individual ships and convoys. Wartime passages were therefore conducted where possible under radio silence. The transmitter was usually sealed and the seal could only be broken in extreme and well-defined circumstances such as when attacked by the enemy. Thus, the radio operator's wartime lot became one of monitoring transmissions and listening out; a boring task even at the best of times, but nevertheless vital to the ship's safety and security.

Not least among the diversity inherent in members of *Capira*'s crew was their polyglot nature. *Capira*'s officers had the challenge of welding men from ten nations and as many languages into an effective team. In war this was even more challenging, considering the heightened tension and additional vigilance required, especially when in convoy. English was the native tongue of just under half *Capira*'s crew; however, only six were British – the remaining English speakers comprising nine Canadians and one each hailing from South Africa, Malta and Belgium. Added to the North American contingent were two French Canadians, but apart from the US Navy Armed Guard who joined the ship in March 1942 there were no Americans in the crew. However, there was one man, William Owens, a British crew member working in the engine room employed as a fireman, who was a United States resident. Excepting a Swedish seaman and the eight Chinese seamen who traditionally serviced the galley and laundry on these ships, the remainder were by now technically refugees or displaced persons, their countries having been overrun by the Nazi war machine. Of these unfortunates, including *Capria*'s Danish master, three were Dutch, three Norwegian, one Belgian (Flemish), one Latvian and finally a

Slovenian Yugoslav who was close to Marshal Tito. Given his communist connections and presumed anti-fascist outlook he remained fearful for his life, and consequently always kept a pistol close at hand. From the crew manifest we know that all of *Capira's* crew could read, or at least claimed they could. Their weights and heights are also recorded, not to mention their physical marks and peculiarities. Taken together the average age of the crew was 32, each with an average of 12 years sea- going service. What is not recorded, however, is the faith, if any, of individual crew members. Those of the Jewish faith were acknowledged as being at significant risk if taken prisoner by the Germans and were offered false names and identities, with the accompanying paperwork, whilst employed as merchant seamen. On balance, therefore, *Capira* was manned by a highly diverse but otherwise experienced, competent, versatile and hardened crew well used to plying their various trades on the world's oceans.

In company with naval vessels, life on board a merchantman was regulated by dividing up the twenty four hours into watches. During their time on watch, members of *Capira's* crew were employed according to their trade and also called upon to carry out the many other activities required to run a ship in peace and now in war. Naturally, maximum effort was required whilst loading and unloading before and after a voyage. However, maintaining the ship, especially its fabric, also required the investment of considerable time and effort throughout the passage, as owners were loath to have their ships spend time in dock for anything but a major overhaul. Preserving the ship from the ravages of seawater was an imperative, therefore painting both the interior and exterior of the ship was high on the list of priorities. Crew members on the SS *Empire Baffin* during its passage to Russia in convoy PQ16 recorded painting masts, funnels and derricks as well as the heads in-between fighting off air and submarine attacks. Washing down the decks and flats (corridors) and squaring away equipment spaces that were always in danger of dislodging their contents in heavy seas became a constant task; one undertaken mostly in cramped, not to mention dangerous, circumstances and invariably in poor weather. Clearing ice from the superstructure to prevent the ship becoming top heavy on Arctic voyages was a particularly hazardous but essential task, especially in heavy weather. Under the watchful eye of a competent officer, some members of the crew took a turn at the wheel, or helped out on other tasks such as maintaining the radio watch or on lookout as the need arose. Before the outbreak of war, crews, including in some cases cooks, began to be trained on the operation of the rudimentary armaments being mounted on merchantmen. This was so that they could assist the specialist gunners drawn from the Army, Royal Marines, Navy and occasionally RAF who were deployed in small detachments on armed merchant ships. Other tasks associated with the weaponry, such as cleaning and filling magazines, as well as servicing the guns during enemy attacks, were also taken on by anyone who happened to be available. Once off-watch, crew members' time was taken up with personal administration, made all the more difficult whilst at sea; especially during wartime. Unless one was in a larger, more modern vessel that had its own condensers, fresh water was at a premium. Sea water showers were common. Messing and sleeping spaces were tight and privacy therefore uncommon. Fresh rations seldom lasted throughout the voyage. Bad weather limited the preparation of hot food, and sometimes sandwiches had to be served instead. Negotiating one's way from the galley to the mess deck with a plate of food also proved impossible on occasions, and it was carried in large metal cans instead. The result was the same, however; the food arrived cold. Although there was no professional barber on cargo ships, there was always someone prepared to take on the task for a tot of rum. Unless someone in the crew had brought along an instrument that they could play, there was very little by way of recreation or indeed the time to indulge in it. Sometimes merchant ships carried passengers who might have something to offer. Such was the case on convoy PQ16 where Alexander Werth, *The Times'* Moscow correspondent and an expert on the Soviet Union, gave talks whilst on passage to Murmansk in the SS *Empire Baffin*. Otherwise, off-duty time was spent in eating and, if possible whilst in hostile waters, sleeping[2].

So, these were men for whom the sea was not only the means of making a living, albeit a difficult and precarious one, but also a way of life. Added to which they now faced the danger of enemy attack from beneath, on or above the waves, and the increased prospect of a watery grave. Even so, a merchant seaman's role was not particularly well appreciated. They were not well-rewarded by the owners, well-served by the authorities, or understood by the public. As previously mentioned, the vast majority were casually employed for a single voyage only. Seamen signed Articles of Agreement when they joined a ship. This designated the point at which their paid employment aboard a ship began and ended. The Articles remained in force until the voyage came to an end and the seaman was duly paid off. His pay then ceased until he signed on the same or another ship again. Understandably, his pay would also cease if he jumped ship in a port during a voyage, or left for any other reason. Any other reason also extended to circumstances where his ship was sunk either by natural disaster or enemy action. If this happened to be his unfortunate lot, then his pay was stopped immediately, the Articles having been deemed to have come to an end. In many cases, this not only affected the seaman but also those to whom he had allotted a portion of his wages. For a married man this was invariably his wife, and the allotment also ceased immediately the ship went to the bottom, potentially leaving his family destitute.

For British merchant seamen, this callous situation was rectified in May 1941 with the introduction of the Essential Work (Merchant Navy) Order. This established a Merchant Navy Reserve Pool, and to ensure that seamen would always be available for service the government paid them to remain in the pool even when they were ashore. As far as British merchant seamen were concerned, therefore, casual employment was replaced by continuous paid employment and a comprehensive system of registration made possible. All those who had served at sea during the preceding five years, plus those intending to serve during the war, were required to register. As a consequence, they were not liable for conscription into the armed services and retained their status as civilians within a reserved occupation, although the majority fought (and many died) alongside their navy counterparts. Official estimates vary slightly, but approximately 30,000 merchant seamen deaths during the Second World War were notified to the Registrar General. This included foreign seamen serving in British ships, and British seamen serving in foreign ships chartered to or requisitioned by the British government.[3] Pro rata, there were more merchant seaman casualties than in any of the three armed services. This pattern of casualties was replicated for the US Merchant Marine which suffered 3.9 percent casualties, a rate that exceeded even the US Marine Corps.[4] Those merchant seamen who served during that conflict, although dwelling in a civilian-cum-combatant twilight zone, deserve to take their rightful place and counted among their brothers-in-arms.

Perhaps no more fitting tribute to merchant seamen has been given than that by Captain Leslie Saunders RN, the Captain of the ill-fated HMS *Trinidad* who wrote:[5]

> My admiration for the sheer guts of these merchant seamen defies description. We in the Navy were trained for war; we were provided with the offensive and defensive means for waging it. They were trained for peace; their ships so vulnerable that a single shell, bomb or torpedo would sink them, or set them on fire. They could not hit back, but no Hun was going to stop them sailing the seas. I felt uncomfortable when I allowed myself to think of it – I so well equipped for, and they so exposed to, the horrors of war, especially in these Arctic waters.

The fact that he was required to stand and serve alongside his navy counterparts did not deter the authorities from continuing to treat the merchant seaman as a civilian, subject to the same controls and strictures as the rest of the civilian population. Two examples serve to demonstrate this.

Essential items such as binoculars were issued as part of the inventory for use of officers and ratings in naval ships. Merchant Navy officers, however, were invited to purchase their own from a limited pool supplied by the Admiralty; and, as a circular from the Trade Division stated, 'It must be clearly understood that this pool of binoculars is very limited and it is not anticipated that any further supply will become available.'[6] It seems remarkable that as radar and sonar were beginning to be installed in naval escorts the merchant seaman, relying solely on keen eyesight to keep watch and keep station even in the worst of conditions by day and by night, was invited to purchase his own binoculars from the Admiralty's parsimonious pool.

The second example involves an element of farce. For many years the Merchant Navy Comforts Service[7] had encouraged charitably-inclined ladies to knit woollen items (comforts) for free distribution to merchant seamen. This was a very practical and personal link between seamen and the wider civilian population, as those producing the items often put a card or message in with the socks, jumpers, scarves, gloves, etc., and the seaman receiving them would reply with a word of thanks. However, clothing was rationed from 1 June 1941 and it was proposed that comforts be put on the ration for merchant seamen. This was challenged by the seamen's unions as well as others, who pointed out that members of the armed services, especially the Royal Navy, who also received a free issue of knitted comforts were not subject to coupon rationing.

Nevertheless, the scheme to include comforts on ration books went ahead, against pressure from the most unlikely quarters. On 1 August 1942, a civilian in the Ministry of War Transport wrote to a colleague suggesting an urgent meeting to '... secure a settlement to the comforts question.' He went on: 'Apparently the minister's wife is interested in the question, and he is badgered at home as well as in the office.' The issue was still being fought over in September of the following year, by which time it had been raised in a question in the House of Commons during a debate on the war situation. Up to this point, the system in use to ration seamen's clothing was based on the issue of certificates by marine superintendents, that could then be exchanged for items of clothing. Unfortunately, the system was subject to lax control and therefore abuse, as evidenced in this extract from a brief to the then Minister for War Transport, Lord Leathers:

> An early settlement of this vexed question is essential. It is holding up the whole rationing scheme for the Merchant Navy. Meanwhile, scandal is rapidly developing about the mis-use of certificates issued by the Mercantile Marine Offices to Merchant Seamen. These certificates are being sold by seamen on a large scale, and are now being forged. Further, owing to the loose way in which the blank forms have been handled in some Mercantile Marine Offices, seamen are able to get hold of considerable numbers of them, fill them in and sell them.

It seems that the black market was having a field day. The outcome was that comforts for merchant seamen were eventually put on clothing ration cards, but the items themselves were issued without charge.

The reasons that motivated these men to sign on were probably as diverse as their individual stories. It was certainly not for the pay and conditions, which even in peacetime were neither generous nor benign. For some, especially those from Scandinavia, it may have been a traditional occupation followed by succeeding generations of father and son. For others it may have been an escape from poverty, unemployment or other deprivation. Others may have fallen foul of the law, and there is some evidence for this on the 27 July crew manifest, where four members of the crew are described as '*malefide*' and had been previously detained and deported. What their offences were, if any, we are not told; but it would be unusual for a crew to be devoid of members variously avoiding the law, seeking some sort of asylum or simply running away.

We can be clear about one man's motivation, however. The young sailor who had walked into the Merchant Marine office at London's Victoria Dock on that cold November morning knew for sure what he was doing. He had been born into a poor working-class family in the East End of London during the last year of the First World War. He was the second youngest of seven children, and when he was 16 his mother died from tuberculosis, a disease that he subsequently contracted. He survived, and following a spell in a convalescent hospital in Surrey went back to the East End. Still in his teens and clearly susceptible to the unhealthy environment, he had returned to he was advised and facilitated by an uncle to go to sea. So, at the age of 19, he joined his first ship; the SS *Grantully Castle* out of London, bound for South Africa as a pantry boy. For the next nine years he never looked back. Not only did it fully restore him physically, it also healed the wounds of an unhappy childhood. It opened his mind to a world far more expansive than that which he had hitherto grown accustomed. Not only was it an enriching experience, it was the first time he had felt entirely free and content. The sea was a friend and he was happy when he was on it.

# 2 WESTWARD

## (6 DECEMBER 1941 TO 29 MARCH 1942)

For while the tired waves, vainly breaking,
Seem here no painful inch to gain,
Far back, through creeks and inlets making,
Comes silent, flooding in, the main.

And not by eastern windows only,
When daylight comes, comes in the light;
In front the sun climbs slow, how slowly!
But westward, look, the land is bright!

From *Say not the struggle naught availeth* by Arthur Hugh Clough

Londoners watching the vapour trails of dogfighting Luftwaffe and RAF planes in the summer of 1940 were unaware of the devastation about to be visited upon their city. The German blitz on the capital, begun in October 1940, was to peak on 10 May 1941 when incendiaries started over 2,000 fires, the House of Commons was destroyed and almost 1,500 people were killed. The docks had been targeted many times, but *Capira* now lay tied up and relatively unmolested. During the past six months the ferocity of German bombing had abated, Hitler's attention having been turned to the east and the attack on Russia launched in July. For Britain as well as occupied Europe, however, attention turned to the west and the United States, wherein their main hope of defeating Nazi Germany lay.

For the young seaman who had signed on less than two weeks before, this was to be a 'Foreign' passage. For reasons of security, merchant seamen were not normally told well in advance of their destination or other information such as convoy numbers. Some, however, found out or thought they knew such details and rumours were rife. The crew knew for certain on joining the *Capira* that they were westward bound for the United States, but were probably ignorant at this time of her ultimate destination before returning to the UK.

On the 6 December, *Capira* slipped her moorings and sailed out into the Thames estuary. The following day the Japanese attacked the US Pacific fleet lying at anchor in Pearl Harbor. Roosevelt's 'day that will live in infamy' did not go unnoticed by her crew as the *Capira* steamed up river to join one of the costal convoys forming up at Southend. Given the nationalities represented, the crew's spirits would have been lifted when they realised that US neutrality could not be sustained for much longer, and it was only a matter of time before America committed itself to engaging fully in the Battle of the Atlantic. They didn't have long to wait. On 9 December, *Capira* sailed into the North Sea in company with a number of other ships bound for the Firth of Forth, anchoring there on 11 December. That day, much to the surprise (not least relief) of all concerned, Germany declared war on the United States. Although the Lend Lease Act signed in March had effectively ended US neutrality, this event put the final nail in the coffin of US isolationism. The full force of American industrial might, as well as its considerable manpower, could now be deployed in the defeat of the Axis powers; it also gave the green light for the US Navy to play a full and active part in the Battle of the Atlantic.

As the far-reaching consequences of these events were being debated, the crew of the *Capira* were busily preparing to navigate their charge around the northern coastline of Scotland and into Loch Ewe, where she would join other merchantmen in convoy for the outward passage to the States. Two days later, *Capira* left the Firth of Forth and sailed north again, rounding Dunnet Head on 15 December[1]. Those on watch who looked landward across to the rugged cliffs at the northernmost tip of the Scottish mainland would have seen evidence of recent naval constructions, adjacent to the lighthouse that had stood sentinel for well over a hundred years. The Admiralty had recently installed a coastal defence radar station there which formed part of the air early warning network around the British coast. Dunnet Head was also home to the northern chain of radio navigation stations, that remained there in various guises until the advent of GPS made them obsolete a generation or more later. The following day, *Capira* reached Loch Ewe and anchored in her final port of call before proceeding across the Atlantic.

Loch Ewe, a natural anchorage eight miles long and three miles wide, is located in the north west Highlands of Scotland about 80 miles west of Inverness. It was of considerable strategic importance in the Second World War, as its north-facing mouth protected the harbour from the prevailing westerly winds. More importantly, its location further west made it less exposed to air attack than the existing naval base at Scapa Flow. Loch Ewe also provided an ideal refuelling base for escorts, and thereby enabled a new Russian convoy cycle to be introduced from January 1942 onwards. In addition, the anchorage was also used as an RV for ships linking up with the ON (Outward North) Atlantic convoys that sailed from Liverpool and had started at the end of July. The loch therefore soon became established as a subsidiary assembly port for convoys as anti-submarine booms and nets were stretched between the Isle of Ewe and the northern and southern shores. Around its shores, several gun emplacements were constructed against attack from both air and sea; and so, in June 1941, the base was duly commissioned as HMS *Helicon*. From then on, members of the local population were required to carry a special resident's permit, as well as the nation-wide identity card. As an additional security measure, photography in and around the loch was strictly forbidden. And so it was that on 17 December, our sailor's 24th birthday, the anti-submarine net across the mouth of the loch was towed back by the boom tender vessel and SS *Capira* sailed out in company with the ships of Convoy ON47 via the North Channel and into the North Atlantic.

ON47 comprised a motley assortment of around thirty tramps and steamers[2]. The oldest was SS *Maycrest*. Laid down before 1913, she was a coal burner and considered so ancient by her crew that she was referred to as the Mayflower. Ancient or not, she joined the convoy from Iceland and arrived safely in the States, whilst seven more modern ships either straggled and joined later convoys or put back with various faults. ON47 also carried some rudimentary air cover in the shape of SS *Empire Gale*, a CAM (Catapult Armed Merchantman) ship carrying an obsolete single use Mk1 Hurricane fighter, whilst rescue facilities, should they be required, were provided by SS *Copeland*. *Capira* took up her convoy position at #84, the eighth column, forth row, bound for Boston. For the next six days, ON47 was escorted by three British corvettes, a Free French sloop and a First World War US destroyer now sailing under the White Ensign. Their task was to counter German submarines, or U-boats as they were more commonly referred to. U-boats were seen as the major threat to communications in the Atlantic; a threat that would have been even more potent had the Commander-in-Chief U-boats had his way.

*Befehlshaber der Unterseeboote* (BdU), Admiral Karl Dönitz[3] was a thoroughly professional naval officer who had operated submarines during the First World War. During his last patrol in the Mediterranean in October 1918, his boat *UB68* developed stability problems and sank. He was taken prisoner by the British and spent nine months in captivity before resuming his naval career. At an early stage he had recognised the potential of U-boats for imposing a stranglehold on sea trade, especially now that improved communications made their targeting in far greater numbers on Atlantic convoys possible. In 1935, and in recognition of the strategic grasp he had on the potential role of the U-boat, Dönitz was given the task of building up the German submarine arm. Although he remained a firm advocate of the U-boat, Dönitz did recognise its vulnerability particularly to emerging technologies for detecting underwater craft such as sonar, or ASDIC[4] as it was then designated. To counter this threat, he developed the tactic of surface or near surface attack at night, and by 1937 his misgivings about the U-boat's effectiveness, given the possibility of acoustic detection, had largely evaporated. He also formulated the concept of '*Rudeltaktik*' (Pack Tactics) that subsequently proved to be highly effective when essential factors such as good intelligence, experienced crews, favourable dispositions and weather conditions came together. However, at the outbreak of war, Germany had only 57 U-boats, of which 23 were effective ocean going Type VIIs; and with such a small fleet, Dönitz was unable to turn his ideas on *Rudeltaktik* into reality at that time. Nevertheless, he considered it vital that by whatever means the U-boat arm must be put to strategic use, i.e. the interception and destruction of trade between the UK and its trading partners, especially the USA. Thankfully his ideas did not at first receive total acceptance by Hitler or the head of the German navy, Grossadmiral Erich Raeder. During the early days of the war (and it has to be said not without some success) they considered U-boats best employed against enemy capital ships. However, following the fall of France and Norway, the U-boat arm had far greater access to Atlantic trade routes and thereafter the BdU attempted to concentrate its efforts there. Nevertheless, U-boat deployment remained subject to some interference from Hitler and the German high command throughout the war[5].

Unbeknown to the ON47 escorts, there were very few U-boats in the North Atlantic at this time. Only four were operating to the west of the British Isles as the convoy sailed in a north westerly arc that would take it close to Iceland. During the next four days, those U-boats that were capable of intercepting ON47, should it have been detected, moved their centre of operations further south[6]. The focus of German naval operations at this time was very much on Mediterranean convoys and those steaming further south along the West African coast. To this must be added two other factors in favour of ON47 reaching its destination unmolested: First, the difficulties facing Germany over U-boat repair, and second the intelligence gained from the Enigma code breakers at Bletchley Park. Dönitz had lobbied for repair priority to be given to U-boats, but could not gain acceptance of this by the Naval High Command, whose focus was on surface ships. Dönitz could not agree and recorded his misgivings over the employment of German shipyard workers on any vessels save those necessary to win the war i.e. the U-boat.[7] Dönitz' initial failure to win the argument prevented the production of sufficient U-boats early on in the war to provide a knock-out blow to trans-Atlantic communications, although it was seen by the allies as a close-run thing at the time. The second factor, decrypts of German naval signals, gave valuable intelligence of their intentions and consequently enabled the timely diversion of convoys away from U-boat concentrations. The combined result of these factors was that only one ship was lost in a direct attack on an ON convoy up to the end of 1941 and only three ships were lost up to the end of April 1942. Thereafter, as so often happens in war, the advantage swung in favour of the U-boat, largely because of the output from the new construction and training programme for U-boats and their crews combined with the cessation of signal intelligence;[8] a situation that pertained until the end of 1942[9].

At this stage in the ON convoy series it was the norm for ships not to follow the shortest, great circle route, but to sail much further north. This kept the convoy in touch with air cover from Iceland, and the escorts could make use of the refuelling base there. However, ON convoys at the end of 1941 were escorted only part way across the ocean and then dispersed. So on 22 December five US destroyers took up escort duty; but the following day, at a point just south of Greenland, the remaining 23 ships in ON47 dispersed to their various destinations.

*Capira* reached Boston on 4 January 1942, but not before running aground at Marble Head. How this mishap occurred or who was responsible is not recorded. Had it been a naval vessel, there would have been a board of enquiry inevitably followed by a courts martial of those officers whose actions or negligence contributed to the grounding. But as a merchant vessel, *Capira*'s officers were not subject to such strictures and she was soon re-floated, but not without some damage having sustained leaks in two of her holds. However, this mishap was not sufficient to prevent her discharging her cargo at Boston, and during the following eleven weeks she underwent extensive repairs in dry dock there. It is apparent that the repairs were not solely occasioned by the incident at Marble Head and had been planned in advance. According to Lloyds List[10] *Capira* had sustained ice damage during the previous November when on a voyage to Archangel, one of the two north Russian ports that were largely ice-free in winter. Plates, hatch covers, floors, ceilings and frames had to be renewed; tanks steam cleaned, the crankshaft lifted and propeller shaft drawn. Finally, her main bearings were re-metalled and the engines realigned. All in all, she underwent a partial refit at a cost of over $185,000.

Towards the end of this period of much needed maintenance, *Capira* had some rudimentary defence equipment installed, and various other modifications made to give her some capability against air and U-boat attack, albeit very limited. In addition to the repairs, mountings were installed for a 4-inch gun aft on *Capira*'s poop deck, together with two 30-calibre Lewis Machine guns. Both of these weapons were of First World War vintage, and by now obsolete, and it could be argued had more of a psychological effect on the ship's crew than any military effect on the enemy. Two more Lewis MGs were deployed forward on the boat deck, with two 50-calibre Browning MGs aft. Finally, two more Brownings were placed on the bridge. Splinter protection was provided for the gun areas and extended to the bridge and radio house. All illuminated areas above decks were darkened so that an effective blackout could be maintained at night. Above-deck sea chests were reinforced with steel straps and concrete, a fire control telephone system was provided, and a sky lookout station was established on top of the pilot house. In addition, she had been fitted with degaussing coils as a protection against magnetic mines. This was apparently a British installation that had been fitted whilst *Capira* was in New York a year previously, and was by no means standard for all merchant ships. Finally, berthing and messing facilities were provided for the US Navy Armed Guard detachment of an officer and twelve enlisted men[11]. *Capira* was now ready to go to war, although in effect she had already been actively engaged for the five months since her passage to Archangel in convoy PQ1.

All of these defensive modifications were initiated by the US War Shipping Administration, who had requisitioned *Capira* on 19 March and it is unlikely that she was taken over in total ignorance of her condition. Requisitioning such ships was a wartime necessity to ensure that the US Government had sufficient mercantile capacity at its command. The British Government had instituted a similar scheme under the Ministry of War Transport (MOWT) which was formed on 1 May 1941 from the Ministry of Shipping and the Ministry of Transport. MOWT not only ensured the husbanding of British-controlled merchant ships already subject to U-boat attrition, but in collaboration with its US counterpart coordinated the passage of vital supplies in protective convoys.

The on-board defence of merchant ships fell either to the US Armed Guard following America's entry into the war at the end of 1941, or British Defensively Equipped Merchant Ship (DEMS) gunners from the outset in 1939. Detachments from either organisation were deployed during wartime passages. The Armed Guard had been raised during the First World War to man the guns on defensively equipped merchant ships. However, this had been a limited operation confined to 384 vessels, and Armed Guard units were disbanded at the end of hostilities. The formation of a similar force at the outbreak of the Second World War was hampered by the US Neutrality Act, which forbade the arming of US merchant ships. The Act was repealed by Congress in October 1941 and work began immediately to enlist and train Armed Guard units to man the guns and radio communications of US-registered merchant ships, or those sailing under a US flag of convenience such as the *Capira*. The Armed Guard unit of around a dozen men was under the command of its officer and not the ship's master, placing the guard commander in a delicate position within the ship's chain of command. The ideal Armed Guard officer was a tactful person who could look after the interests of his men and at the same time keep relations smooth between the navy complement and the master, officers and crew of the merchant ship. He was a man who could get along with people who were under great mental strain and who could win their confidence. His relationship with his gunners was close. He was a kind of doctor, chaplain and commanding officer all at the same time. On the *Capira* this daunting task fell to Ensign Raymond E. Combs USNR, as he and his Armed Guardsmen joined the ship in Boston on the 26 March.

Like the United States the British had Defensively Armed Merchant Ships (DAMS) in the First World War. The organization was resurrected just before Britain entered the Second World War, and in June 1939 the Admiralty Trade Division established the DEMS Organization. Unlike the US system, however, the DEMS gunners were transferred from existing units, typically the Royal Artillery. In addition, often retired men or reservists were recruited from the Royal Navy and Royal Marines. On troopships transporting RAF personnel, troops from the RAF Regiment manned the guns. For administrative and pay purposes most naval DEMS personnel were attached to HMS *President*, a naval drill ship; their record was then supplemented with the name of the merchant ship they were serving on. All members of the armed forces serving on board a DEMS ship were required to sign the merchant ship's Articles of Agreement and received a nominal wage of one shilling per month from the ship's owners. This was an internationally recognized legal requirement that allowed them to visit neutral ports without fear of being interned as armed forces personnel. Therefore, in many respects, they were treated as merchant seamen and were therefore unlike the Armed Guard technically under the authority of the ship's master. Finally, some merchant seamen were also trained on the guns that had been fitted to their ships and qualified as Merchant Seaman Gunners, for which they received additional payment. The term 'DEMS Gunner' was commonly used to cover all such personnel. The United States, however, was unable to assign prime responsibility for manning guns to merchant seamen. It was argued that since there was no control over them from the time they completed one voyage until they agreed to sign on for another, there was no means of requiring them to undergo gunnery training. Nevertheless, many did.

Austin Byrne, a naval DEMS gunner from Bradford called up in 1941, recalled undergoing six weeks basic training at HMS *Glendower*,[12] a naval shore-based establishment at Pwellhi. There he was taught the use of a lead-line, tying knots, gas attack practice and learning the parts of an anchor; none of which would prove of any use to him in the months ahead. Only once was he given any training in the handling of small boats; skills that proved to be essential when his ship was torpedoed. Ironically, or fortunately, he had already acquired such skills whilst in the Sea Cadets before the war. DEMS Gunnery training followed and was conducted at HMS *Wellesley*, another shore base formerly the Royal Southern Hospital in Toxteth, Liverpool. Here he was trained on the 4-inch deck gun and a range of anti-aircraft machine guns including the Marlin, Hotchkiss and Lewis MG. Training in the use of the 4-inch gun began with wooden shells, but Austin missed the chance of practice with live ammunition when fog descended on the Mersey and the exercise was called off, for fear of shelling a vessel in one of the many incoming Atlantic convoys. He did however get to fire the Holman Projector. This was a makeshift weapon designed to fire hand grenades into the path of oncoming enemy aircraft, but was probably feared more by those using it than any attacker. Having fired five rounds from each of the MGs (he never did get to fire the 4-inch), he was pronounced trained and sent to his first ship the SS *Induna*. She was a coal- burning cargo ship and his first passage on her was up to Russia in PQ13[13]. Life onboard was dominated by the watch pattern of 4 hours on and 4 off, manning weapons either on the open bridge or in the gun pits. In spite of being issued with cold weather clothing[14] the only way to keep warm was to keep moving, by pacing up and down the bridge and gun pit decks. Living conditions were Spartan. A two-foot-wide bunk was provided with one straw mattress, known by seamen as a 'Donkey's Breakfast', and in Austin's case this louse- infested item was immediately thrown overboard. In addition, he was issued with a blanket and a pillow, both of which were filthy. Sleeping in one's clothes was the norm and they were seldom, if ever, taken off whilst at sea, and then only for very good reasons. The ten gunners shared one toilet and a small hand basin. There were no showers, and one had to go from the gunners' mess deck aft to the galley amidships to get hot water. Heating was provided from a coal-burning stove situated on the mess deck, but again getting fuel for it involved a long and arduous journey negotiating ladders, narrow corridors and the freight stored on deck. The gunners' mess deck had a composite floor made of an ash-like substance that had not set and turned to mud after a few days at sea. Three meals were provided each day which one had to collect from the galley and carry to the mess deck. They were invariably cold before they could be eaten. And as to the quality of the food? 'Nowt to brag about' was Austin's comment.[15]

It isn't clear if all the crew of the *Capira* were kept on the payroll during the ship's protracted refit. However, some of the ordinary rates were, and so it is assumed that the officers and those involved in operating the ship's systems continued to be employed by the US War Shipping Administration. They would have probably assisted the repair work and refit whilst she was in Boston, and during their free time the crew would no doubt have taken advantage of the delights of that bustling city. The refit also allowed others time to travel further afield and visit places such as New York. Life in US cities was in stark contrast to the wartime deprivations that British sailors had become accustomed to back home. In March there had been a further reduction in the coal ration in Britain, a ban on pleasure driving had been introduced in an attempt to conserve petrol reserves, a reduction in the flour content of bread had been announced, and double-breasted suits were banned. All of these unwelcome but necessary economic measures reflected the increasing rate of merchant shipping casualties. In stark contrast, however, the wealth and progress driven by the American Dream were everywhere in evidence on this side of the Atlantic, and the sheer vitality of American cities, especially New York, was intoxicating. Many a British sailor related or recorded their impressions of the New World. One such was Able Seaman J. Hawkins, a DEMS gunner aboard the SS *Bridgepool,* who arrived in the States on Sunday 26 July having just crossed from Liverpool in convoy ON110. During his stay in the city and passage back to the UK in convoy SC97 he kept a diary[16]chronicling the day's events. New York must have come as somewhat of a shock to this young man from the sleepy village of Sawston in Cambridgeshire. Seeing skyscrapers for the first time, dining at Jack Dempsey's restaurant, going to see Broadway shows, going on to Brooklyn night clubs where the shows were 'very hot' and being fêted by New Yorkers in the many bars that he visited, appear to have occupied most of his time ashore; as it must the crew of the *Capira* when they were able to take their leisure. Once the delights of the city had been sampled, shopping became a priority and items that were practically unobtainable in Britain such as nylons could be purchased relatively cheaply in the States and brought back as presents or sold on at a profit.

In addition, New York and Boston were safe havens from the carnage that was occurring off the Eastern Seaboard at that time. Less than a month after Germany had declared war on the United States, the *Kreigsmarine* were already geared up for their 'Second Happy Time' (*Glückliche Zeit*)[17]. Soon after the attack on Pearl Harbour, Dönitz wrote: 'An attempt must be made… to strike a blow at the American coast with a drumbeat.' Operation *Paukenschlag* claimed its first victim on 11 January when *U123* sank the British merchantman *Cyclops* 125 miles south east of Cape Sable, Nova Scotia. The next day, off Rhode Island, *U123* sank two tankers and damaged a third. On 19 January she sank three more ships off the coast south of New York. By the end of January, a handful of U-boats had sent 100,000 tons of shipping to the bottom, and in February and March a further 250,000 tons were sunk, one fifth of which were tankers. Such destruction was facilitated to some extent by the reluctance of the US Naval and civil authorities to initiate a convoy system along the Eastern Seaboard, or to implement a coastal blackout so that merchantmen would not present easy targets silhouetted against the bright lights[18] of the coastal resorts.

Kapitänleutnant Reinhard Hardegen recalled how he had stood on the bridge of *U123* on 14 January, hypnotised by the sight before him. He had surfaced in shallow water just outside New York's inner harbour. The undimmed lights of Manhattan seemed to emit a warm glow that hung in the night sky. Hardegen drank in the view and then invited other crew members, including the embedded propogandist photographer Alwin Tolle, to see it too[19]. 'We were the first to be here and for the first time in this war a German soldier looked on the coast of the USA,' he wrote in his memoirs. 'I thought it would be a big surprise for the Americans that a submarine would be there. There was no blackout, also no dimming. I could see on Coney Island the houses, lights and motor cars. Therefore it was very easy navigation for me.'[20] Hardegen's success in reaching and operating off the US coast was in spite of the Admiralty sending daily updates to the US Naval Staff in Washington on his progress across the Atlantic. In a later interview, Hardegen put this down to much more than good luck, attributing his success largely to the American's culpability in ignoring the intelligence supplied by the British.[21]

Much of the blame for such inactivity has been placed at the door of the then C-in-C Atlantic Fleet, Admiral Ernest King USN. And much of the controversy has been clouded by the poor relationship between King and the British naval authorities, as well as King and his own contemporaries in the United States. He had a combative nature and was described as '... perhaps the most disliked Allied leader of World War II. Only British Field Marshal Montgomery may have had more enemies...'[22] Admiral Charles Little, Head of the British Naval Delegation in Washington, observed King at first hand and regularly forwarded his impressions to the First Sea Lord. Variously he described King as '...not a clever man ... conceited... and bearing the "ancient grudge" against the British.' Little also described him as having 'the mind of a warrant officer who fills his store with paint or holly stones with great reluctance to use them!... notoriously rude and unnecessarily abrupt.'[23] King was also said to be a heavy drinker and womaniser, characteristics that were guaranteed not to go down well with the more puritanical outlook of others in the US Navy at that time. Nevertheless, Little conceded that King was approachable and easy to talk to if tackled in private[24]. It was when he was with others that he became belligerent and awkward. However, he retained the confidence of the President and in December 1942 became C-in-C US Fleet, an appointment that in March 1943 was combined with that of Chief of Naval Operations. Part of the problem, no doubt exacerbated by King's belligerence towards the British, was the Admiralty's belief that the US Navy had much to learn from the experience of those who had already been engaged in fighting the war with Germany for the past two years or so. King thought otherwise and endeavoured to keep his officers from any influence that might emanate from the Royal Navy. While content to take British naval assets under command, he remained adamant that no US naval personnel should be under the command of the Royal Navy. On the subject of naval tactics his mind was similarly closed, and he rejected categorically the formation and passage of convoys along the Eastern Seaboard without the means of effective naval escort; a protective measure that could not be fully provided at that time. Some measure of air cover was available, however, but its pattern of deployment was not varied; with the result that observant U-boat captains avoided it without undue difficulty. Further despatches from Admiral Little summed up the situation:

> Losses of merchant ships in the Caribbean and North Atlantic are bad and there is no cure in sight. Escort craft will come available slowly and air and surface co-operation will also gradually be developed, but evidence of the Admiralty's justifiable anxiety causes irritation. Efforts... to bring about frank discussion and joint planning to meet the shipping situation to best mutual advantage have failed. I'm afraid combined planning is not developing... the real reason is that honest examination of almost any problem leads to revelation of the need for U.S. assistance or support to us. There is no immediate prospect of the machine working as it should – a matter is not first discussed and then drafted with a combined paper; one "side" has to put something up and the other produces a counterblast. The final paper is like the dialogue of rough and tumble comedians and leaves little for the C.O.S. to do except examine for anything objectionable to one partner or the other. [25]

Little's pessimism on the prospects for the future of Anglo-American cooperation in this arena slowly evaporated as US neutrality in the European conflict became undermined and disappeared completely after the attack on Pearl Harbor. In the meantime, merchant ships continued to be picked off one by one, usually at night, as they made their lonely passages unguarded and silhouetted by the lights of the coastal resorts; a needless loss of shipping, materiel and above all merchant seamen's lives.

*Capira* was fortunate enough to remain under repair in Boston during a large part of the period when the *Kreigsmarine* was causing havoc off the US coast, but by the 24 March she was fully armed with the naval detachment embarked. On 27 March 1942 she left fully loaded with war materiel for Nova Scotia, at her full speed of 9 kts [16.7 km/hr], eventually to join convoy SC77 forming up at Halifax. This short passage of two days gave the Armed Guard crew an opportunity to shake down and test fire the guns, only to discover that the .50 calibre Brownings were defective and could not be fired. This appeared to be a common defect experienced by other ships but was quickly rectified by DEMS gunners on arrival at Halifax. We do not know how much or indeed how little the merchant crews knew of the number of ships now being sunk off the US coast. However it is unlikely that the high toll being exacted by the *Kriegsmarine* could have been kept under wraps, and *Capira's* crew must have had some very tense and nervous moments during this passage[26]. If they did, they would discover that was nothing to the mental strain they were to undergo in a matter of weeks in an Arctic convoy.

# 3 CONVOY

For the king had at sea a navy of Tharshish with the
navy of Hiram: once in three years came the navy of
Tharshish, bringing gold, and silver, ivory, and apes,
and peacocks.

1 Kings 10[22] (KJV)

Ever since King Solomon's navy sailed the Red Sea, merchant ships have
gathered together in convoys for mutual protection. As both a tactic and a
strategy it has served the British well throughout their history. At the Battle
of Pulo Aura fought in the Strait of Malacca in 1804, a large convoy of
well-armed East Indiamen sailing in convoy under Nathaniel Dance drove
off and chased a powerful French naval squadron. The historical record
supplies many other examples of convoys being used tactically as protection
against the country's enemies, as well as fending off marauding privateers.
However, it was during the First World War when the system was used to
counter the potential stranglehold that German submarines had over the
Atlantic routes supplying foodstuffs, armaments and raw materials to the
allies. A strategic lifeline carrying essential materiel, in stark contrast to
King Solomon's exotic cargoes. The many hard lessons that had been learnt
during the First World War were swiftly applied by the British government
at the outbreak of the Second, and in September 1939 the convoy system
was reintroduced in anticipation of the German U-boat threat. Soon the
majority of merchantmen, including those flying the flag of neutral nations,
were being marshalled into convoys and the *Capira* was no exception.

In late August 1939[1] before the outbreak of hostilities, the Admiralty took
control of all British merchant vessels. Central control of these precious assets
had long been seen as necessary, even more so as the threat against them had
taken on new dimensions during the inter-war years. The rapid development
of aviation opened the way for long range naval reconnaissance aircraft and
bombers to interdict shipping. Torpedo bombers, for example, based in
Norway and Finland covering the North Atlantic between 1941 and 1943,

presented a particular menace to ships proceeding to Russia. In addition, Germany's small but powerful fleet of pocket battle ships provided another headache for the convoy planners to grapple with. Although the threat presented by the *Graf Spee* (scuttled off Montevideo in December 1939) and the *Bismark* (sunk in the North Atlantic in May 1941) had been eliminated, the most powerful ship in the *Kriegsmarine*, the *Tirpitz*, continued to present a very potent threat to Allied shipping, even though she spent most of her wartime career sheltering in Norwegian fjords, seldom venturing onto the open sea. Developments in aircraft and naval forces were accompanied by technological advances in sonar and radar that greatly enhanced target location. Radio communications and signals intelligence also began to play an increasingly important part in both enabling the concentration of German submarine forces into 'Wolf Packs' and for both sides deciphering and reading each other's intentions. Dominating all operations, however, was the ever-present factor of the weather especially that encountered in the North Atlantic; sometimes capricious, often hostile but always indifferent to friend and foe alike. Thus, convoy operations throughout the Second World War became hostage to the ebb and flow of either side's fortunes as technology, tactics, intelligence, the elements and pure chance played their respective roles.

The rapid introduction of a convoy system on the outbreak of war served to underscore the vital importance of imports to Britain's survival and her determination to continue the war effort. Maintaining the bridge across the Atlantic not only protected the population from starvation but also ensured the build-up of men and materiel for the eventual liberation of continental Europe from Nazi domination. Just how important the convoys were in sustaining the British Isles can be captured in a few statistics. In 1939 Britain needed to import 55 million tons of goods. Over two-fifths of imports came from British Empire ports, imposing very long passages on the merchant fleet[2]. These long hauls were lengthened further in the early years of the war by the effective closure of both the English Channel and the Suez route to the east. Bombay voyages, for instance, increased from 6,000 to 11,000 miles. Protecting this lifeline was of utmost priority; to put it into perspective, if all the supplies carried by just one average sized Atlantic convoy of 35 ships were gathered together, they would fill a line of ten-ton trucks spaced 50 yards apart which would stretch from Inverness to Southampton via Carlisle.[3] As a consequence of its overwhelming reliance on imports and its need to service an empire, Great Britain maintained the world's largest merchant fleet, made up of 3,000 ocean-going vessels and 1,000 large coastal ships.

More than 200 convoy routes existed during the war, each known by two or more letters. Not all of these were concerned with trade to and from the United Kingdom; some were troop carriers, whilst others were concerned with trade to the Empire and other friendly countries, whilst yet more were concerned with coastal movements around the British Isles. The letters sometimes indicated the departure and destination ports, i.e. the 'AB' convoys sailed from Aden to Bombay and 'A' convoys returned from Bombay to Aden. 'ON' stood for 'Outward North' i.e. Liverpool to North America. The 'HX' designation meant 'Home from Halifax (Nova Scotia)'. The North Russian PQ convoy series, however, were named after Commander Philip Quellyn Roberts, a planning officer in the Admiralty. During *Capira*'s time convoys returning from Russia were designated QP. Convoys were divided into slow convoys for ships that could not maintain a steady speed of 10kts [18.5km/hr], and fast convoys for ships capable of speeds between 10 and 15kts [18.5 and 27.8km/hr]. Those ships, like the ocean-going liners of the inter-war years that could make more than 15kts, usually travelled alone as they were well capable of outrunning U-boats. Convoys travelled at the speed of their slowest ship. Sometimes the lettering also indicated the convoy's speed. 'HX' convoys were always fast and the 'SC', Sydney (Nova Scotia) were slow. Convoys also received a number when they left harbour, e.g. SC97 or HX348. *Capira*, having been employed almost exclusively in the North Atlantic sailed mainly in ON, SC, PQ and QP convoys.

Typically, a convoy of around 35 ships would steam in nine to twelve columns. Before 1943 ships sailed in column at two cable [370m] intervals. This was increased to three [555m] or four [740m] cable intervals to accommodate inexperienced masters. The distance between columns was set at three cables [555m] by day and five [925m] at night. Operational research (OR), which was in its infancy at this time, showed that five cable spacing of columns presented a lesser, more open, target and the formation was therefore eventually set at five cables. A nine-column convoy would therefore be four nautical miles [7.4km] wide and one and a half nautical miles [3.4km] deep. When accompanied by well-trained and coordinated air and surface escorts the convoy system was very effective. However, due to shortages of escort vessels and suitably trained crews this was seldom the case during the early years of the war. OR also showed that the number of ships in convoy could be increased significantly without the necessity to increase naval vessels in the escort. The guiding principle was that the enlarged convoy should sail on a broad front, because in such a formation a numerical increase in merchant ships would not result in a significant increase in the convoy perimeter requiring protection. Convoy numbers therefore increased to beyond 60 ships in up to 12 columns whilst maintaining the column length. However, later operations in 1944 with far more than 60 ships in convoy did eventually necessitate increasing the length of columns[4]. By this time, however, Allied navies had expanded dramatically and sufficient escorts were available for their effective protection.

Between the outbreak of war in September 1939 and the entry of the United States in December 1941, the task of protecting the vulnerable merchantmen in the North Atlantic was shared primarily by the Royal Navy and the Royal Canadian Navy (RCN). The extent and complexity of the task that both navies faced on the outbreak of war was monumental and required a massive and speedy increase in their size. This was particularly the case with the RCN[5] where the rate of expansion was fifty to one and in the Royal Navy it was eight to one. The challenges that such an unprecedented expansion posed for training and equipping a modern navy in an era of rapid technological development were formidable. At the beginning of the war, both navies' resources were too widespread to provide continuous and effective protection all the way across the Atlantic. Ideally, a convoy's escorts would consist of two destroyers; one each at front and rear of the convoy; assisted by a mix of about five smaller escorts such as corvettes, sloops and frigates that would keep watch along the sides and rear of the formation. Aircraft, and to a lesser extent submarines, were also vital components in the naval mix protecting the convoys; but again, at the outset of the war they were few and far between, as well as lacking in capability. For example, the range of maritime aircraft was limited and therefore vast areas of the ocean could not be patrolled, leaving convoys prey to U-boats under no threat from either observation or attack from the air. And, as will be discussed later, the reluctance of Bomber Command under Air Marshall Sir Arthur Harris to release air assets from the bombing campaign over Germany effectively starved Costal Command of suitable airframes; this almost certainly resulted in the unnecessary loss of many Allied ships.

Apart from the collective measures being put in place to protect convoys, there was much that could be done to ensure individual merchant ships were less prone to enemy attack. This was especially the case at night and in poor visibility, where an effective blackout could reduce detection by enemy submarines and surface ships. Such requirements for all British, Allied and neutral ships sailing in British convoys were set out in various Admiralty Instructions and Memoranda preceding the outbreak of war. A Shipping Defence Advisory Committee was also set up and as early as July 1937 it had begun to lobby shipping owners to consider the requirement for items of convoy equipment to be provided immediately on the outbreak of hostilities. By October 1938 the Committee reported that the supply of Admiralty items of convoy equipment had been approved and that stocks were beginning to be built up. The following month equipment details were published in addition to the general principles for darkening ships at night. Regulation of these protective measures fell to Naval Control Service Officers and later their Convoy Equipment Inspection Officers (CEIOs) set up in October 1941. However, inspectors were few and far between to begin with and supporting facilities such as communications and transport to cover their large areas of responsibility were almost non-existent. As a result, few shipping owners carried out the Admiralty recommendations and failed to have their ships adequately equipped. In reality it was the effective blacking out of ships that proved to be the most difficult problem to be solved. Admiralty estimates of the cost of blackout materials falling to ships' owners proved to be unrealistically low at £10 per ship, and therefore no provision was made by owners to blackout their ships before hostilities began. There was the odd exception, however. One CEIO inspecting a ship failed to detect any vestige of light and asked the master how he had achieved such a feat. He replied: 'After dark the dynamo is stopped and it's more than anyone's life is worth to light even a match. She's blacked out all right and actually I'm saving money for the owners.'[6] Nevertheless, this parlous state of affairs continued until the early part of 1941, during which time merchant ship losses were numerous. In response the inspection regime was strengthened and provided with the appropriate resources to ensure owners' compliance. However, resistance from some of the 'hard' owners persisted until inspecting officers, supported by the Director of Trade Division in the Admiralty, refused to grant one merchantman a certificate to sail in convoy. A list of the work required to be carried out was sent to the owners and not surprisingly it was completed in record time; but even so delayed sailing by a few days. Once news spread, resistance to the regulations began to evaporate and from then on a marked improvement was noticeable. One inevitable consequence of blacking out ships at night, however, was the increased risk of collisions. During the first six months of the war the number of incidents had almost doubled; consequently, some of the provisions, especially around the use of navigation lights, were relaxed. All of these measures both collective and individual were seen as vitally defensive at the time. As the war progressed, the convoy, especially a large one accompanied by a strong escort, having attracted the attention of a number of U-boats, would adopt a more offensive posture especially if accompanied by an escort carrier. This tended to be the case beyond May 1943, when there was a decisive change in Allied fortunes in the Atlantic. However, this was far from the case in early 1942, when the advantage lay very much with the U-boat.

Ironically, the first merchant ship to fall victim to U-boat attack was neither in convoy nor a prize vessel. The liner *Athenia* was sunk by *U30* on the very day Britain and France declared war on Germany; 3 September 1939. Although the *Athenia* sinking was a mistake on the part of the German *Kriegsmarine* (Hitler had ordered his U-boats to abide by international law) the Admiralty believed that unrestricted submarine warfare had been initiated, justifying their rapid implementation of the convoy system. Even so, the U-boat menace was to demonstrate its potency and point to the struggle ahead to overcome it. Twenty-five merchantmen were sunk by submarines in September alone, followed by a further 14 in October. However, as the convoy system got underway the rate of sinkings slowed to a trickle, with only 21 being lost to submarine attack during the first five months of 1940[7]. During the same period, from the outbreak of war until the fall of France in May 1940, the Germans lost 24 of their submarines. This was an unacceptable loss rate, when it is considered that there were only 57 U-boats capable of going to sea in September 1939. Clearly such attrition was not sustainable by Germany; however, she was already radically gearing up U-boat production. Fifty boats were launched in 1940 and a further 1,040 came off the ramps between 1941 and the end of the war[8]. However, it is a sobering thought to reflect on what might have happened had Dönitz, whilst Commander-in-Chief U Boats, had more assets at his disposal during the early months of the war. Following the fall of France in May 1940, the Germans gained access to the French Atlantic ports and their facilities. This made U-boat access to the UK trade routes much easier and also provided bases for German aircraft to range out over large parts of those routes too. So after May 1940, Allied merchant ship losses began to mount again and thus began a period known by German submariners as the 'First Happy Time'.

The British Prime Minister, Winston Churchill, was in no doubt about what was at stake and made clear that the most important theatre of the war for Britain lay in the Atlantic:

> In order to win this war Hitler must either conquer this island by invasion or he must cut the ocean lifeline which joins us to the United States... Wonderful exertions have been made by our Navy and our Air Force... and, need I say, by the officers and men of the Merchant Navy, who go out in all weathers and in the teeth of all dangers to fight for love of their native land and for a cause they comprehend and serve. Still, when you think how easy it is to sink ships at sea and how hard it is to build and protect them, when you remember we never have less than 2,000 ships afloat and 300 to 400 in the danger areas, when you think of the great armies we maintain... and the world-wide traffic we have to carry, can you wonder that it is the Battle of the Atlantic which holds the first place in the thoughts of those upon whom rests the responsibility for procuring the victory?[9]

Sixteen months on from Churchill's speech, the situation remained precariously balanced. Many of the successes enjoyed by either side owed their genesis to emerging technologies, especially in the areas of radar and signals intelligence. Well-established technologies such as sonar were also being developed and further improved. However, it must be borne in mind that for every measure introduced by one side it was highly likely that it would not be long before an effective counter-measure would be put in place by the other. During the period under consideration here, from late November 1941 to September 1942, many of the technical advances were in their relative infancy. Moreover those that were beginning to show results often suffered severe setbacks due to the introduction of effective counter-measures as related below.

## Allied Radar, HF/DF and German Countermeasures

The science of detecting objects by means of reflected radio waves had been understood for some time. Inevitably the technology required to realise the possibilities predicted by scientists took time to develop. By the beginning of the war, the British had invested considerable effort in developing and implementing a system of radar early warning stations around those parts of the British Isles considered most vulnerable to air attack. This system, known as 'Chain Home' was fully operational in the summer of 1940, in time for the Battle of Britain. Thankfully it proved highly successful in locating the distance, bearing, altitude and speed of enemy attacking formations in sufficient time for the RAF to respond effectively. The technological challenge involved in the manufacture and construction of Chain Home at this time should not be underestimated. It required the transmission of radio waves at an appropriate wavelength and with sufficient power capable of reaching the target and being reflected back to be detected by a receiver. In addition, transmission had to be in short bursts or pulses so that the time taken for a reflected pulse to arrive back at the transmitter could be measured and hence the range of the target calculated. Furthermore, the radar beam had to be focussed into a very narrow arc so that the direction and altitude of the target could also be calculated accurately. To measure the speed of the target relative to the transmitter, a comparison of the slight change in frequency between the transmitted and reflected pulse would be made. From this change in frequency, known as the Doppler effect, the relative speed of the target could be arrived at. Perhaps the greatest challenge of all, however, was training sufficient technicians to maintain such high-tech equipment and operators to interpret the results accurately. For the output from all this technology upon which so much depended was a series of spikes on a fuzzy green line, running across the centre of a round screen barely 20cm in diameter[10].

In stark contrast to Austin Byrne's experience as a conscripted gunner, the Royal Navy's Radar Mechanics underwent a comprehensive and intense training regime. Tom Heley was one such mechanic and following a few weeks basic training at HMS *Ganges*, a shore-based naval establishment at Shotley, he was posted to the signals school at Portsmouth. There he underwent basic and further trade training eventually gaining a 'Wireless Telegraphist' rating. He then completed a preliminary course at Rugby Technical College in the theoretical aspects of radar, or Radio Direction Finding (RDF) as it was then known, before going to HMS *Valkyrie* another of the navy's shore-based establishments on the Isle of Man, to be trained on the full range of radar equipment he would be maintaining at sea. This was highly classified work and not surprisingly so as the British had, at that point in the war, developed radar to a far higher degree than the Germans or indeed the USA. Some thirteen months after joining the navy, Tom Heley finally completed his radar equipment training and was promoted to Leading Radio Mechanic (Radar). After a short stint back at Portsmouth he joined the cruiser HMS *Nigeria* on 19 March 1942[11]. It is worth noting that the equipment on his training certificates covered practically all naval radars then in service. These included surveillance, both air and sea target acquisition, ranging and fire control. Some of these radars were also linked to electro-mechanical analogue computers, so the equipment he was working on was very much state of the art and hence highly classified[12].

Tom would have been well aware that, in general, the smaller the target the shorter the radar wavelength had to be in order to detect it. Also, the maximum range at which the target could be detected depended on the power of the transmitted pulse. For example, the operating wavelength of Chain Home was around 6 meters, sufficient for detecting formations of aircraft, determining their strength, altitude, speed, range and direction. With such information, fighters could then be vectored on to the formation. It also proved possible to replicate early warning and target acquisition radar on larger warships and during 1940, Type 279 radars operating at a wavelength of 7.5m and Type 281s operating at 3.3m were installed on larger warships of the Royal Navy to counter the threat from the air. They were also used in a secondary role for sea surveillance but the maritime surface environment presented far more challenges for radar than the detection of aircraft against the background of a relatively benign sky. As we shall see later, the Type 281 mounted on HMS *Nigeria*, and no doubt maintained by Tom Heley, played a significant part in the defence of convoy PQ15. However, the ability of radars then available to detect small targets on the ocean such as a submarine conning tower or periscope against surface clutter was very limited. Much shorter wavelengths of a few centimetres were required to achieve this and more compact equipment was required if such radars were to be deployed on aircraft or submarines.

The *Kreigsmarine* had also been experimenting with shipborne radar and by 1939 had installed an early surface target acquisition and ranging radar in a handful of its warships. Photographs of the scuttled *Admiral Graf Spee* just outside Montevideo show the German *Seetakt* naval radar mounted on the ship's optical rangefinder. Operated at a wavelength of 60cm, it was in advance of anything mounted on Allied ships at that time and had been used to great effect by the *Graf Spee* against merchant shipping in the Atlantic. However, it was large and therefore, like British systems, not suitable for mounting on submarines or aircraft at that time for surveillance or targeting. Germany therefore concentrated on developing early warning and countermeasures to protect its U-boats against attack from ships and aircraft. Therefore extensive development of surveillance radar for use on German submarines did not get underway until later in the war. Another reason for such delay was a belief shared by German scientists that it was not possible to produce compact radars operating in the centimetric band with sufficient power to detect smaller targets such as aircraft. Only after German scientists had examined a centimetric radar from a British bomber downed over Rotterdam in February 1943 were they able to produce radars with far greater resolution that were sufficiently compact for use in submarines and aircraft[13]. But by then it was too late to catch up on all of the technological and scientific development enjoyed by the allies during the intervening years. The *Kreigsmarine* also tended to overestimate the value of passive versus active detection and thereby adopted a philosophy of 'radar silence'. The aim of this was to avoid detection from radiating sources in the same way as radio silence was intended to prevent signal detection, interception and direction finding. The effort applied to this aspect throughout the war in defence of U-boats was therefore considerable when compared with the development of active submarine measures.

British scientists were the first to develop a compact centimetric radar capable of locating a submarine periscope. This was due to the invention of the cavity magnetron, a breakthrough shared with the United States and kept out of the hands of the Germans until the unfortunate incident over Rotterdam. Such technology was embodied in the British Type 271 radar and its variants fitted to RN anti-submarine ships during the first half of 1941 and, much later, to RCN ships. The RCN were not so far advanced, and were still deploying metric radar systems such as the Types SW1C[14] and SW2C that were far less effective in locating small targets, especially close in. These sets, considered by some to be a menace due to their frequent ability to produce false echoes, were being installed in RCN ships in 1942 long after the RN had begun installing the far superior Type 271 into its vessels[15]. Nevertheless, and as will be covered later, the SW1C played its part in the defence of convoy SC 97, scoring a notable success. Early in 1940 a few British maritime aircraft were fitted with a metric radar, the ASV1[16]. This gave them a limited capability against submarines on the surface but was mainly used to locate larger objects like the convoy itself. The ASV1 was also limited, especially at night, by its long minimum range. This was partially compensated for in June 1942 by combining its operation with a high intensity searchlight, the 'Leigh Light'.

However, German countermeasures introduced in August 1942 in the form of the 'Metox' radar detector, temporarily cancelled this particular edge. Metox, named after its French manufacturer, was essentially a receiver suitably tuned to detect when a U-boat was being illuminated at metric wavelengths and therefore enabled the boat to dive before the aircraft got within visual range. Its antenna, nicknamed the Biscay Cross, resembled a simple cross mounted on the conning tower that had to be rotated by hand and withdrawn when the boat dived. In spite of its somewhat awkward deployment and operation, it was effective; and so for a time the odds moved once more in favour of the submarine. That was until centimetric radar, undetectable by Metox, was developed and manufactured in sufficient quantities to be installed in Allied aircraft from January 1943 onwards. Fortunately, this coincided with the introduction of maritime aircraft capable of ranging longer distances over the ocean to protect convoys and therefore provided a much-needed edge to the Allies. Also fortunate was the fact that the news of the capture of a British centimetric radar in February proved slow to reach the *Kreigsmarine* and for a time the apparent ineffectiveness of Metox was attributed to Allied aircraft somehow homing in on the weak signals that receivers of that era produced. It was not until late 1943 that German U-boats began to be equipped with effective measures to counter Allied centimetric airborne radar. Thus the baton was passed once again in the technological race but by now it was too late as the Allied ascendency in the Battle of the Atlantic began to be felt by the *Kreigsmarine*.

In addition to centimetric radar, the introduction on board Allied ships of High Frequency/Direction Finding equipment, also known as HF/DF or more colloquially as 'Huff Duff' gave the allies a distinct edge from the middle of 1942 onwards. On destroyers especially, HF/DF enabled escorts to react quickly to a submarine transmitting on the surface and accurately run down the bearing. As Huff Duff was a purely passive device, the U-boat crew did not know that they had been detected. This resulted in many a U-boat captain being surprised and having to crash dive, thereby neutralising his effectiveness either to attack or summon other members of the pack. The Germans' First Happy Time was effectively ended by the introduction of radar and HF/DF, which enabled convoy escorts to locate and 'see' U-boats in the dark and during poor weather[17].

Therefore, during *Capira*'s last voyage, only British naval escort vessels had radars capable of reliably detecting small surface targets such as U-boat conning towers and periscopes; while others also had the ability to detect airborne targets. The gradual introduction of HF/DF also gave the RN the added advantage of surprise attacks on U-boats. Allied aircraft, on the other hand, whilst having the means to detect a surfaced U-boat, still lacked the ability to detect smaller targets – especially at night.

### Direction Finding, Signals Intelligence and German Countermeasures
Either side also routinely intercepted naval communications for intelligence

purposes and to locate shipping. In this respect, the Allies had the advantage of the use of radio stations located throughout the British Empire and along the American coast. German signals traffic, detected concurrently by several stations some distance apart, enabled the traffic's approximate location to be triangulated.

Much of the signal traffic broadcast by both sides in the conflict was encoded and further encrypted. Great efforts were expended in protecting one's own transmissions and trying to read the opposition's. British, US and Canadian ships operating in the Atlantic used a system designated RN Cypher No 3. Like all cypher systems it was not immune and, depending on the effort and ingenuity expended, it could be broken. Thus from February 1942, the German security service, B Dienst, was regularly reading Allied signals traffic. However, such intelligence has to be gathered and disseminated within a timeframe so that it can be put to effective tactical use and this was not always the case.

The Kreigsmarine, in addition to German ground and air forces, used the 'Enigma' cipher machine to protect its communications[18]. This was an electro-mechanical device that utilised various settings on a plug board and rotors to encrypt messages. Combined with pre-coding and frequent changes of settings the Enigma presented a formidable nut for the Government Code & Cipher School at Bletchley Park to crack. However, on 7 May 1941, action was taken to capture a German weather ship, the München, and with it the Enigma settings for June[19]. Two days later on 9 May, and by an extraordinary piece of good fortune, U110 was captured complete with its Enigma machine and code books[20]. These two events enabled Enigma naval signals traffic to be read within 6 hours of its interception, and consequently provided timely intelligence for the Admiralty to re-route convoys around German wolf packs. A successful operation to intercept another German weather ship, the Lauenberg, on 28 June provided further material enabling German naval signals to be read and disseminated quickly. Other methods and equipment developed at Bletchley Park, largely by the mathematical genius Alan Turing, enabled Enigma to continue to be broken even without the information provided by raids on German weather ships. But this took longer, about two days, which was still sufficient time in some cases to take effective action. This situation lasted until February 1942, when the introduction of a fourth rotor to German Naval Enigma machines prevented further intelligence being gleaned by that means. It took the following eleven months for Alan Turing and his fellow scientists and intelligence officers at Bletchley Park to work out the means of cracking the encrypted code again. This prompted the Admiralty's Operational Intelligence Centre to admit at that time that little could be said with any confidence in estimating the present and future movements of U-boats.[21] As will be recounted later, this eleven-month black out of U-boat intelligence probably contributed to the eventual fate of the *Capira*.

Such naval intelligence blackout only applied to the Atlantic, however. German ships and U-boats in Arctic waters continued to use the three-rotor version of the Enigma machine, enabling some convoys to Russia, most notably PQ12, to be diverted away from concentrations of U-boats. Nevertheless, the time taken to decrypt German naval signals, especially following a change of Enigma settings, diminished their utility and, as in the case of PQ17, failed to prevent a tragedy.

The intelligence war was not all one-sided, however, and as already mentioned the German *B Dienst* was also successful in breaking Admiralty ciphers and occasionally was able to use this to devastating effect in operations against convoys. What is remarkable, however, is that the *Kreigsmarine*, even when armed with the British 'U-boat Situation Report', never suspected that the Enigma had been compromised. In his Memoirs, Dönitz wrote:

These 'Situation Reports' were of the greatest value to us in our efforts to determine how the enemy was able to find out about our U-boat dispositions and with what degree of accuracy he did so. The conclusion we came to was that: ... British conclusions are based on data... readily available to them, on U-boat positions and on their own plotting of the U-boats' movements, combined with a quite feasible process of logical deduction. The most important result that has emerged from this investigation is the all but certain proof that with the assistance of his airborne radar the enemy is able to discover U-boat dispositions with sufficient accuracy to enable his convoys to take evasive action.

The German High Command repeatedly checked and rechecked their cyphers to assure themselves that they were unbreakable. After much deliberation, the head of the German Naval Intelligence Service concluded that it would be impossible for the enemy to decipher traffic encrypted by Enigma. When the work of the Bletchley Park code breakers was eventually declassified and made public in 1974, long after Dönitz had published his Memoirs, his reaction was:

> So that's what happened! … I have been afraid of this time and again. Although the experts continually proved – with conviction as it seemed – that there were other reasons for the suspect observations, they were never able to dispel my doubts completely …[22]

A salutary lesson in the danger inherent in underestimating one's opponent's capabilities, because challenging the impossible is not factored into one's thinking. The fourth rotor incorporated into *Kreigsmarine* Enigma machines in February 1942 effectively blacked out Allied intelligence on the BdU's intentions for nearly a year. The fact that any correlation between the rotor upgrade and U-boat successes in the Atlantic was not apparent to the BdU was probably due to other factors that carried greater weight in the minds of BdU analysts. Among these is undoubtedly the significance the BdU placed in the capability of Allied radar, not to mention the 'Second Happy Time' taking place off the US coast at this time.

## Sonar and its Counter-Measures[23]

Unlike radar, early sonar equipment (or ASDIC as it was referred to) had been fitted to and was operational in some British warships during the inter-war years. The physical principles upon which sonar was founded were very much the same as those of radar, but using sound rather than radio waves transmitted under water. By propagating directional underwater sound waves[24] from a ship, and thereby receiving an echo bouncing off a submerged object, the range and bearing of the object could be calculated. Sound waves also exhibit the Doppler Effect, and therefore can be used to calculate the relative speed of the target and offensive measures taken if it were shown to be hostile. The trick was in differentiating between myriad underwater objects and sound waves reflected from differing layers of seawater from a single U-boat with hostile intent. The key to achieving this lay in the skill of the sonar operator in distinguishing one echo from another and focusing on those characteristic of a submarine.

At the outbreak of the Second World War, the Royal Navy had five sets for different surface ship classes, and others for submarines, incorporated into a complete anti-submarine attack system. Type 123 and 124 sets were the most prolific in the defence of convoys and were fitted into corvettes and destroyers respectively. These were very much based on early 1930s technology and were not able to gauge target depth accurately. This was a severe limitation because to be effective a depth charge had to detonate with 20m of the target. The effectiveness of early ASDIC was further limited through its loss of contact with the target as it got close and passed over it. Depth-charge attacks mounted from the stern or sides of the vessel were therefore fired blind. During such a blind period an experienced U-boat commander could take evasive action. This unsatisfactory situation pertained at the time of *Capira*'s final passage and was not resolved until the development of weapons such as 'Hedgehog' and later 'Squid' that projected warheads at the target ahead of the attacker while still in ASDIC contact.

German submarines were fitted with a number of microphones, arranged in various patterns either side of the bow. These were used offensively to gain an indication of target, range, speed and bearing before coming to periscope depth to refine these parameters and arrive at a firing solution. They could also be used defensively to listen out for hostile surface or sub-surface threats. As with radar, German tactical doctrine emphasised the passive use of sonar and, although active sonar devices were available, they were not routinely fitted. U-boats were equipped with a rudimentary sonar countermeasure, however. This was a simple canister containing calcium hydroxide which produced clouds of bubbles when opened in the sea. These canisters, referred to by German submariners as '*Bold*'[25], were ejected from the boat via a chute and as seawater seeped into the canister the resulting bubbles produced an acoustic echo resembling that of a submarine, hopefully confusing the enemy's sonar returns and hence allowing the U-boat to slip away unnoticed. Experienced U-boat captains were also able to hide behind varying saltwater and temperature conditions that produced false echoes and hence confused sonar operators.

## The Convoy Conference

Before a deep-sea convoy sailed, significant logistic effort was required to ensure that the maximum amount of appropriate materiel was shipped aboard and all necessary arrangements made for the convoy's safe passage. This process culminated in a conference[26] held some hours before sailing. It was presided over by the Royal Navy and brought together the essential players. The convoy commodore, the RN close escort commander, RAF Coastal Command representatives, DEMS officers and merchant ship masters, accompanied when possible by their chief engineers and navigating officers, all attended. Simultaneously, radio officers would hold a separate conference. Enjar Jensen, master of the *Capira,* and Thomas Kinnear his chief engineer, would have been regular attendees at these events before sailing. The conference usually began with the chairman asking if there were any doubtful starters. Then he would draw attention to the manner of identification when at sea and to the list of radio beacons likely to be encountered. Sailing orders were covered next. These gave the time of departure, speed, distance between ships, and so on. Emphasis was placed on keeping closed up especially when passing through the boom. The dangers of straggling behind, abeam or in front were also reiterated. Reference was made to sheets of formation designs and others headed: 'Stop Press'. All convoys, the Chairman would point out, may be used for practice attacks by our own aircraft and gunners must be warned accordingly!

At the far end of the conference room, models of aircraft were slung from the roof. Behind the chairman, a printed notice asked, 'Have you got a blue bulb in your stern light?' and another notice reminded ships' masters of the requirement to have two white rockets ready to fire. The atmosphere was generally easy and informal. Some of the masters, like Enjar Jensen were relatively young, but unlike him they were not all stamped with the sea. A number had undoubtedly followed other careers in civilian life. Not many were in uniform but a few wore blue naval mackintoshes over their civilian clothes. Attaché cases contained all the information they needed for the forthcoming passage and so charts, documents and papers were spread before them and continually referred to as the briefing continued with the Chairman reading out the latest intelligence summaries. Known positions and strengths of U-boat patrols, likely air interdiction and known movements of surface ships. Allied force dispositions including minefields were also gone through as an essential item for, as will become apparent later, the number of self-inflicted casualties was high.

Next to rise and address the conference was the commodore. Next to the escort commander, his was the key appointment in the convoy. He was in overall command and the compliance of independently minded masters to his instructions depended heavily on his ability to impress his personality on them and for them to have confidence in him and his judgement whilst at sea. To assist him in this task, the commodore had a small staff comprising a yeoman of signals, a leading signalman, three signal ratings and a chief petty officer telegraphist. The latter was usually a retired Royal Naval man, but the bulk of the signallers were 'Hostilities only'.

Commodores for ocean-going convoys were usually ex-Royal Naval captains or admirals, all volunteers from the retired list. Before the outbreak of war they had been identified and listed for this very task. Each one had been contacted asking if they were prepared to take on the task and there was an undoubted note of enthusiasm in the majority of replies[27]. A high sense of duty and a liking for responsibility, that found expression in treading a deck again must have driven their eagerness to get going. Gilbert Stevenson, a retired vice admiral telegraphed his reply as follows: 'YES YES YES HOPE LACK OF UNIFORM NO OBSTACLE'. He followed this up with a letter:

> Please inform Their Lordships that I am willing and ready to serve in any capacity they may desire. I have sent two monkey jackets and watch coat to Gieves Portsmouth and await instructions as to alterations of rank.

He of course remained their obedient servant.

Others were more measured in their replies but nonetheless keen. Another retired admiral wrote that he would be greatly honoured and happy to be employed as commodore of convoy and that he was prepared to take up such duties immediately in an emergency. He then went into some detail on the state of his health, assuring Their Lordships that he had recently had his teeth overhauled by a Harley Street dentist who declared them to be exceptionally good, he had been examined by a first-rate Winchester doctor who had informed him that he was a strong healthy man; and his eyesight was also first class. He ended: 'It is quite clear that I am physically fit for sea service.' One wonders if his medical self-certification was accepted or if he had to present himself before an Admiralty medical board before he was appointed. Occasionally the invitation was turned down, and with apparent good reason bearing in mind that those approached were around sixty years of age. One wrote:

'I regret I do not feel justified in accepting an appointment which calls for mental and physical qualities greater than I possess. The last war showed clearly, that with very few exceptions, men of my age failed to act with sufficient speed in emergencies, nor had they the requisite power of endurance... It is perhaps worth recalling that I and my contemporaries are two years older than was Lord Jellico at the outbreak of the last war'. Nevertheless, he ended: 'Should it be possible to make use of my services in a subordinate capacity in connection with the defence of Cromarty or Invergordon I should be glad to offer them. My local knowledge might be of use.'[28]

Those who volunteered and were accepted were appointed Commodores 2nd Class in the Royal Naval Reserve. They retained the right to revert to non-active service at any time, whilst the Admiralty retained the right to retire a commodore from service. Following a short course of instruction at the Admiralty they awaited their convoy appointments. Without doubt, these were men with vast experience and skill and they were held in high regard and listened to intently during the convoy conference.

From the Commodore's perspective the task of looking after 50 or 60 or more ships is one of unceasing vigilance. The Commodore who takes off his clothes after the first night at sea is rare. There are times when the hours are studded with signals received and given, signals by Aldis lamp to and from the naval escort and to ships in convoy; signals by documents coming over by rocket fired from the naval escort. Decisions must be made whether to take evasive action and of what sort; and sometimes the hardest decision of all must be reached— whether or not to leave behind a straggler. The Commodore's main problems lay in the heterogeneous nature of the convoy. This diversified assembly of ships new and old, oil-burning and coal-burning; of ships' masters with varying degrees of skill and experience, each with his own idiosyncrasies; masters of several nationalities, whose readiness to follow or ability to interpret instructions was open to question, comprised the commodore's greatest challenge. Among the ships in convoy there will always be those masters with two or three knots 'up their sleeve' who are tempted, in a crisis, to make use of them. Technically, a master is responsible for his own navigation and if he decided to leave a convoy could do so. However, such action was most rare. The Commodore's decisions, based on wisdom and experience, are usually accepted, and gladly. 'In ice you're better loaded than light, for your Achilles' heel is the rudder and propellers – loaded, they're below the ice and safe from damage; light, they may strike it.'

A convoy's good station-keeping depends largely on the Commodore's ship keeping her revolutions steady. In his part of the briefing he would reiterate the need for individual ships to keep closed up. Because of the need to maintain radio silence, communications from the Commodore would be made using signals flags and crew members became adept at reading them. Austin Byrne recalls one such incident on the SS *Induna* during the passage of PQ13:

> I remember one day the Commodore put something up and so I picked the glasses up and turned to the mate and said 'Keep closed up.' What I didn't realise was that the Skipper was at the side of the mate, and the mate said, 'What did you say, gunner?' I said, 'Keep closed up. That's what it says.' and the skipper burst out laughing. He said 'At least we're teaching you boy.' I said, 'I'm sorry sir.' 'No, that's what you're here for. Keep a good lookout and help.'

But during the dark winter months flag signalling was ruled out and greater use was made of the Aldis lamp. However, this was slow and open to faulty transmission or reception. Sound signalling was also considered but could not be used for signalling more complex orders such as a change of route. One solution to this particular problem was for all ships in the convoy to keep a constant radio watch and for any changes of route to be transmitted direct from the Admiralty. Pre-planned route changes, however, could be made by means of sealed orders that were to be opened by ship's masters at a certain point in the voyage, or on receipt of a signal.[29]

Losses often resulted from ships straggling, sometimes by only half a mile astern. Bad weather and poor visibility also militated against good station-keeping. With visibility falling and low navigation lights, the tendency for those at the helm of each merchant ship was to err on the side of caution. For ships in the outboard columns this meant a gradual drift out of position. Intermittent sightings of other vessels would then give a false impression for the next columns inboard and gradually the convoy dispersed. Ships which could not keep course at all because of steering or loading problems further exacerbated the situation. Each ship handles differently in bad weather depending on its load, draught, speed and aspect presented to the prevailing wind. Therefore, each ship has an optimum speed and course to weather a storm. Without the commodore's command to override such considerations each master could take action to reduce damage to his ship, ultimately resulting in the convoy becoming scattered. Although a commodore would endeavour to nurse stragglers as much as possible there comes a time when the safety of the entire convoy takes precedence; and that safety lies in speed. Having made this point he would then cover a number of contingencies such as action on meeting bad weather, especially fog. Commodores would often exercise convoys on sound signals in clear weather to get ships accustomed to keeping station by that means. Procedures on encountering ice and procedures for avoiding U-boats would be covered, as well as switching time zones as the convoy proceeds eastward or westward. The need for good blackout discipline whilst steaming at night would also be emphasised as what to do if a ship is seen inadvertently showing a light. Finally, he would cover the circumstances in which radio silence may be broken. This was an essential point, for the direction of stray transmissions could be picked up by a number of enemy listeners and a ship/convoy's position easily triangulated. Once under attack, radio silence became unnecessary. However, sometimes ships might detect a 'sitter', a U-boat intent on observing the convoy in preparation for an attack or busily mustering other boats for an ambush. In such circumstances, simple and effective procedures were required for passing the information to the escort where the need for speed of action and hence transmission had to be balanced against compromising security.

The DEMS Officer is next to come forward and address the conference, reminding masters how to achieve the best from their largely obsolete armaments, no doubt covering the use of low-angle guns against torpedo or other bombers and their 4-inch gun against submarines on the surface. He brings them up to date on lessons learnt from recent engagements. How to use their guns as pointers against suspected U-boat periscopes to help the escort locate them and similarly the use of tracer at night. He goes over again the orders for using illuminating flares, commonly called 'Snowflake'; at night as they can aid an enemy attacker as well as illuminating him. Test firing of guns is also covered as well as the need to conserve ammunition. This was a particular necessity on Russian convoys where, due to the proximity of German airfields in Norway and Finland, ships at sea and in harbour in Murmansk were subject to especially high volumes of air attack and ships would run out of ammunition.

An RAF flight lieutenant is next up to explain the air picture, such as it is. He would remind masters and ships' captains that that if they did not always see Coastal Command aircraft, it did not mean they weren't there. He would emphasise the danger of making too much smoke, that it can be seen by aircraft 50 miles distant, and that air crews have reported that the smallest chink of light in the dark can be spotted at that distance too. Finally, he urges that all gunners and observers become experts in aircraft recognition to avoid 'home goals', especially at night when approaching aircraft should not be engaged unless the ships' crews are absolutely certain it is an enemy.

The next briefer eases the tension by suggesting that ships' officers and men wearing dentures should keep them in their mouths or handy in their pockets because men in open boats have suffered much from having left them behind. No doubt good advice, bearing in mind the consistency of emergency rations stowed on rafts and in lifeboats. He is the master of the rescue ship, a small ship that sails at the rear of the convoy and is equipped with spare accommodation for up to 150 survivors, a sick bay and operating theatre complete with a doctor and compliment of medical staff. What he says is to the point. 'When a ship is torpedoed, we must have some indication where it is, and which ship it is. If it is possible, and I know sometimes it isn't, get a rocket or a wireless message away.' He then asks them to ensure that all lifejackets are checked and have their lights and whistles attached and are in good order. He explains that the whistle is essential, because if it is blown continuously the rescue ship can get a direction. He also reminds masters that coloured sails in the lifeboats are important too, because it is almost impossible to see a grey boat on a grey sea. 'If you've abandoned ship then stay around it or the wreckage no matter how long,' he urges. 'If we have to steam over hundreds of square miles looking for you it takes a long time but wreckage helps us to find the place.' He goes on: 'If men on rafts or in boats can't help themselves when they get to our ship, my men will come over the side on to the rafts and boats to help you. They go over with a bowline already in a noose and before you know what is happening you will be aboard.' He then explains two further points: first that his ship has scramble-nets attached to booms which are thrust out, nets which prevent men from drifting past, and to which they can cling; and second, that ships' boats approaching his vessel should lower their masts. He ends reassuringly, 'Believe me, you won't be left.'

Finally, the Senior Officer commanding the escort gives his brief, emphasising again the dangers of straggling and many of the other points of convoy procedure and discipline already covered.

This brings the conference to a close. The RN chairman requests them to hand in their confidential papers before leaving the meeting (they will be returned before sailing), informs them the times of boats to take them back to their ships, and concludes: 'That's all gentlemen. I hope you'll have a successful and pleasant journey'.

It is against this background that we now return to the *Capira,* her onward passage to Iceland, and the context of the Arctic convoys.

# 4 HALIFAX TO HVALFJÖRÐUR

## (29 MARCH – 14 APRIL 1942)

Lo from our loitering ship a new land at last to be seen;
Toothed rocks down the side of the firth on the east guard a weary
  wide lea,
And black slope the hillsides above, striped adown with their desolate
  green:
And a peak rises up on the west from the meeting of cloud and of sea,
Foursquare from base unto point like the building of Gods that have
  been,
The last of that waste of the mountains all cloud-wreathed and snow-
  flecked and grey,
And bright with the dawn that began just now at the ending of day.

From *Iceland First Seen* by William Morris

Long before Europeans established a foothold in Nova Scotia, the Mi'Kmaq Indians fished its lakes and long coastline. They would have been familiar with the wide sweep of Bedford Basin that has since become the area's main harbour, and major reason for founding the town of Halifax. Halifax itself has had a long acquaintance with military and naval history, going back as far as 1749 when the British established the city as a counterbalance to the French presence in Nova Scotia. The British continued to use the city and its harbour as a military base throughout the eighteenth century and well into the nineteenth. Its geographical location and proximity to the New England states made it an ideal base in support of activities during the American Revolution and later, in the War of 1812. Well into the twentieth century, Halifax and the neighbouring port of Sydney remained strategic facilities but this time in support of wars on the other side of the Atlantic. For during both world wars, these ports became the major staging areas for convoys proceeding directly to the United Kingdom or Iceland where, in the latter case, they formed up with ships coming from Scotland before venturing into the icy waters of the Barents Sea, en-route to the north Russian ports of Archangel and Murmansk.

On 29 March, *Capira* picked up the pilot at the entrance to Bedford Basin, proceeded through the anti-submarine nets and anchored in the harbour. The following day she sailed in company with 50 other ships in convoy SC77 bound for Iceland and thence to Russia. Being one of the last ships to leave the Basin in the late afternoon, she took her place near the rear of the convoy in position #75. One eyewitness remarked that her decks were loaded with tanks, greenish grey with some bright blue, the greatest number he had ever seen on a freighter.[1] Several other ships in SC77 also had deck cargoes of tanks and crated aircraft bound for Russia. However, it was not just crated armaments that were being shipped to support the Soviet forces. A typical cargo manifest of this time is given at Appendix I and displays the vast array of materiel necessary for the conduct of war and the logistical support essential for its sustainability. Of the 51 merchantmen in the convoy, only 34 were proceeding to the UK, the remaining 17, including *Capira*, were to sail to Iceland and await convoy PQ15 to Murmansk. SC77 did not sail out directly into the North Atlantic but took the safer passage through the Belle Isle Strait between the Labrador coast and Newfoundland. At a convoy speed of about 6 knots [11km/hr] the passage to Iceland took over two weeks, giving the US Navy Armed Guard ample time to slip into their routine of keeping an anti-submarine watch at all times with an extra watch on the 4-inch deck gun at sunrise and sunset, the men standing four on and eight off.[2]

For obvious reasons, the various meeting points for escorts remained under wraps by the Admiralty until the convoy was at sea. In this particular case, the Iceland Ocean Meeting Point, or ICOMP as it was better known, was signalled to the Mid Ocean escort commander by C-in-C Western Approaches on 4 April. For the first part of the passage, SC77 was given a local escort of a British destroyer and four Canadian corvettes.[3] The Mid Ocean Escort took over on 4 April. This was an all-Canadian force led by HMCS *Assiniboine*, a River Class destroyer and five Flower Class corvettes.[4] HMCS *Assiniboine* had joined SC77 on the evening of 3 April. She was commanded by Lieutenant J.H. Stubbs RCN, and was immediately tasked to form a striking force 20 miles ahead of the convoy. On the evening of the following day, 4 April, *Assiniboine* took over from HMS *Walker* as Ocean Escort. Five days later, USSs *Leary* and *Decatur* joined the convoy and took station 4 miles astern to await the arrival of USSs *Schenck* and *Badger*. The convoy made very bad time and on the 9 April a gale blew up and lasted through until the afternoon of the following day. There was also fog, and inevitably the convoy became badly scattered. Visibility then improved and the escorts set about rounding up the convoy, but according to the escort report five ships remained unaccounted for,[5] emphasising how difficult command and control had become under such conditions.

Just after midday on 10 April, tension in the convoy rose dramatically as SS *Empire Franklin* signalled that she had sighted a submarine. HMCS *Amhurst* was ordered to investigate but under the prevailing weather conditions she failed to make contact with the *Empire Franklin* or make any submarine contacts. It later transpired that the master of the *Empire Franklin* thought he had sighted a periscope close to the ship about 1½m above the surface. It was subsequently established that HMCS *Assiniboine* had lost her starboard lower boom in the gale, and as it would float upright in the water it was assumed that this was what the *Empire Franklin's* master had mistaken for a periscope; amply demonstrating how easy it was for errors to occur under conditions of poor visibility, heightened tension and pressure. The false sighting was corroborated later by Admiralty intelligence, reassuring the convoy commodore and escort that no U-boats were thought to be in the area at that time. An examination of the German U-boat war diary or *Kreigtagesbuch* (KTB) also confirms the fact. About midday on 11 April, USSs *Schenck*, *Badger* and *Decatur* met the convoy at the ICOMP and proceeded with their charges, including the *Capira* and 14 other merchantmen to Iceland. Early on 14 April, USS *Schenck* had a contact off Iceland and mounted an attack that eventually proved to be another false alarm. Notwithstanding these minor incidents, this element of SC77 arrived safely off Reykjavik on the evening of 14 April and anchored in Hvalfjörður to await the arrival the following day of the 17 ships of convoy PQ15 that had set out from Oban on 10 April[6].

Hvalfjörður is the Icelandic for 'Whale-Fjord', and takes its name from the large number of whales that were located and hunted there during the whaling heydays. At about 30km long and 5km wide, it was exposed but ideal for forming up convoys before they put to sea. Consequently, the British and Americans established a naval facility there and one of the piers built by the United States Navy remained in use until commercial whaling was shut down in the 1980s; nevertheless, small scale whaling still takes place there today. Hvalfjörður is some way from Reykjavik and a road tunnel now runs under the narrow entrance, giving easy access to its farther shore. Today it remains a lonely place, with only the odd dwelling or smallholding dotted around its perimeter and in many respects has remained as it was in 1942. Even the prefabricated huts built by British and US soldiers still serve their purpose for those who carry out their living there. Back then Olly Lindsay, an Apprentice on the SS *Botavon*, which was also awaiting the arrival of PQ15, was taken by the stark beauty of the scene and wrote that:

> The Icelandic mountains with their mantle of snow looked very picturesque in the sunshine but the wind blowing off them was perishing. After darkness fell there were plenty of lights in the city, the headlights of cars could be seen, we were surprised at the lack of a blackout. No shore leave was allowed, apparently the Icelandic people were not very friendly disposed to the occupying forces.[7]

One did not have to look far for the source of the Icelander's apparent unfriendliness. On 10 May 1940, following unsuccessful attempts to persuade the Icelandic government to join the Allies in the fight against Hitler, a small force of British and Canadian troops violated Icelandic neutrality and occupied the country. This operation, codenamed 'Fork', was aimed at forestalling a German invasion and the dire consequence for Atlantic convoys that would follow had the *Kreigsmarine* established a base there for its ships and U-boats. As it later transpired, the Germans had planned such an operation but had abandoned it by the time of the British occupation. So, for the rest of the war the Allies maintained its presence on the island and built up a substantial infrastructure that proved to be vital to the staging and protection of convoys on route to Russia.

From his Enlightenment perspective, Carl von Clausewitz, the Nineteenth Century German military theorist and author of *On War*, would probably have applauded the occupation of Iceland under such circumstances. Although he could not have anticipated the global scale of mid-Twentieth Century warfare, he would have fully appreciated the dilemma facing Churchill and his admirals at that time, when neither the USA or the Soviet Union were actively engaged in direct hostilities with Germany. His dictum, that war is the continuation of political intercourse with the intermixing of other means, neatly encapsulates Britain's actions then and a year or so later when Hitler invaded Russia. Great Britain's successful continuation of 'political intercourse' with Germany relied on keeping Russia in the war whilst the industrial power house of the USA was mobilized onto a war footing. The occupation of Iceland proved to be an unforeseen strategic benefit in pursuing this policy.

Thus, following the launch of Operation Barbarossa on 22 June 1941, and the subsequent early defeats suffered by the Soviet Forces, Stalin's requests for US and British military aid did not go unheeded; though the two camps were ideologically at odds with each other. Roosevelt and Churchill met in early August 1941 and gave assurances of industrial and military aid to the Soviet leader. The preceding month, Churchill had already reached the conclusion that the Soviets must be helped and he had directed the First Sea Lord, Admiral of the Fleet Sir Dudley Pound, and Commander-in-Chief Home Fleet, Admiral Sir Jack Tovey, to begin planning a northern convoy system to Russia through Archangel on the White Sea and Murmansk on the Kola Inlet. With Iceland already in Allied hands, one potential problem had already been resolved – but many more presented themselves.

Pound and Tovey were thoroughly professional sailors, who now found themselves in the unenviable position of having to follow orders that made little tactical sense but were born out of a politico-strategic necessity. Both were fighting sailors, ever-ready in the spirit of Nelson's last signal to close with the enemy. In fact Tovey had done just that in May, when he had led the force that sank the *Bismark* and was subsequently appointed KBE for his outstanding leadership. Pound had commanded HMS *Colossus* at Jutland, sinking two German Cruisers and fending off two destroyers whilst under fire. Tovey had also won a DSO for the persistent and determined manner in which he had attacked the enemy ships during the same battle when commanding HMS *Onslow*. However, both were also realists, well aware of the stress that the navy was already under protecting the United Kingdom's strategic life line across the Atlantic. They were not minded to further endanger this endeavour by running another, perhaps even more dangerous, gauntlet during the perpetual daylight of an Arctic summer or an Arctic winter, when the choice of sea lanes was limited and where opportunities for concentrating U-boats were more frequent and air attack from land-based *Luftwaffe* squadrons in northern Norway more likely.

But by this time, Pound was not in the best of health and it is said that Churchill found him easy to dominate. Such a judgment, however, seems somewhat at odds with Pound's undoubted reputation as the architect of victory during the Battle of the Atlantic, where strident determination was the order of the day. Tovey was also somewhat unbending when the situation demanded. During the inter-war years he had been reported on by his immediate superior as '…sharing one characteristic with me. In myself I call it tenacity of purpose; in Captain Tovey I can only describe it as sheer bloody obstinacy'. A well-regarded officer, Tovey's preference was to lead from the front. As C-in-C Home Fleet he was very much a sea-going admiral, ever-ready to share the privations of those whom he commanded.

However, Tovey was no gung-ho leader and he was convinced that it was wrong to try to run the Russian convoys from Iceland during the long daylight hours of summer, particularly given the Allies lack of long-range air cover at that time. Tovey thought that the concept was fundamentally unsound and said so. This brought him into conflict with Churchill, who considered him obstructionist. Although they did not always see eye-to-eye, Dudley Pound agreed with Tovey and acknowledged that the establishment of regular convoys to Russia via this route using Iceland as a staging post would be the most hazardous of operations especially in summer. Nevertheless, they were required to carry out Churchill's bidding in pursuit of the politico-strategic objective. Fearing a Soviet accommodation with Hitler in exchange for Ukrainian territory and the potential consequences for the UK, Churchill was clear in his judgement that Russia must be kept in the war and therefore insisted that the Arctic convoys go ahead.

And so the first Russian convoy, code-named 'Dervish', arrived in Archangel at the end of August 1941, and was followed by the PQ series in October, at the rate of two convoys per month. By the end of 1941, the system was well-established and Churchill wrote encouragingly to Stalin in March that he had '…given express directions that the supplies promised by us shall not in any way be interrupted or delayed. The continuing progress of the Russian armies and the known terrible losses of the enemy are naturally our sources of greatest encouragement in this trying period.'[8]

Given that only two vessels had been sunk and around 50 lives lost on the Russian run at the time of Churchill's letter, this was not an unreasonable position to take. However, from the end of March, German attacks began to intensify and the rate of sinkings increased significantly. By the time PQ15 sailed at the end of April, a further 14 merchantmen had gone to the bottom of the Barents Sea, with the loss of over 200 lives and countless tons of war materiel proving how prescient Tovey had been in his tactical assessment.

But there remains a tragic irony in all of this. In spite of Tovey's prescience concerning allied loss of life and shipping due to enemy action, the fact remains that decisions taken by the British Admiralty and commanders on the spot led to two disasters of our own making as convoys PQ17 and QP13 crossed in the Barents Sea. These tragedies were part of what Clauswitz termed the 'friction' borne of the circumstances inherent in war. The case of QP13, the returning convoy in which the *Capira* sailed will be explored later. But first let us examine Tovey's other major concern, the lack of effective air cover.

# 5 THE 'BATTLE FOR THE AIR'

'The bomber will always get through'

Stanley Baldwin *A Fear for the Future*, 1932

The debate over the deployment of air power in support of naval operations that took place between October 1940 and April 1942 serves to illustrate the very real tension consequent upon the competing strategic and tactical imperatives that applied at that time. The debate covered the period when *Capira* sailed for Murmansk in PQ15, when the attrition of merchant shipping in the North Atlantic and the Barents Sea was about to become critical.

The source of that tension lay in the advocacy of strategic bombing as a means of knocking Germany out of the war. This would be achieved, it was thought, through the destruction of industry and infrastructure and the consequent deleterious effect on the will of the German population to continue the fight. Since the means to prosecute such a strategy had not been available previously, it had remained largely an article of faith; influenced in large measure by post-First World War strategic thinkers such as the Italian, Douhet. However, Douhet's analysis was based on very little evidence of the effect of strategic bombing in the First World War. Although some attacks had been made on German industry, (ironically by the Naval Air Service) and German zeppelins had indiscriminately bombed the British mainland with some loss of civilian lives, no concrete conclusions could be drawn from these experiences.

However, the bombing and partial destruction of Guernica by the German Condor Legion during the Spanish Civil War kept the debate alive, and also raised the spectre of the possibility of mass gas attacks from the air on civilian populations. It is therefore understandable how the concept of strategic bombing and faith in its ability to win wars became ingrained in the psyche of some politicians and their service acolytes. And so, after the fall of France, strategic bombing was undertaken with the few bombing assets then available. Not that there was any assumption that it would bring an immediate end to the war, but it was the only means available at that time of taking large scale offensive action against Germany. And in the early part of the war, its only positive effect was to raise the morale of the British population in the knowledge that they were somehow striking back. Quite naturally, this policy found great favour with Churchill, and in spite of his acknowledged fear of the devastating effect that a U-boat blockade of the Atlantic would have on the country's ability to continue the war, he was keen to pursue it although it meant prioritising the provision of aircraft for Bomber Command over those for convoy protection.

Writing to Chief of the Air Staff (CAS), Sir Charles Portal, in October 1940, Churchill was adamant that the policy of creating the largest possible bombing force and using it to impair the enemy's morale would not change. Nevertheless, he added a note of caution:

> Even if all the towns of Germany were rendered largely uninhabitable, it does not follow that the military control would be weakened, or even that war industry could not be carried on... The Air Staff would make a mistake to put their claim too high... The only plan is to persevere.[1]

Having advocated bombing Germany and Italy to the greatest extent possible the means to achieve such an objective was not at hand by the end of 1940. Churchill wrote to his Air Minister 'I am deeply concerned at the stagnant condition of our bomber force... I consider the rapid expansion of the bomber force one of the greatest military objectives now before us.'[2] Such strong direction, from a leader rapidly growing in confidence following the Battle of Britain, could not be disregarded. Nevertheless, the fact remained that the successful outcome of the Battle of the Atlantic and the need to support the Soviet Union through the Arctic convoys could not be achieved without sufficient and appropriate air assets being procured or, if so needed, current assets redeployed against the myriad threats that the convoys were exposed to.

But, given Churchill's stance, it is not surprising that even a singular request such as that by C-in-C Costal Command, Sir Philip Joubert de la Ferté, in early 1941 to bomb the U-boat bases on the French Coast, was turned down by the Air Ministry. Joubert was not one to be deterred, however, even though he lacked the Prime Minister's support, and persisted in pressing his case. Later that year, on 3 March, with the full support of Dudley Pound, the First Sea Lord, he put a paper before the War Cabinet Defence Committee calling into question the strategy of bombing Germany whilst pointing out the truly strategic nature of the war at sea. In doing so, he had put his finger on the central issue in contention between the Naval and Air staffs.

The problem faced by the Air Ministry was that there was little evidence to validate the strategic bombers' claims for their strategy. However, this did not deter the air staff, whose reports to the War Cabinet were invariably upbeat. For example, the Air Situation Report for the week of 30 August 1941 majored on the strategic campaign against German industry and communications (major attacks on German cities were not being carried out at this point in the war). In spite of the comparatively short time that the offensive had been going on, plus the unusually unfavourable weather conditions experienced by the attackers, staffs still maintained that 'reliable' reports arriving in increasing numbers indicated that the effect of the campaign was being felt. Later analysis showed this not to be the case. The report also couched (it could be said justifiably) all other air activity in terms of its contribution to the main objective:

> A complement to our offensive against land communications is provided by attacks on ports and by those of our light bombers on shipping; the considerable measure of success achieved has undoubtedly increased the pressure on Germany's inland communication system, and so enhanced the value of our main offensive... the attack of targets likely to influence the Battle of the Atlantic is undertaken when necessary and attacks on other objectives in Germany are carried out as tactical and other considerations dictate.

The report also concluded that a valuable factor in the dislocation of communications in Germany was the interference with supplies for the Eastern Front, and that the strategic offensive was, therefore, an important contribution to Russian resistance[3].

The complete lack of effectiveness of so-called precision bombing against German industry and infrastructure became apparent following the unfortunately titled Butt Report delivered in August 1941[4]. David Bensusan-Butt was a civil servant tasked by Lord Cherwell, the cabinet's chief scientific advisor, with reporting on the effectiveness of Bomber Command's night bombing activities. Based on 650 photographs taken by attacking aircraft between 2 and 25 June 1941, and relating to 28 targets over 48 nights on 100 separate raids, he concluded that less than a third of those aircraft that dropped their bombs got within 5 miles of their targets. This figure was much lower for specific raids over the German industrial heartland, where natural obfuscation and defensive measures were much more in evidence. In short, precision bombing was not having much effect on the German economy, which at this stage in the war remained largely on a pre-war footing but was continuing to supply Germany's domestic as well as war requirements. As part of the response to the Butt Report, Harris was appointed C-in-C Bomber Command in February 1942.

The situation on the strategic bombing of Germany had not changed appreciably eight months later when two assessments dealing with it were produced. The first was a short note to Dudley Pound from the Director Naval Intelligence (DNI) and the second a lengthy report from the Joint Intelligence Committee (JIC).

The note[5] dated 8 April, written by Rear Admiral John Godfrey, DNI, gave his views on the use of the bomber force in light of the JIC Report. It was classified MOST SECRET and began: 'The correct use of the bomber force to give maximum aid to Russia during the summer is the most urgent question of our war strategy today.' It contrasted the two, then prevailing, views that the bomber force should continue to be used primarily for night bombing of Germany versus being partly diverted to other operations such as anti-U-boat, anti-shipping and land forces support. Night bombing was perceived as the only offensive action that could be taken against Germany at that time. Godfrey asserted that 'all serious estimates of the effect... of our campaign to date, show that it has been extremely small, and hitherto has been of negligible assistance to Russia.' He went on: 'What it can hope to achieve in the future must be to some extent a matter of speculation, but careful weighing of all the factors involved make it extremely unlikely that anything decisive will be achieved.'

He also cited the British experience of the Blitz in refuting the notion that bombing alone could lead to a decisive result. In dismissing the argument that night bombing of Germany should continue, Godfrey acknowledged the factors that had led to it being adopted almost as an article of faith by the cabinet and RAF. These, in the main, he believed to be psychologically-based resulting from the perceived impotence in hitting back at Germany between the fall of France and Germany's invasion of Russia. The reasons that led the RAF to over-egg the effect of strategic bombing may have also been a result of inter-service rivalry, in which the RAF saw itself as 'the decisive service, leaving the Navy with the defensive role of guarding our communications, and the Army with that of occupying the country of an enemy, already defeated from the air.' Godfrey cautioned against reinforcing failure in the strategic air campaign against Germany, as it could lead to the complete failure to render important aid to Russia; not to mention serious embitterment between the armed services and, perhaps, dismemberment of the Air Force itself. This would, of course, be disastrous and it was therefore in the interests of all, not least the RAF, to rethink the strategy. However, he acknowledged that it was '…difficult to change the habits of thought of years in a few weeks.' He concluded: 'The Air Force can contribute vitally… to the winning of the anti-U-boat campaign and by doing so, can make many other kinds of offensive action against the enemy possible which are now impossible owing to the prospect of a shipping shortage.'

The JIC paper on the effect of bombing policy, with special reference to assistance to Russia during the summer months[6] was considered by Dudley Pound and his fellow chiefs of staff two days later, on 10 April. The report was lengthy but inconclusive, due to a lack of good intelligence on the effect British raids were having on German industrial capacity and morale. The tentative conclusions that it arrived at were therefore heavily caveated. The issue of assistance to Russia was cast in terms of the effect that strategic bombing of Germany may have on forcing a diversion of German fighter and air defence effort from its eastern front to protect the Reich. By this time the programme of Arctic convoys was well under way; however, air cover for the close protection of the Russian convoys was not considered. Furthermore, strikes against German shipping, port facilities, shipyards and other targets affecting the Battle of the Atlantic covered in the report were considered a diversion from the main strategic effort. Therefore, in the absence of definitive intelligence, the report recommended that an independent enquiry be undertaken to relate the lessons learnt from the German blitz on Great Britain (on which there was considerable information) to future attacks on Germany.

Before the JIC Report was taken by the Chiefs of Staff (CsOS) that morning, they considered the first item on the agenda; convoys to Russia. Dudley Pound opened the debate by casting doubt on the strategic benefit of the convoys, especially in the face of the scale of air opposition likely to be encountered. However if the supplies were essential, then every effort would be made to deliver them. Alan Brooke, Chief of the Imperial General Staff (CIGS), concurred and said that they were taking a great military risk when they themselves were in urgent need of the same equipment. It was agreed that they would represent their views to the War Cabinet. On the subject of the JIC Report, Alan Brooke considered that it did not bring out what could be achieved by bombing, whilst Portal supported the recommendation and the contention that aerial bombing was of assistance to the Russians. Reference was then made to a mathematical assessment by Lord Cherwell of the effect of bombing civilian targets in large urban areas and the concomitant effect on morale[7]. Written at the end of March, it concluded: 'There seems little doubt that this (i.e. the mass bombing of German cities) would break the spirit of the people.' According to the minutes, Dudley Pound did not offer a view on the JIC report; however, the Committee pointed out that the object of the assessment of the effects of aerial bombing was to see if British bombers could be employed more effectively. The Committee then instructed the secretary to submit a minute to Churchill in light of their discussion.

In light of subsequent events, there seems little doubt that the Cherwell Memorandum, supported by the failure of precision bombing detailed in the Butt Report, only served to strengthen the Prime Minister's resolve to employ area bombing against German cities as a way of hitting back at the enemy more effectively. It is strange, especially following DNI's comments on the JIC Report, that there is no record in the minutes of the meeting of Dudley Pound expressing a view or putting forward any arguments for the redeployment of aircraft for the protection of convoys, especially those to Russia. Quite apart from the shipping losses being sustained in the Atlantic, he was acutely aware of and concerned about the threat to Russian convoys; although losses had been relatively light up until then, with 9 merchantmen sunk, a further 48 were to go to the bottom going to and coming from Russia during the following three months. Twenty-eight of those sinkings during this period were due to attacks by German aircraft and 20 due to U-boats. Without suitable accompanying platforms upon which to mount effective fighter cover in the convoy, there was little that could be done to counter the direct threat from German torpedo and dive bombers. However, the use of long-range bombers for reconnaissance and the suppression of U-boat activity, as well as the interdiction of German airfields in northern Norway during the passage of Arctic convoys, would have no doubt gone some way to reducing casualties. It could be that Dudley Pound was persisting in the hope that the Arctic convoys would be abandoned if Stalin could be persuaded that the difficulties and risks were too great to justify the benefit to Russia; a view he expressed at the CsOS meeting. However, even this was secondary to the more strategic issue of the RAF playing a far more prominent role in the protection of our own lines of communication.

Returning specifically to the protection of Arctic convoys there was also the possibility that the Russian air force could play a more active role; it had been hoped that the lack of air cover for the Russian convoys would be compensated in part by Soviet Naval and Air support especially as they approached their destinations.

But this had not materialised, a fact that was also borne out by the Senior British Naval Officer (SBNO) based in Murmansk, in some notes he penned following his relief.[8] In them, Rear Admiral Bevan reiterated his belief that Soviet long-range fighters could not be made available in sufficient numbers to provide adequate or reliable convoy escorts. The reasons for this, however, were not to do with a lack of willingness or competence on the part of the Soviets, but a lack of capacity. The needs of the Soviet Army were predominant and he concluded that, difficult as it may be, the provision of British fighter escorts was an essential part of the convoy system to North Russia – just as much as that of surface escorts.

Rear Admiral Commanding First Cruiser Squadron, Fredrick

Dalrymple-Hamilton, was of the same view, as far as the covering force was concerned. He wrote to Tovey in February 1942,[9] voicing his concern over the lack of air cover, arguing that the Germans would attempt to emulate the recent Japanese attacks on HMS *Repulse* and *Prince of Wales*. Both ships had been sunk by shore-based aircraft 400 miles from the scene of action. He also discounted any assistance provided by the Americans, who were just about to augment the Home Fleet, because they would take some time to get up to speed; in any case, their interests at that time lay chiefly in the Pacific. Furthermore, Dalrymple-Hamilton pointed to the fact that the Germans now had a window of opportunity to severely disrupt Russian convoys before the arrival of the spring claimed aircraft for a renewed offensive in Russia. His suggested solution was to continue to deploy the Covering Force, comprising a fleet carrier and heavy cruisers, escorted by destroyers and other warships, between Scotland and Iceland and to ensure that the aircraft carriers (he wanted more than one) were equipped with the latest Sea Hurricane fighters. On the assumption that the convoys were of real value to Russia he also opined that she: 'should help us to take Northern Norway now and make aerodromes to the southward as far as, and including Bodo, unusable by the Germans.'

Although such a proposition was out of the question at that time, it was a view often expressed by officers of the Russian Northern Fleet to the SBNO. They believed that the only means of securing comparative safety for the north Russian convoys was the occupation of Northern Norway by British ground and air forces; the aim being to obtain local air superiority, and deprive the enemy of submarine bases and airfields. Bevan was quick to point out the conditions required for attaining and sustaining such an expedition. Local air superiority was a *sine qua non,* as was abundant shipping; not only to transport the troops required but to keep them sustained thereafter. Bevan enquired of the Soviet C-in-C Northern Fleet, Vice Admiral Golovko, if the Soviet Government could undertake to supply say 10,000 men and their equipment. Quite naturally, Golovko would not commit himself confirming Bevan's undoubted view that the Russians could not support such an undertaking with any reliability.

The use of air assets for the bombing campaign on Germany also began to be debated outside the upper echelons of the Cabinet and Chiefs of

Staff Committees, and it became a shared concern throughout the Navy. This is evidenced by another Dalrymple-Hamilton letter, this time to his mother whom he addressed as 'My dear old mum'. On 11 April 1942 he wrote:

> The war is looking extremely black at the moment and will continue to do so I am afraid for some time to come. As you know, I have always maintained that the lack of a proper Naval Air Service was the greatest handicap we fought under. It has now become an urgent requirement if we are going to win the war. It makes me mad to see the Air strength of the country being devoted to killing a few women and children in Germany, whilst our fleet and Empire are being lost to the Japanese daily. There is no mystery about the Japanese succession of victories, they are <u>entirely</u> due to sea power brought up to date by making use of the aeroplane, which is the new weapon at sea exactly similar in principle to any other new weapon in the past, such as the submarine.

In that respect he was spot on, but he took the argument one step further and continued:

> To say that the air has done away with Battleships is absolute & uneducated nonsense, it has done away with <u>our</u> battleships because we have been starved of fighter protection; but it has not done away with the Japanese battleships because they have taken the elementary precaution to provide themselves with a trained well-equipped Naval Air Service.

One can only speculate on the extent to which such strategic musings impacted his mother. However, the reality was that the aircraft had, in effect, become a long-range gun capable of hitting capital ships above and submarines diving below the surface at distances far greater than any deck-mounted ordinance then in service could reach. It had made the battleship obsolete, as the Battle of Midway about to be fought in the Pacific was to demonstrate so conclusively.

Unbeknownst to Dalrymple-Hamilton, Tovey, C-in-C Home Fleet, was also making an impassioned and hard-hitting bid for more air assets to be deployed in defence of, among other maritime assets, Arctic convoys.[10] In his despatch covering the period 1 April to 30 June 1942, he reported on the grave shortage of aircraft for cooperation at sea and the fact that he had raised the matter at the C-in-C's meeting at the Admiralty on 1 June to little effect. He reiterated that the whole strategy of the war was governed by sea communications, and that disasters had resulted and would continue to result from failure to protect them whilst interrupting the enemy's. Until now the Navy could not carry out its much-increased task without adequate air support and such support, repeatedly asked for, had not been forthcoming. Since Coastal and Fighter Commands were fully committed and unable to meet the Home Fleet's requirements for reconnaissance, anti-submarine and convoy escort duties in the Barents Sea and elsewhere, the only other source of aircraft for these essential duties was Bomber Command, currently engaged in 1,000 bomber raids on German cities. It was Tovey's contention that this force had long enjoyed absolute priority in the design and supply of aircraft and crews. Tovey went on: 'Whatever the results of the bombing of cities might be, and this was the subject of keen controversy, it could not of itself win the war, whereas the failure of our sea communications would assuredly lose it.' He therefore proposed reducing the scale of the bombing offensive sufficiently to allow the Navy and the Army the support without which they could not play their part; adding that it was difficult to believe that the population of Cologne would notice much difference between a raid of 1,000 bombers and one of 750[11].

Tovey ended his despatch with the chilling words:

I realised that Their Lordships had for a long time been pressing for increased air support; but it had not materialised, and I informed Their Lordships that in my opinion the situation at sea was now so grave that the time had come for a stand to be made, even if this led to Their taking the extreme step of resignation.

In spite of Tovey's call for a stand to be made, substantive air cover for Arctic convoys throughout their passage from Iceland to the Murman coast was not made available until an escort carrier, HMS *Avenger*, was deployed with PQ18 in September 1942. Even though its planes were effective in breaking up attacking formations and keeping U-boats below the surface, it could have been of more utility had it carried more up-to-date aircraft, and its crew had more experience in deploying them tactically. Meanwhile, the strategic night bombing of Germany continued unabated and was later supplemented by the US taking on high level daylight raids.

# 6 UP TO RUSSIA

## (25 APRIL TO 5 MAY 1942)

..................... Lest man know not
That he on dry land loveliest liveth,
List how I, care-wretched, on ice-cold sea,
Weathered the winter, wretched outcast
Deprived of my kinsmen;
Hung with hard ice-flakes, where hail-scur flew,
There I heard naught save the harsh sea

From *The Seafarer*, adapted from the Anglo-Saxon by Ezra Pound

Much has been documented about the appalling conditions experienced by ships and their crews during the passage of Arctic convoys. Mountainous seas, the blizzards, the fog, pack ice and icebergs, not to mention the fear of sudden and devastating attack from above or below the waves; all conspired to make the wartime passage to Russia one of the most unpleasant and dangerous a sailor was likely to encounter. The most significant feature of the Arctic Ocean that set it apart from any other area of naval operations in the Second World War was its proximity to the northern ice cap. In summer the ice cap, warmed by the Gulf Stream, recedes well north of Jan Mayen and Bear Islands, hence opening up a larger expanse of sea room for convoys to operate in and thus provide more options for evading detection. However, such advantage was partially offset by long weeks of perpetual daylight that greatly assisted enemy reconnaissance and targeting, especially on those rare occasions when the weather was good.

There was also a downside to the effect of the Gulf Stream when its warm, more saline waters mixed with the cold ice-melt of the Arctic, producing thermoclines at various depths in the ocean that, in turn, produced false echoes on sonar equipment and hence provided a potential hiding place for U-boats. In winter, sea conditions presented less of a problem for sonar, but the advancing pack ice encloses both Jan Mayen and Bear Islands, so the routing of convoys was severely restricted and driven a lot closer to the North Cape, leaving them prey to enemy aircraft and warships lurking in their Norwegian bases. Also, in winter as in spring, cyclonic winds whipped up, blowing in from the Kara Sea to blast snow across the Barents Sea in violent storms, resulting in the dangerous build-up of ice on ships' superstructures. This rendered them top heavy, so crews were kept constantly busy with picks and steam hoses removing ice from decks, equipment and exposed cargoes. The perpetual darkness of the Arctic winter also heightened navigational hazards, especially for ships in convoy where navigation and communication lights were of necessity kept to the bare minimum. Arctic conditions, coupled with the constant threat of attack, inevitably resulted in frequent malfunctioning of equipment and machinery. Routine maintenance and servicing often having been delayed or not carried out at all because of the weather or operational commitments.

Arctic conditions also demanded special maintenance regimes to prevent the malfunctioning of guns, torpedoes, radar and sonar equipment consequent upon the extreme cold. Atmospheric conditions in the far north often interfered with radio communications, and magnetic compasses became unreliable. Gyro compasses were therefore an essential requirement, but not all merchant shipping companies invested in such equipment at that time.

Personal administration and safety also became problematic. Regardless of the season, convoy duties, especially for those on watch on open bridges or going about their business on deck, demanded high levels of personal insulation, as this excerpt from a RN officer's letter home demonstrates:

My rig for the morning watch, 4 – 8 a.m., was underwear, thickish socks, seaboot stockings and flying boots, pyjama trousers, fleece-lined corduroy trousers, shirt, fisherman's sweater, woollen scarf round middle, fleece waistcoat, light leather jacket, wool muffler, fleece lined overcoat, fleece-lined helmet, mittens and fleece-lined gloves. At the end of an hour both feet and hands were freezing, but that was all except the nose which seems to catch it a bit. This is due to the wind, the actual cold is nothing much without the wind, but keep watch in it is rather like having to wait four hours on a railway station in mid-winter.[1]

Simply standing up or attempting to lie still in one's bunk was exhausting during bad weather, especially in the smaller ships. Sleep was impossible and, for those prone to it, seasickness was an added discomfort. Injuries caused by being thrown against bulkheads or equipment were not uncommon; and in the galleys only the most rudimentary of meals could be prepared. The pressures and stresses that all of these factors placed on those manning ships in Arctic convoys were enormous. Everyone was required to be constantly vigilant and ready to react whilst going about their daily tasks, in the face of an unrelenting enemy and a climate that could be just as unpredictable and violent. It is no wonder that, even for many a hardened sailor, one passage to Russia was enough.

The convoy conference for PQ15 was held on 25 April and was subsequently reported on enthusiastically by the Flag Officer Commanding 10th Cruiser Squadron (FOC 10th CS) to the C-in-C Home Fleet thus:

> As a result of convoy conference today I am convinced attendance of SO Ocean Escort at such conferences is of utmost value… Thanks to your successful efforts to provide reasonable escort whole tone of conference was one of optimism and while I still consider an adequate supporting force should be available in offing you may be assured PQ 15 will sail with full confidence in its ability to frustrate knavish tricks of enemy.[2]

As it later transpired, it was not so much the enemy's knavish tricks but the 'home goals' that frustrated PQ15, its escorts, and the return convoy QP13.

PQ15 left Iceland on 25 April[3] under the watchful eye of its commodore Captain H.J. Anchor RNR. Herbert Anchor was in his late forties, and had already had a distinguished career at sea. He had just been awarded the OBE in the 1942 New Year Honours, and was mentioned in dispatches at the end of the war for his services with ocean convoys that had occupied him continuously between 1942 and 1945. FOC 10th CS was particularly impressed by the manner in which the Commodore addressed the assembled ships' masters at the convoy conference, dealing patiently and firmly with the questions they raised[4]. In addition to the commodore, it is worth reflecting on the nature and task of ship's masters, who guided their charges through such dangerous waters under his watchful eye. In this we are fortunate to have the eyewitness account of Walter H. Hesse, the third assistant engineer on SS *Mormacrey,* a First World War vintage American freighter loaded with various armaments and 300 tons of explosive[5]. In his memoire of PQ15, he paints a vivid picture of the ship's master:

> During periods at sea, our captain never left the bridge, eating his meals there and catching short catnaps on a cot as conditions permitted. Average in height, middle-aged, and with a trace of grey in his hair, he was usually seen with a stubble of beard and red-rimmed eyes from lack of sleep. He lived every minute with the burden of his responsibility and was dedicated to bringing his ship safely to port.[6]

Although Ejnar Jensen in the *Capira* was probably at the younger end of the spectrum of masters in the convoy, like his older colleagues he was at the top of his profession, competent and committed to his charge. As with any command, it was a lonely task where ultimate responsibility for the lives of the crew rested on his shoulders, and it took a special type of seaman to accept it; especially in wartime, with all its attendant risks.

Captain Anchor raised his flag in SS *Botavon,* a former Blue Funnel Line ship carrying 2,600 tons of government stores, and launched in 1912 but still capable of 12 knots. At the beginning of April, *Botavon* had already made one abortive attempt to get to Russia in PQ14[7]. Severe weather conditions had forced her and several other ships in the convoy to return to Iceland, and they were now incorporated into PQ15. There were 25 ships in PQ15[8] and these are listed in Appendix II. Unfortunately, there is no complete record of the sailing order, so individual convoy positions are vague. However, Captain H. Austin, the master of SS *Southgate,* records in his post convoy report that they were formed up in columns of five line ahead and five line abreast, *Southgate's* position being the leading ship in the port column. The commodore's ship was the leading vessel in the centre column, the vice commodore's ship lead the column on her starboard side and SS *Empire Morn* a Catapult Aircraft Merchant or CAM ship lead the outside starboard column.[9]

The convoy also contained three other specialist ships. SS *Krassin*[10] and SS *Montcalm* were icebreakers, and SS *Empire Bard* a heavy lift ship. The inclusion on SS *Empire Morn* was an innovation for PQ15 and was hastily recorded in a handwritten copy[11] from the Admiralty to the Senior British Naval Officer in Russia. CAM ships attempted to give convoys some air cover, but were in fact no substitute for an escort carrier. They had a rocket-powered catapult fitted over the forecastle head. Mounted on this was an obsolescent Mk1 Hurricane fighter. If the plane was launched, there was no return. Instead, the pilot would have to bail out once the sortie was completed, and hopefully be picked up immediately by one of the convoy's escorting vessels. In the freezing Arctic waters, a few minutes meant the difference between the life and certain death of the pilot. Alternatively, if a friendly airfield was in range, the pilot would make for that. Stowed in the hold of the CAM ship was another airframe. This would be assembled and mounted on the catapult for the return passage should the first one have been used. There was an added irony in all of this; some ships were carrying the latest fighters destined for Russia, crated in their holds, but the convoy had to rely on a single out-dated aeroplane for their own defence. Consequently, the effectiveness of the CAM ship lay more in its veneer of deterrence than fighting capability. As we shall see, and in spite of being attacked several times from the air, PQ15 never launched its Hurricane during the passage to Russia. Nevertheless, an eyewitness[12] on PQ16 one month later reported the launch of a fighter from a CAM ship which engaged several German planes attacking the convoy, and claimed one hit before the pilot ditched next to a destroyer and was successfully recovered from the sea. So the system could be effective against single aircraft, but was of little use against a mass attack[13].

The close escort from Hvalfjörður comprised four Halcyon class minesweepers, led by Captain J.F.H. Crombie in HMS *Bramble,* and four trawlers that would double up as rescue ships. Three days later, on the 29 April, the convoy was joined by a further six destroyers[14] and Force Q. Force Q centred on SS *Gray Ranger,* a fleet oiler, with HMS *Ledbury,* a brand-new Hunt class destroyer, as its close escort. Both ships had left Seidisfjord on the eastern side of Iceland in the early hours of 28 April. They were accompanied by the submarine HMS *Sturgeon* and HMS *Ulster Queen,* a former Irish Sea packet steamer that had been converted to an anti-aircraft role before being commissioned into the Royal Navy. Force Q was there to provide fuel for the smaller, limited range escorts accompanying the convoy[15]. Although destroyers carried sufficient fuel for the passage to Russia, as it was expended the ships became lighter, sat higher out of the water and hence became less stable. This adversely affected their performance, especially when carrying out high speed manoeuvres. Therefore escort destroyers would ideally be refuelled at the mid-point of the passage to remain at their most effective throughout.

*Sturgeon* took up position 4 cables astern of *Gray Ranger,* and during the short passage of 19 hours to join PQ15 she was attacked by a Northrup seaplane. *Sturgeon's* captain ordered her to dive and *Gray Ranger* opened fire, but several machine gun bullets fired from the plane hit the submarine's bridge before the pilot realised his mistake, ceased firing and apologised to the Captain of *Ledbury*[16]. It later transpired[17] that owing to the very secret nature of Force Q, the Air Officer Controlling did not think it advisable to pass the information about the presence of the force or HMS *Sturgeon* to aircraft operating from the Icelandic airbase at Akureyri in support of PQ15. Because the convoy left seven hours later than expected, he thought that the aircraft would not encounter the submarine, but did not realise that Force Q had altered course to intercept the convoy and consequently had put itself within the operational area of planes flying operational sorties from Akureyri. Following this potentially disastrous home goal, procedures were put in place to ensure full information was given to aircrews whether they were likely to encounter other friendly forces or not.

Beginning early on 30 April, *Gray Ranger,* stationed at the rear of the second column, trailed a floating hose and began refuelling. Having successfully oiled *Badsworth*, *Venomous*, *Boadicea*, *St Albans* and *Somali,* she began refuelling *Matchless* early the following morning. However, the hose parted, and further refuelling was abandoned as by then *Matchless* had her tanks three quarters full. At 0700 on 1 May, Force Q parted company with PQ15, zig zagging for the first two hours to shake off any shadowing U-boats. Its next task was to refuel destroyers from QP11, the return convoy, which had left Murmansk on 28 April. Meanwhile, *Ulster Queen* remained with the convoy while *Sturgeon* departed for another patrol area. In his report following the encounter with PQ15, Lieutenant Commander Roger Hill commanding HMS *Ledbury* commented most favourably on the station-keeping of ships in the convoy, in spite of periods of fog and course alterations. He also reported that the oiling at sea had been carried out most ably, particularly for the five destroyers from PQ15 that had taken 24 hours to refuel, during which time the hose had to be repaired twice. Having made the RV with QP11, Force Q returned to Lerwick but not before *Ledbury* came across a small rowing boat just north of the Shetlands. It contained five survivors from the Norwegian ship the *Froya,* which had been sunk by German bombers on 2 May, five days previously. Hill reported:

> They had plenty of food left but little water; one had serious 'survivors' feet, but the remainder were remarkably fit considering they had sailed (with a blanket) and rowed 250 miles. It was difficult to understand them but their ship, which was bound for Norway, had not sunk at once, and the remaining four of the crew, including the Captain, Lieutenant Bvadland, had had time to construct a raft on which they had last been sighted on the evening of Saturday 2 May... These men had saved everything of value – sextant, chronometer watch, binoculars and a large sum of Norwegian money. They knew the exact position where they were sunk and picked up; and had kept afloat and fit in a very small boat. Their one anxiety was for their Captain who had elected to remain on the raft, confident of rescue by British planes and ships.[18]

The survivors' boat was towed to Lerwick, where it was handed over with the Norwegians to the relevant authorities[19]. Hill ended by reporting that his crew then picked up two weeks' wages and had a good run ashore, both beer and a dance venue having been located by Jolly Jack.

Since leaving Iceland, Ensign Combs had increased vigilance on the *Capira* and watches were now posted four hours on and four off, adding an extra man to the 4-inch gun crew during the short period of twilight that passed for night in such northern latitudes at that time of year. Late on the 29 April, other forces were also being prepared for battle. Fliegerfeuhrer Lofoten ordered all serviceable aircraft to be armed with 500 and 250kg bombs for operations against shipping. However, it was not the merchant ships in convoy that held the Fliegerfeuhrer's attention. British radio intercepts, combined with shipping movements and vigorous offensive activity of the

Russians in the North Finnish area, convinced the Germans of a large-scale enemy action against northern Norway. As the following Enigma intercept from Fliegerfeuhrer Lofoten to operational headquarters at Bodø shows, the Germans expected an aerial offensive as well as naval attack, and were on maximum alert for a combined British and Soviet operation against them[20]:

> Increased enemy air raids on Central and Southern Norwegian area on the one hand, and heavy enemy attacks on the Norwegian Mountain Corps and in Central Finnish area on the other, make it appear there will be combined offensive operations (from north west) Russia. Reports about embarkation and disembarkation exercises which took place on 24 and 25/4 in Aberdeen, Wick and Orkneys – by (Canadian) and also Norwegian troops – strengthen this assumption.
>
> In this connection we can expect the approach of enemy naval forces to the Norwegian coast and air raids on aerodromes. All measures are to be taken which facilitate the widest possible dispersal of aircraft on dispersal grounds.[21]

The interpretation of such intelligence gathered by the Germans was obviously flawed but indicates that their feelings of vulnerability within the Arctic Circle, reinforced by Hitler's fixation that the Allies would invade Norway at some point, was just as acute as the convoys that plied those dangerous waters.

The following day the cruiser HMS *Nigeria*, flying the flag of Rear Admiral Borough, FOC 10th CS, took up station with HMS *London* and kept company with the convoy until it reached the vicinity of Bear Island. All in all, this was a formidable escorting force and it allowed a screen to be established forward and along the port and starboard sides of the convoy. The rear of the convoy was not considered as vulnerable, as with a speed of around 7 knots it could outpace a submerged U-boat; but there were occasions when ships in the escort were surprised by the speed of U-boats on the surface. At this point in PQ15's passage, however, the threat from U-boats was minimal. Those that were operating in the Barents Sea were targeted further east against QP11. There were seven U-boats in the pack[22] and one, *U436*, successfully located the escorting cruiser HMS *Edinburgh*, torpedoing and crippling her on 30 April. Thereafter, *Edinburgh* was repeatedly attacked by German aircraft, surface ships and U-boats until she was finally abandoned and sunk by HMS *Foresight* on 2 May. She went to the bottom carrying 465 ingots of gold bullion, Stalin's payment for the military aid convoys such as PQ15 were shipping to Russia[23].

Fortunately, U-boat operations against QP11 were not successful, and *U405* plus *U703* were redirected to the north east during the night of 30 April to intercept PQ15. These were joined later by *U251* and *U376,* and all four formed a shortened patrol line across the anticipated track of PQ15 following its detection and reported position on 1 May[24]. Coincidentally, on the morning of 30 April, the Covering Force had assembled off Seidisfjord to give long-range cover to PQ15 as far as the vicinity of Bear Island, before turning back to do the same for QP11 on its return to Iceland. The threat from German capital ships such as the *Tirpitz* breaking out from their protected fjords in Northern Norway and causing havoc in a convoy was ever present; and it had been reported two days earlier on 28 April that four such ships had been sighted in Trondheim. These were attacked by about 30 RAF bombers on the nights of 28 and 29 April. Due to the German smoke-screen, only minor damage was sustained by the berths and none to the enemy ships, save that *Prinz Eugen*'s transmitters were hit by bomb splinters. The German Admiral Commanding Battleships at Trondheim was also looking for the Allied Covering Force, and had sent out reconnaissance flights to locate it[25]. By late in the afternoon of 29 April he had identified the Covering Force, but his first concern was the protection of the *Tirpitz* from low-level torpedo attack by the aircraft aboard HMS *Victorious,* and consequently set about reviewing the state of the anti-torpedo defences in his area. Later that day, however, he realised that the Force was covering the passage of PQ15;[26] nevertheless, he was still concerned about the possibility of further air attacks and ordered that during the course of the imminent clear, full-moon nights, all ships would operate outside Aasenfjord, retaining a smoke-screen over their normal berths and then return to them by day[27].

Meanwhile, PQ15 had enjoyed an unimpeded passage until the early hours of 30 April, when fog intervened for about eight hours. This was long enough for the convoy to become somewhat dispersed, but by 1000 hours it had reformed. At 2145 hours, an enemy 'shadower' appeared and according to the convoy commodore accompanied the convoy for the remainder of the passage. The shadower was a long range Bloehm & Voss reconnaissance aircraft based in Norway. These flying boats remained in visual contact with the convoy but kept well out of range of the escorts' guns. Their task was to continuously report the convoy's position until German bombers could be mustered and vectored for an attack. Captain Leslie Saunders, commanding HMS *Trinidad* on an earlier convoy, PQ13, that had been severely mauled by the *Luftwaffe,* recorded an exchange between a cruiser captain and the pilot of a shadower. '… the cruiser captain called the flying boat by signal lamp, and getting a reply, signalled, "Please go round the other way for a change. You are making me dizzy." Back came the answer in English, "Certainly. Anything to oblige." – and he so obliged.' [28]

Sailors on the *Capira* also recalled how the convoy would signal the shadower and challenge it to come in and have a go. It would acknowledge the request but declined to oblige. In spite of the banter, the shadower's intent remained deadly as it relayed the convoy position to other, more potent forces. Those forces in the shape of six JU88 bombers appeared at 2200 hours on 1 May, when the convoy was about 250 miles south west of Bear Island. Fortunately, HMS *Nigeria*'s Type 281 radar picked up the raiders while they were still some way off and the escort was well prepared for their arrival; all ships were in the first degree of readiness. As soon as the formation was sighted it came under a controlled 4-inch barrage from *Nigeria* and the *Ulster Queen,* and spasmodic fire from the rest of the escort and other ships in the convoy. The *Ulster Queen*'s Commanding Officer reported[29]:

> Enemy aircraft immediately split up and thereafter manoeuvred separately and futilely around the convoy, dropping a few bombs near the A/S trawler astern of the convoy, but never, with one exception closing to a bombing position on the convoy. The one exception attacked through cloud on Port bow of 'Ulster Queen', received the full benefit of all this ship's close-range weapons, some from 'Nigeria' and machine gun fire from another of escort, and was shot down two cables from 'Ulster Queen'.

Captain Anchor's log of important incidents reported the attack with consummate brevity; 'Enemy bomber attack. Cloud base approximately

1000-1500 feet, light snow flurries. Bombs dropped all wide and attack poorly carried out on Convoy. One bomber brought down by gunfire.'[30] The master of the *Botavon* was slightly less prosaic in his report: 'Three bombs were dropped but no ships were damaged. The ships of the convoy and our escorts opened fire. We opened fire with every available gun and either HMS London or my ship were responsible for destroying one of the enemy aircraft which crashed into the sea in flames ahead of us.'[31]

However, the master of the *Empire Bard* thought that it was the combined fire of all the ships that had scored this particular success, whilst Captain Austin on *Southgate* saw 'three distinct flashes as the bombs exploded but no hits were scored. The escort and our vessel opened fire causing it to bank; it then dropped dead ahead of us and crashed into the sea. We altered course slightly to avoid the wreckage which passed close to the ship's side, but saw no survivors.[32]

The captain of H Nor MS *St Albans* had a front row seat as:

> ... one plane approached from my port bow and passed directly overhead at a range of about 1000 yds... Hits were obtained and one close burst from the 12 pdr. was seen to remove fragments of the plane which sheared off to port and a few moments later crashed ahead of the convoy; during the intervening time it received further heavy punishment from other escorts and the convoy.[33]

Walter Hesse also recalled this attack, and from the perspective of a merchant seaman had a very different view:

> On deck was chaos. Gunfire erupted from the ships. Germans darted in from every direction. Only four planes attacked us, but it seemed like many more. Most of the action concentrated on the vulnerable corners of the convoy. Our position was better protected. Despite this, one plane showed disdain for our defenses and flew low between our column and the adjacent column. This was the gun crew's first opportunity to fire in combat and it revealed how ineffective our firepower was. No planes were downed. Several bombs were dropped, but no hits were scored. As suddenly as the raid began, it ended.[34]

SS *Capira* with another ship behind her and when sailing under
her former name SS *West Campgaw*

(Author's collection)

Merchant ships on northern convoy duty passing through Arctic fog, which gives the impression of a boiling sea due to the difference in sea and air temperatures

(© IWM A15356)

A liberty ship rides out the storm in a convoy to Russia

Admiral Sir John Tovey on the quarterdeck of the flagship
HMS *King George V*
(© IWM A14845)

The First Sea Lord, Admiral of the Fleet Sir Dudley Pound on the bridge of
SS *Queen Mary* en route to the USA

(© IWM A16722)

Oiler and escort in Whale Bay, Iceland

(© IWM A9182)

An obsolete Mk1 Hurricane being mounted on a merchantman CAM ship
(© IWM A9421)

Sailors clearing the decks of snow on board HMS *King George V* whilst
she was in Arctic waters

(© IWM A15424)

In all probability, it was HMS *London*'s directed firepower that brought down the JU88, but not before HMS *Nigeria* had claimed it as well. The remnants of the attacking force were eventually driven off by the volume of fire put up by the convoy and its escort. One can only imagine the relief and elation the crews on the merchantmen must have felt, having come through this first encounter unscathed and with some modest success. We now know from Enigma intercepts[35] that a second wave had been planned against PQ15, to follow half an hour after the first. The second wave comprised three JU88s and four He111 torpedo bombers, but this attack never developed; probably because it failed to locate the convoy in the prevailing weather conditions. PQ15 proceeded unmolested on its lawful occasions, for the time being at least.

Soon after this attack on 2 May, HMS *Nigeria* left the convoy, leaving instructions that the *Ulster Queen* was to remain stationed between columns 3 and 4. With her Type 279 radar operating continuously, the *Ulster Queen* now took responsibility for early warning of an air attack on the convoy, whilst a Bloem & Voss and Dornier 18 shadower continued to accompany it. As usual, the shadower continued to keep well out of range of *Ulster Queen*'s guns, which she used whenever potential targets appeared within her armament's maximum range of 16,000 yards [14.6km]. There was an expectation that the *Ulster Queen*'s radar would provide early warning of an attack, but as the Commanding Officer reported later, the Type 279 completely failed to give any warning of aircraft approach at any time in these mountainous Arctic waters. This was especially the case with low-level attacks, and was to have dire consequences later in the convoy's passage to Murmansk. Meanwhile, some 350 miles east of Iceland, the force of Allied warships covering PQ15 had just sustained a severe blow.

## The sinking of HMS *Punjabi*

In addition to the close escort protecting the convoy, the Home Fleet, complemented by a number of US warships, was providing a heavy covering force some miles to the south of the convoy's passage. The covering force had been fully constituted since the sailing of PQ12 early in March. Its primary function was to guard the Arctic convoys against the threat of German surface ships, especially the heavily armed *Tirpitz* that had established itself at Trondheim in mid-January. From there, it could deploy rapidly with its escorts to cause havoc among the convoy routes, as the *Admiral Scheer* had demonstrated in the North Atlantic in October 1940 when, in addition to the armed merchant cruiser *Jervis Bay*, it sank five other merchantmen sailing with convoy HX84. Thus, the very fact that the Germans had a fleet based on the Norwegian fjords was enough to tie down the bulk of the Home Fleet based at Scapa Flow in convoy protection. Up until the attack on Pearl Harbor in December 1941, US escorts had been restricted to protecting convoys steaming from the Eastern Seaboard to Iceland. From there the Royal Navy, assisted by Canadian, Free French, Polish and Norwegian ships, assumed sole responsibility for convoy protection into Russian waters. Following Pearl Harbor and Germany's declaration of war on the United States, a few days later all this changed and the USN participated thereafter in both close escort and covering force duties.

The heavy element of the Covering Force comprised the battleships HMS *King George* V and USS *Washington*, the carrier HMS *Victorious*, the cruiser HMS *Kenya* and the US Cruisers *Wichita* and *Tuscaloosa*.[36] There was also a destroyer screen comprising six British and four US ships. As already mentioned, this substantial force had been spotted by German reconnaissance planes two days previously; although its purpose of covering PQ15 had been correctly interpreted by the Germans, they were wary of the presence of the carrier HMS *Victorious*. Fearing an aerial attack launched from her, they had ordered an immediate review of anti-torpedo protection around Trondheim where the *Tirpitz* was berthed[37].

Admiral Tovey, C-in-C Home Fleet, had raised his flag in *King George* V, the first of the five KGV class battleships laid down in 1937. The US component under Rear Admiral Robert C. Griffen flew his flag in the USS *Washington*. Both capital ships had formidable main armaments that comprised 10 x 14-inch guns on *KGV* and 9 x 16-inch guns on the *Washington,* ideally suited to defeating the armour plating of German pocket battleships. However, the immediate threat to the covering force came from a most unexpected quarter. Kenneth Tipper, a sailor on HMS *Punjabi*, a covering force destroyer, takes up the story:

At 15:45 on 1 May a thick fog descended on the fleet. I was in the main wireless cabin in the forward part of the ship, prior to relieving another telegraphist in the cabin aft where we conducted our interception work. Suddenly there was a tremendous crash, the *Punjabi* heeled over sharply on its side, and all the lights went out. First thought was that we had been torpedoed, but our nemesis turned out to be one of our own ships – the 34,000-ton battleship *King George* V had rammed and cut in half our 1,850-ton destroyer.[38]

*King George* V's bow was severely damaged around the waterline and worse was to come. The aft portion of HMS *Punjabi* passed down the starboard side of the *KGV,* and as her ready-use depth charges rolled overboard they detonated, sinking the afterpart of the *Punjabi* and further damaging *KGV* below the waterline, flooding two of her compartments. The forepart of the *Punjabi,* which remained afloat, passed down the port side of *KGV* causing considerable damage to the plating forward, in addition to the bow damage caused by the collision. The exploding depth charges also killed those unfortunate enough to have been thrown into the water. Mercifully, the bow section of the destroyer remained afloat for around forty minutes; long enough for the ship's whaler and some floats to be launched, and to evacuate some of the crew before the destroyers HMS *Martin* and HMS *Marne* arrived on the scene, picking up those survivors in the water and taking off the remaining crew members still on board *Punjabi*.[39] Forty-nine of the *Punjabi*'s crew were lost in the disaster from a complement of 256 officers and men. *King George* V was out of the order of battle for two months, undergoing repairs at Birkenhead. The incident was kept secret until the end of the war, but that did not prevent the Navy from arraigning the captain, the officer of the watch and the rest of the ship's company on charges of losing the *Punjabi*.

The courts martial[40] was held a mere six days later aboard HMS *Tyne*, a destroyer support ship based at Scapa Flow The Navy docs not look kindly on those who put its ships in unnecessary danger and the penalties for doing so are consequently severe. Since the incident involved not only issues of navigation and seamanship occasioned by its officers, but also issues around the state of the ship's depth charges, the whole ship's company was arraigned before the courts martial. *Punjabi*'s captain was found guilty of negligently or by default hazarding his ship, whilst the officer of the watch was convicted of negligently or by default losing the *Punjabi*. Both were sentenced to forfeiture of seniority, dismissal from their ship (strange, since it was by now in two halves resting on the bottom of the Barents Sea!) and to be severely reprimanded. All other surviving officers and members of crew were formally acquitted, their conduct judged by the court to have been in the best traditions of the Service. The courts martial proceedings, however, demonstrate just how fine a thread the turn of events hangs on, and how two highly-regarded and respected officers can be seduced into making wrong decisions seemingly for all the right reasons. Both officers committed their recall of events to paper the following day whilst aboard HMS *Martin*. These accounts formed the basis of the narrative at the courts martial:

The covering force had been steaming in line at 18 knots [33km/hr] with *KGV* in the lead. A screen of five destroyers on the port and starboard sides of the column had been deployed. *Punjabi* was in the starboard screen with *Inglefield* ahead of her and *Martin*, *Oribi* and *Marne* astern of her in that order. Visibility had been variable all day with occasional fog patches. Unusually for these northern waters there was little wind but a heavy swell was running. Because of the variable visibility the destroyers in the screen had been ordered by Tovey to take up night cruising dispositions if the visibility shut down. In clear conditions the screen on either side of the column fanned out such that the entire force took on an arrowhead formation. At night or when visibility closed in, however, the destroyers closed in towards the column and manoeuvred into line astern on either side of the capital ships. Although Captain D.3 in *Inglefield* commanded the starboard screen, the destroyers had changed their dispositions with and without orders from him as the conditions dictated. About two hours before the collision whilst closed up in fog Captain D.3 signalled the starboard screen to ' take up station as soon as visibility permits without further signal.' During the afternoon watch, before the collision, there had already been two changes; at about 1520, Captain D.3 ordered the screen to close in as visibility was quickly deteriorating. About ten minutes later, this order was rescinded as visibility suddenly improved again and visual contact was established between *Inglefield* and

*KGV*, and between *Inglefield* and *Punjabi*. The respite was brief, however, and about 15 minutes later the covering force ran into another fog bank. At this juncture the commanding officer of the *Punjabi*, Commander the Honourable J.M.G. Waldegrave DSC RN, was uncertain as to Captain D.3's intentions but in view of the C-in-C's earlier signal, plus the fact that the fog persisted, gave orders to the officer of the watch, Lieutenant L.R. Hollis RN, to make a slight increase in speed and close *Inglefield* gradually, anticipating that an alteration of only a very few degrees would be necessary. Before altering course, Hollis told the Second Officer of the Watch, Mr A.J. Smith, to tell the anti-submarine cabinet's crew to pass *Inglefield*'s range and bearing to the bridge. This had become standard procedure, and as the A/S crew were well aware of the disposition of the destroyer screen the captain and Hollis would have had confidence in the reply 'Echo bearing 195 degrees.'. Unfortunately, no range was given but Hollis, confident that he knew where *Inglefield* was, ordered the A/S crew to 'Hold that echo' and altered course to port using 10 degrees of wheel. By this time HMS *Martin*, astern of *Punjabi*, was observed to be closing in also, and as Waldegrave had previously given instructions to Hollis on how he wanted *Punjabi* to close on *Inglefield* he left the bridge.

Given the variability of the conditions and the uncertainty of Captain D.3's intentions, it was a mistake for the captain to leave the bridge at this time. Nevertheless, there comes a point in any officer's command when relatively complex but routine manoeuvres can safely be left in the hands of competent and well-practised subordinates. Not to do so runs the risk of placing undue pressure on the captain and through unremitting fatigue, subjecting him to conditions where wrong decisions are taken. In the event, however, it is a difficult call to make.

Yet all may have been well for the *Punjabi* and her crew were it not for Hollis' subsequent actions following the almost simultaneous receipt of two pieces of information. First the A/S crew reported 'Bearing drawing left, left cut on 140 degrees' followed by 'Bearing steady'. Having established that the echo was some 1,200 yds [1km] distant, and having previously given the order to hold the bearing, Hollis assumed that this information referred to *Inglefield* and that she had slowed down and, as a consequence,

*Punjabi* was now slightly ahead of her but still well to the starboard of both *Inglefield* and the track of the main body of the Task Force. Just as Hollis was absorbing this information, a mine was spotted by the Signalman of the Watch off *Punjabi*'s starboard bow. This further distraction prevented Hollis from completing the initial course alteration, and *Punjabi* continued to swing slowly to port. Hollis had just given the order 'Midships' but had not yet steadied *Punjabi* on a bearing that he assumed to be more oblique to the track of the main body of the Task Force. Hollis immediately informed the captain of the mine, and made to HMS *Martin* astern of him 'Monkey starboard'. The mine was now clearly visible to Hollis and he judged that maintaining its present course *Punjabi* would run it down, so he ordered a further turn to port of 15 degrees and increased speed to around 18¾kts [35km/hr]. In ordering such a bold manoeuvre, albeit considered necessary given the circumstances, Hollis must have calculated that he had sufficient sea room to execute it without hazarding his ship. Such confidence would no doubt have been based on his interpretation of the ASDIC information, and a consequently assumption that *Punjabi* was not in imminent danger of crossing the track of the Task Force's capital ships on his port side. Tragically it would appear that Hollis had mis-appreciated the significance of the ASDIC information that referred to another vessel and not as Hollis assumed the *Inglefield*. The cumulative effect of Hollis' well-intentioned but falsely-informed actions had placed the *Punjabi* on a collision course with Tovey's flagship.

There can be few sights more terrifying for a destroyer captain and his crew than to have a battleship suddenly appear from out of a fogbank and bear down on them, with no chance of either craft taking effective avoiding action. The port forward lookout was the first to spot *KGV* and raise the alarm. Hollis saw *KGV*'s black shape approaching *Punjabi* from the port side and gave the order 'Hard a-starboard, full speed ahead.' As Hollis was giving his order, the captain appeared on the bridge. Waldegrave judged that Hollis' action was all that could be done, as they awaited the inevitable collision which occurred at about 1545hrs; around three minutes since Hollis had given the order to turn 10 degrees to port. *KGV*'s bow scythed through *Punjabi*'s superstructure, on the port side between X and Y mountings, cutting the destroyer in two. According to Waldegrave's statement, *Punjabi*'s stern floated for a minute or two, but some depth charges (known to be set to safe, but dislodged by the shock of the collision) exploded. The USS *Washington* passed close by *Punjabi*'s stern as it sank, and more of her depth charges detonated. The carrier HMS *Victorious* followed and altered course to port, narrowly missing *Punjabi*'s fore part which remained afloat. The rest of the Task Force steamed past without further incident.

There can be few experiences more terrifying than being below decks in a rapidly sinking ship. This befell two officers who survived, and subsequently recorded statements received by the courts martial. Sub Lieutenant Stuart Lawrence RNVR was in the wardroom when the collision occurred, and Sub Lieutenant Symonds RAN, an Australian officer, was in his cabin adjacent to the wardroom. Their somewhat understated accounts provide us with a small window through which we may glimpse the terror facing those below decks in the after part of the ship. As *KGV* hit the *Punjabi* Sub Lieutenant Lawrence heard:

.... the engines rapidly increase in revolutions. Within a matter of seconds, the ship violently lurched to port, and I was flung across the wardroom table against the ship's side. The ship seemed to right herself for a few seconds, and during this time I was able to make my way towards the ladder leading up to the after flat. I observed four people ahead of me in the process of climbing the ladder, and had myself started to climb when the ship listed heavily to starboard, making exit difficult. On reaching the after flat, I appeared to be the last up the ladder when a large explosion occurred which at the time I assumed to be the detonator locker. This explosion threw me into the starboard corner of the after flat. I managed to scramble over the debris on to the port side of the quarter deck and the ship sank under me. As the stern disappeared, 'Y' gun passed very close to me. The fuel oil at this time was very unpleasant, and I was now completely covered. I had great difficulty seeing anything owing to the oil but I did recognise Sub Lt. D. McNaughton R.N.V.R., and we remained together for a short period. Suddenly there was a large explosion underneath me which fortunately lifted me clear of the water. After falling and being immersed another explosion occurred; this having unpleasant reactions to my body. For a short time after this I felt that I had not the strength to move about. I then observed a US cruiser bearing down on me at what I took to be a terrific speed. The bow wave of this vessel pushed me aside and I passed a few feet away down its port side. The second US cruiser passed at a greater distance away and caused me no worry. I now saw some distance away the foremost part of the '*Punjabi*' but had not the strength to reach it. After floating around for what seemed a very long time, I was hauled into the stern sheets of '*Martin*'s' motor boat. I then lost consciousness.

As the ship lurched violently to starboard and started to go down, Sub Lieutenant Symonds ran from his cabin and, with some difficulty, got onto the quarter deck where he could see that the ship was rapidly sinking. His assumption was that the *Punjabi* had been torpedoed.

I removed my seaboots and several others came up the Wardroom hatch, the only one I remember being Sub Lieut. Piggin RNZVR. By this time the water had reached my feet and I fell in, the stern sinking immediately afterwards. There was a little suction. When I came to the surface there were several heads, unrecognisable from oil fuel, nearby; most were able to grab some piece of flotsam. I rested on half a splinter mat. A large explosion now occurred which shook me badly. At this moment I saw the stern of USS *Washington* pass, leaving me a cable or so clear to starboard. Several seconds later another similar explosion occurred. At this moment we were on the starboard beam of HMS *Victorious*. When the confusion cleared, the group from the stern had been scattered. Looking up, I saw USS *Wichita* bearing down on me from about 70 feet away. I struck out to get clear but was only about six feet off when she came up to me. I remained at about this distance on my back all the way along the starboard side experiencing very little wash. Shortly afterwards USS *Tuscaloosa* passed fifty yards off leaving me to port. She appeared to alter course to port because her fog buoy wire passed over me. By this time there was no one nearby. I rested my chest on a cork lifejacket and kicked with my legs towards the remainder of the ship where I could see rescue work by '*Martin*' in progress. As I got near the ship, I heard the encouraging words of the Captain to some men in difficulties, telling them of '*Marne*'s' approach. Shortly afterwards I was picked up by 'Marne's' whaler and later hoisted inboard by an ingenious canvas jacket with rope attached.

Symonds ended his account by paying tribute to Marne's crew who treated all survivors excellently and left nothing to be desired. He also added an interesting detail gathered during his ordeal; the kapok suit (service issue) he was wearing at the time held up extremely well and kept him to some extent warm.

Miraculously the fore part of the ship remained afloat, albeit with a 35 degree list to starboard. However as the list increased it rapidly became apparent that it could not remain afloat for much longer. Waldegrave gave the order to lower the ship's whaler which got away safely full to capacity. The only other available boat was the ship's sailing dingy, which was swamped in an attempt to launch it over the side. However, Waldegrave remained focused on saving lives while the fore part was still afloat, and did not give the order to abandon ship. Instead, those still aboard turned their attention to launching the Carley floats and cutting adrift available timber to assist those survivors that Waldegrave now observed in the water. These, he assumed, had been in the after part of the ship, or had jumped from the fore part when the collision occurred. Most of these men were picked up by the whaler or the Carley floats later to be taken on board by other destroyers. The sea was also littered with the bodies of those who had been killed by the concussion from the exploding depth charges. HMS Martin was now approaching. She lowered her boats into the water to pick up survivors who were coated with a thick covering of Punjabi's fuel oil, that had by now spread over the site of the collision. HMS Marne also joined in the rescue and boats began to approach what remained of the Punjabi. After picking up a few men still in the sea the remainder of the ship's company embarked from the Punjabi; and not before time, as the list had continued to increase and the last survivors to leave waited on the bilge keel. Punjabi's fore part sank at 1621hrs, thirty-one minutes after the collision and within seconds of the last man being rescued.

In retrospect, and bearing in mind the enormity of the disaster, it seems incredible that from a complement of 12 officers and 242 ratings only 7 officers and 42 ratings were lost. Waldegrave's report paid tribute to the behaviour of the ship's crew after the collision, recording that it was beyond praise. Special mention was made of Lieutenant Hollis and Mr Smith who were of great assistance to him throughout the rescue. Waldegrave concluded: 'It is with the most profound regret that I have to record the sinking of H.M. Ship under my command and the loss of valuable lives.'

It is debatable whether or not there would have been a different outcome had Waldegrave remained on the bridge throughout. His absence could not have amounted to more than four minutes. During that time, Hollis made two course alterations towards the track of the Task Force. The first alteration had not been completed and the ship's heading stabilised on safe bearing before the second emergency course alteration had to be made. Moreover, the second alteration was carried out on Hollis' false appreciation of the ship's position. Would Waldegrave, given the echo information and with only seconds to act before hitting the mine, have appreciated his true position relative to *Inglefield* and the main column of the Task Force and given different orders? What other options were there given the heat of the moment and the pressure to do something? Reducing speed would have been unwise given the visibility and proximity of HMS *Martin* astern of the *Punjabi*. Perhaps Waldegrave would have judged that a less than 15 degree turn to port was necessary to avoid hitting the mine and at the same time avoided colliding with *KGV*. Speculation apart, however, the court were of the opinion that Hollis displayed a negligent lack of appreciation of the tactical situation, by altering course to port an amount which exposed the ship to certain danger of collision, and that that was the immediate cause of the disaster. The court were also of the opinion that in the conditions of bad visibility prevailing and in view of the fact that *KGV* and *Inglefield* were not in sight, Waldegrave should not have left the bridge after ordering Hollis to close on *Inglefield* and was therefore also negligent.

At the end of proceedings, both Waldegrave and Hollis received glowing reports on their record and ability in mitigation of punishment. The court had been convened on the orders of the C-in-C, Admiral Tovey, who also signed the court proceedings before their dispatch to the Admiralty. Although Tovey's views on this incident are not recorded, there is a hand-written letter[41] in his archive residing in the National Maritime Museum from 'Shorty' Carlisle, someone who knew him well, that may well throw some light on what Tovey's reaction might have been. In it, Carlisle writes about the art of ship handling and manoeuvring and says of Tovey:

> He was always scrupulously fair.... I once had occasion to report to him the results of a Courts Martial on a rather stupid collision which had occurred when visibility was 15 miles. It had been obvious from the beginning where blame lay, but Jack Tovey said: 'You know it is very seldom one can attribute 100% blame in any collision: there is nearly always something that the other fellow could have done to avoid it.'

It could be construed that in this case the other fellow was Tovey himself, although in all probability he would have delegated the operation of his flagship to its captain. Indeed, *KGV* did all it could, if not to avoid but certainly to mitigate the effects of the inevitable collision as the *Punjabi* appeared almost directly in front of her from out the fog. Circumstances had certainly conspired against Hollis and Waldegrave, and although bad luck is by no means a defence, in this case there is some evidence to believe that they may have had some unspoken sympathy from their peers and seniors. There but for the grace of God.

There is a final sad footnote to this incident. Following a short stint ashore, Commander Waldegrave was assigned to another ship that was torpedoed whilst on patrol. As part of his damage control duties, he entered a flooded part of the ship and, having secured a line to himself, he was then lowered into the compartment through a hatch because the ladder been blown away. Whilst attempting to ascertain the extent of the damage there was an explosion that killed him instantly. As one of his friends attested: 'He died as he lived, a source of inspiration to all with whom he had come in contact.'[42]

Having successfully survived one assault, the ships and escort of PQ15 remained at a state of high alert. Feelings of vulnerability were further intensified after the cruisers *Nigeria* and *London* left the convoy at 0745 on 2 May, whereupon Rear Admiral Borough handed over its safe conduct to Captain Crombie in HMS *Bramble*. Their departure spawned a rumour that

PQ15 was now being used as bait to lure German capital ships into the area, as Walter Hesse wrote some years later:

> Following the first raid the two British cruisers left the convoy at full speed. Rumours ran rife. Scuttlebutt had it that the convoy was to be bait to try and lure the German pocket battleship, TIRPITZ, out of her lair where she was skulking in the Norwegian fjords. Supposedly tailing us was a British aircraft carrier and an American battleship which, along with cruisers and other naval craft in the vicinity, were determined to sink or seize the TIRPITZ... The rumor was never confirmed.

The reality was quite different. It was pre-planned that the 10th CS would part company at this point, as its assets were considered too valuable to be risked east of Bear Island. Shortly after assuming responsibility for PQ15, Crombie made contact with the returning convoy QP11. Keen to glean all he could from QP11's passage thus far, he despatched HMS *Somali* to liaise with QP11's escort commander who was in HMS *Bulldog*. However, there was little new intelligence to be gleaned except that QP11 had been attacked in daylight by four torpedo bombers. Fortunately the attack, like the one PQ15 had sustained the previous evening, was poorly coordinated, and had been fought off without loss.

## The loss of the *Jastrzab*

As PQ15 got closer to the North Cape, enemy surveillance of the convoy intensified and Crombie reported that half an hour after passing QP11 the convoy was continuously shadowed by Bloem & Voss or Focke-Wulf aircraft and U-boats. Just after 1800 hours, H Nor MS *St Albans* had an ASDIC contact some 2,000 yards off the port beam of the convoy. As she followed up, it became apparent that the contact was indeed a submarine. It was assumed to be a U-boat, and attacked –- but only with a single depth charge, as communications with depth charge control had momentarily broken down and there was no facility for the captain to fire a full pattern from the bridge. At that point, HMS *Seagull* made contact with what was now positively identified as a submarine and joined in the hunt, whilst *St Albans* lined up for another attack, this time dropping a full pattern of six depth charges. As the water settled following this attack, Commander S.V. Storheill, Royal Norwegian Navy commanding H Nor MS *St Albans*, saw a yellow flare on the surface. This he assumed was a calcium flare used to mark the point of attack. The flare was also seen by Lieutenant Commander Pollock, the captain of the *Seagull,* just before he mounted an attack with a pattern of five DCs. Following the third pattern of depth charges, the submarine was severely damaged and forced to the surface. What followed is best described in Storheill's words:[43]

A few minutes after *Seagull's* attack the submarine surfaced about 700-800 yards [640-730m] away between 45 and 55 degrees on my starboard bow, on a course roughly at right angles to mine and her bow pointing left. She was turning rapidly to port, which I feared was an attempt to torpedo me. I accordingly put both engines full ahead and ordered 'Hard Starboard'. I could not open fire because H.M.S. *Seagull* was directly in line, but I opened up, with 0.5 and 12 pounder as soon as she was clear. My reasons for opening fire were; firstly, to prevent another attack. Knowing the Germans as I do, from the war in Norway, I consider them quite capable of torpedoing one ship whilst crying '*Kamerad*' to the other. Secondly, I wanted to create panic and so prevent them using the forward gun; I also wanted to force the crew to remain on board and thus stop any ideas they might have of scuttling their ship. In the meantime I intended sending my boarding party away, knowing the importance of capturing an enemy submarine and her secret documents. Just as I opened fire I saw a flash from the conning tower. The range was now between three and four hundred yards [270–370m]. Just after fire was opened my liaison officer pointed out that the submarine was British. I ceased fire at once and then made the terrible discovery that I had been firing at an Allied submarine.[44]

It was in fact *P551,* the *Jastrzab,* a Polish submarine that had inexplicably closed with the convoy and been mistaken as hostile. By the time the action was ended five people including two British ratings seconded to the *Jastrzab* had been killed. Six others including the submarine's captain and the British liaison officer were wounded. It soon became apparent that the *Jastrzab* was too badly damaged to be salvageable. There was damage in the control, motor and engine rooms, both battery compartments and the torpedo compartment[45]. In addition, the bridge was full of holes from the escorts' machine guns. As a consequence of such a severe battering, the *Jastrzab* began to sink in spite of the efforts of those on the ballast pumps to save her. Whilst on the surface, her main ballast had to be blown several times to keep the submarine afloat. Once the crew were taken off, there was no other option but to sink her, and so HMS *Seagull* opened up with its main armament and the ill-fated *Jastrzab* slipped beneath the waves. The dead and wounded were taken on board *St Albans* which then proceeded with all speed to re-join the convoy, with the intention of transferring the wounded to the *Ulster Queen* which had a well-equipped sick bay. Unfortunately, the constant threat of air and U-boat attack prevented the transfer, and two of the wounded died during the night. The dead were buried at sea, the usual ceremony being observed. The wounded were eventually transferred to a hospital at Vaenga Bay. What appears strange by today's standards was that there seemed to be no recrimination from the Polish crew towards those who had sunk their boat. They were later transferred to HMS *London,* keen to get back on patrol in a replacement sub. It is also remarkable that *Jastrzab's* Captain, Lieutenant Commander Romanowski, in spite of receiving no less than five gunshot wounds to his legs, retained the presence of mind to bring the boat's confidential code books off with him.

At the subsequent board of inquiry, the commanding officers of all three vessels involved in the incident were exonerated. This finding no doubt turned on the assumption that the submarine was hostile as no other Allied submarines were reported to be in the area. However there is also no doubt that Romanowski had deployed a yellow signal flare indicating that the submarine was friendly. This was clearly seen by those on *St Albans* and *Seagull,* but in the heat of battle either ignored or, as Storheill reported, mistaken for something else[46]. As the *Jastrzab* surfaced there was a desperate rush by the British liaison personnel on board to signal that this was a friendly vessel. T Sub Lieutenant Maurice Hanbury RNVR, accompanied by the British signalman and telegraphist, made for the bridge in the face of intense machine-gun fire to assist in passing the recognition signal. Hanbury was severely wounded. On reaching the bridge, Leading Signalman Thomas Beard RN managed to light a smoke flare to indicate a friendly boat. As it blazed in his hand, he received severe burns in an attempt to place it on its bracket, but before he could do so he too fell victim to the fire from the escorts and was killed. The same fate awaited Leading Telegraphist Martin Dowd RN as he operated the Aldis lamp, following Beard's failed attempt with the smoke flare. In fact, *Seagull* had picked up part of Dowd's signal but could only make out the letters 'ISH'. All three received immediate mentions in despatches, and later, the Polish Cross of Valour for their actions that day. The valediction written by Lieutenant Commander Romanowski some weeks later encapsulates his total lack of rancour at being sunk by the escorts and the high regard in which he (and no doubt the vast majority of Polish sailors) had not only for the Royal Navy, but also for a country that had gone to war on their behalf.

> Once more we could admire the fine spirit and high training of the Royal Navy. It is impossible for me, in words, to express my sincere sorrow that the liaison officer was badly wounded and that the Signalman and the Telegraphist lost their lives. Their blood mingling with ours symbolised once more the great friendship and understanding between our countries and of the readiness to fight for the freedom of all nations.[47]

The fact that *Jastrzab* was off-station only served to emphasise how difficult it was to navigate in Arctic conditions[48]. Crombie later received information that the *Jastrzab* had not been able to fix its true position for the previous six days. However, the fact that the convoy had been set a new course by FOC 10th CS to avoid the ice south of Bear Island before HMS *Nigeria* parted company with the convoy about eleven hours previously was undoubtedly a contributory factor in closing with the Polish submarine[49]. This tragedy was followed swiftly by another, as the *Luftwaffe* struck PQ 15 again just before midnight.

Like the first aerial attack, individual accounts of the second vary considerably in their detail[50]. However, there is general consensus over the number and type of aircraft involved, their direction, and altitude. The account given by Captain Crombie, the escort commander, best encapsulates what happened:

At 2327.Z/2 May in position 073⁰ North 019⁰ 41ʹ East an attack by torpedo aircraft developed. Six aircraft came in low on the starboard bow of the convoy; some torpedoes were seen to be dropped outside the Screen and some while they were passing through the Screen. One machine was hit and crashed just ahead of the convoy in flames. Another was apparently hit and passed down the starboard column of the convoy and there is evidence now that what was reported as a possibility... could now be considered almost a certainty although this machine was not seen to crash. S.S. *'Botavon'*, S.S. *'Jutland'* and *'Cape Corso'* were hit by torpedoes. *'Cape Corso'* blew up and *'Jutland'* sank very quickly. *'Botavon'* settled down by the bows and sank more slowly and I ordered *'Badsworth'* to sink her by gunfire[51]. The Commodore and one hundred and thirty seven survivors were picked up by HMS *'Badsworth'*, trawlers and HMS *'Chiltern'*.

*Jutland* had been carrying 1,560 tons of military stores, including 500 tons of cordite and 300 tons of small arms ammunition, and was therefore lucky not to have suffered the instantaneous fate of *Cape Corso*.[52] *Jutland*'s Master, Captain J Henderson, gave the following account of the action as he witnessed it from the bridge of his ship[53]:

I saw five Heinkel He111s flying low over the water at some distance along the starboard side of the convoy. I noticed they were painted dark green and when they were ahead of the convoy they turned sharply to port and flew at right-angles to our course, passing from starboard to port across the bows of the leading ships at a distance of about 100 yards [90m]. The convoy was putting up a very heavy barrage but nothing seemed to deter the enemy, who came on in single line ahead at a height of only 20 feet [6m] above the water. Each plane as it drew level dropped two torpedoes simultaneously, alongside each other, apparently from under the fuselage. I noticed one torpedo jump out of the water, like a porpoise, then steady on its course. Another one I watched as it struck the water about 100 yards [90m] off our starboard bow, and 100 yards [90m] ahead; I could see the bubbles of the wake quite clearly as it crossed our bows, then it turned to port in a semi-circle, with a radius of about 150 yards [135m], finally striking the ship on the port quarter, the opposite side from which it had been released... When the torpedo struck there was not a very loud explosion but the after part of the vessel was violently shaken, breaking some glass in the saloon; the poop was completely wrecked and the 4″ gun and 12 pounder, which were aft, were blown over the side. The propeller was blown off, causing the engines to race, but the Engineer on watch immediately stopped them. Very little water was thrown up but a great deal of debris from the poop, there was no flame, no smoke and no smell... The ship settled very rapidly by the stern... We launched all four boats without any trouble everything worked well, and all the crew and passengers, with the exception of one passenger, got safely away. The vessel sank... within 12 minutes of being torpedoed...

Captain Barnetson was on the bridge of the *Cape Race* and, as one of the lead ships, had an excellent view of the action. He was also very lucky to have survived the attack a torpedo having crossed under the stern of his ship before it hit the *Cape Corso*. He recalled the moment:

The sea was dead calm, wind force 0/1 with a hazy visibility and snow flurries... As the aircraft drew nearer they dived to 100 feet [30m] in order to release their torpedoes. One of the aircraft carried straight on its course and flew across the leading ships in the convoy, just clearing the forefoot of my vessel as it passed. The 'plane offered a target so large that it filled our gun sights and it banked on its side in an endeavour to edge away but the range was so short that our tracers could plainly be seen entering the fuselage of the machine. Immediately afterwards it crashed into the sea on my port bow. I am absolutely certain that our ship's gunfire brought this 'plane down, although I realise the possibility that other ships in the convoy may also have hit it.

As for the merchant seamen observing the attack from the decks of their ships, their perspective was somewhat different and mixed. Jack Drummond, a sailor on the icebreaker *Montcalm*, recalled that:

...the torpedo just missed our bow and we watched it carry on to hit the sternpost of the 'Cape Corso', the ship in the lead of the next column.

She was loaded with ammunition and drums of fuel. There was a terrific flash, and in seconds as we watched, the ship seemed to melt away into nothing and disappear. We all dropped to the deck and seconds later a terrific explosion followed, debris started falling, and then the wave of heat hit us… it was all over in a minute. One ship and crew, the next minute, nothing! All gone. It was a shattering experience. We were all very quiet, silent.[54]

The *Capira* was immediately astern of *Cape Corso* which gave Ensign Combs a good view of the action. He observed that three hits were made by torpedoes. SS *Cape Corso* blew up immediately, the flames reaching several hundred feet into the air, and the ship sank before *Capira* came abeam.[55] However, these accounts were somewhat at odds with John Barrett's recollections witnessed from the bridge of the SS *Expositor*:

A German bomber came down low into the middle of the convoy and was shot down but not before it released its torpedo. Some minutes later this struck the *Cape Corso*. There was an subdued explosion that burst through what I would call the #2 hatch cover. The ship began to sink slowly going down stern first. I saw no lifeboats lowered and assumed no one survived …[56]

However, John Barrett's assumption was incorrect. *Cape Corso*'s Second Engineer, Mr G. Waddingham, was one of the few survivors, and it is his account to which we now turn:

We saw six torpedo 'planes approaching the convoy on the starboard side, they circled round for some time without attacking the convoy. I decided things were dying down and went down to my cabin for a rest. Before I actually turned in I went up on deck to have a final look round. I heard the Mate shout that he had sighted the track of a torpedo approaching the ship on the starboard side. I looked and saw the torpedo making straight for the ship amidships, and a second later saw the 6 'planes in line abreast approaching the Convoy. They had apparently dropped their torpedoes whilst behind a cloud and were just rising to about 500 feet [150m] when

I sighted them. All the ships were firing and our Marlins opened fire too. I made a dash for the port side and a second later was thrown off my feet as the torpedo struck between the engine room and No. 3 on the starboard side… The Gunners on the Marlins were still firing after the ship had been struck. I did not see a flash with the torpedo nor had I any time to notice any column of water thrown up, for in a very few seconds the whole of the after part of the ship was a blazing inferno. … I saw one of the sailors rushing from the after part of the ship, his duffel coat pulled well over his head, he reached the after part and dived overboard, a second later a fireman came from aft his clothes ablaze like a human torch. I tore his clothes off him then decided it was time I dived overboard too. I did not see this fireman again. I dived overboard and when I came up I saw the deck was under water and the poop just an island, I saw the 3rd Mate trying to lower the port jolly boat and a second later I saw the ship sink… just 2 minutes after the explosion. There was one sailor in the port jolly boat, he had his leg caught in the wreckage strewn all over the boat and as the wreckage came to the surface the sailor came up too, he managed to get clear of the wreckage and swim away. While I was swimming in the water I saw one of the planes crash into the sea in flames just ahead of me.[57]

Without a life jacket, Waddingham swam around for another half hour[58] before being picked up by one of the escorting anti-submarine trawlers. Another two survivors were also picked up by this ship and three more by a destroyer. These were the only survivors.

Captain Austin in SS *Southgate* separately claimed to have shot down the aircraft that sank the *Cape Corso* as it skimmed across the fo'c'sle head and his gunners opened fire shooting off its port wing. It is not surprising, therefore, that Crombie's report did not stop short of criticising the screening vessels for not picking up the attackers more quickly and disrupting what became a well-coordinated attack, before the German planes got among the merchantmen. He noted that it was HMS *Bramble* from the central position of the screen that had opened fire with her Oerlikon guns first, but that *Somali* and *Matchless* should have been a few seconds quicker on the trigger. Had their reactions been slicker, he felt that the attack might have been hampered and more enemy aircraft brought down. Nevertheless, he conceded that it was unlikely that the loss of ships in the convoy could have been prevented, since the visibility was variable and that the half-light of the Arctic night, combined with haze, made the aircraft very difficult to see. Another disappointment was that HMS *Ulster Queen*'s Type 279 radar failed to detect the raiders. This was not unexpected, as detailed in the Commanding Officer's report, and was probably exacerbated because, unlike the first attack, the enemy flew in low and were probably camouflaged electronically by sea clutter. *Ulster Queen*'s position at the centre of the convoy (she had been placed there by FOC 10th CS) also meant that she could not bring her formidable anti-aircraft armament to bear on the attackers, who went for the lead ships in the convoy. The *Ulster Queen*'s commanding officer commented:

> The Torpedo aircraft were first sighted by '*Ulster Queen*' distant about 6 miles [11km] on Starboard bow of convoy, coming in very low (at 20 to 30 feet [6-8m] above Sea). '*Ulster Queen*' blew long Fog-horn blast hoisted signal for 'Air attack imminent' and commenced 4" barrage. Owing to '*Ulster Queen*'s' station between the columns this 4" barrage could not be fired low enough, and, in fact, had to be checked almost at once as the field of fire was so badly masked by two Merchant Ships that the approaching aircraft could not at times be seen above the line of the upper works of the intervening Merchant Ships.

Commenting on his ship's position in the convoy he added:

> The correct stationing of the A/A Ship is outside, but close to, the wing column of the Convoy on the side on which attack is expected. Preferably the A/A Ship should have sufficient flexibility of speed to vary frequently her position from ahead to astern on that side. In this position the A/A Ship has scope to use her long-range weapons effectively through 180 degrees and anything that gets past and over the Convoy can be tackled by her close-range weapons. I am convinced that had not German reconnaissance aircraft on May 2nd noted, for fourteen hours, the A/A Ship of P.Q. 15 boxed up in the middle of the Convoy (against my wish), the Torpedo Aircraft that night would not have attacked in a bunch, all on the one bearing most favourable to themselves and least favourable to us.[59]

It has to be said that, once Crombie had assumed command of the escort, he had considered moving *Ulster Queen* to a position where her gunfire against low-flying aircraft could be more effectively employed which, in his view, was ahead of the convoy but inside the screen. In the end he decided to leave her where she was. The risk of losing her to torpedo attack was considered to be too great and, in any case, he fully expected a full-scale air attack to be mounted by the Germans as they approached Murmansk, and thought it more prudent to husband her firepower for the anticipated battle. The balance of caution versus risk is always a close call in such situations, but in this case it would seem that the advice of the *Ulster Queen*'s Commanding Officer should have been heeded, as he had already gained considerable experience in convoy protection in the Southern Irish sea during a very active period. The Director of Gunnery and Anti-Aircraft Warfare's later comments on the convoy report also agreed that the decision to place *Ulster Queen* within the convoy was wrong.[60] That said, it is doubtful if a change of position of the A/A ship would have made much difference to the warning time, given the limitations of the Type 279 radar in these conditions against a low-flying enemy. Crombie's criticism of *Somali* and *Matchless* being slow on the trigger may therefore have been unfounded, especially if they had also at that time been alerted to the presence of a U-boat in the area which, as we shall see, remained a possibility.

For most of the crew and gunners these attacks were their first taste of close quarter action and losing ships in convoy. Barnetson's comments on their reaction to being under fire for the first time makes interesting reading:

> When first attacked the guns crew were a little nervy, but soon shook down to it and gave the enemy aircraft a warm reception. With the exception of the gunlayer it was their first experience of being in action. All the guns crew, including the Naval and Army personnel were very good and gave me great satisfaction, especially the Naval gunlayer. He was only a youngster but very keen and efficient, and had it not been for his leadership I do not think the others would have stuck to it as well.

Barnetson also mentioned in his report that all his officers and the catering department had been trained in gunnery, so they had a full gun crew and plenty of spare members. On the *Capira,* Armed Guard gun crews had also had a baptism of fire. They had been very vocal in their longing for action on the passage across the Atlantic, but following their experience in PQ15 they were no longer as enthusiastic. Although Barnetson was upbeat about his crew on the *Cape Race,* Walter Hesse on the *Mormacrey* reflected on another reaction to combat:

> None of us were the same after the first raid. Even the Chief Mate, ever the optimist, had deep lines of stress in his face. The slightest sound, a dropped hammer, the sound of running feet, sent shivers of dread through each man. We slept with our clothes on, never undressed except to shower. Mealtime was no longer leisurely nor a time for conversation. We deserted the officer's mess as soon as food was bolted down. Four hours in the engine room was an eternity. We lingered no longer in the engine room than was necessary. Conversations were whispered. We became introspective as events forced us to consider our own mortality.

There is no doubt that the German torpedo bombers, in all probability He111s, had exacted a considerable blow on PQ15. Even Tovey, in his covering note to the post-convoy report, paid tribute to the *Luftwaffe's* feat, attributing its success to the efficiency of the navigation and homing organisation of the German Air Force in bringing an attack to bear on the convoy 240 miles [400km] from their air base in moderate to poor visibility and the half-light of the Arctic night. It was also apparent that the inclusion of a CAM ship in the convoy was a wasted effort, as the Hurricane she carried on the catapult was never launched. Given that it would not have been of much use against the shadower, it could, however, have had some effect in breaking the formation of the torpedo bombers in the second attack, if it could have been launched in sufficient time. As it was the poor visibility and the poor performance of *Ulster Queen's* radar meant that the convoy's sole air asset was doomed to remain on its launch ramp. The Commodore, Captain Anchor, was under no illusions about effective air defence, even if his solution was out of the question at this time. After all it was his ship SS *Botavon* that had been sunk under him. In his post operation report he wrote:

It is considered if small aircraft carrier was in Convoy the 'shadower' could have been disposed of and therefore enemy would not have been continuously informed of the position of the Convoy. It is doubtful with the weather experienced if the Convoy could have been located in such poor visibility and low clouds. Merchant ships in Russian Convoys should have at least six Bofors. The present armament is inadequate to deal with Aircraft torpedo attack.

However, there is good evidence from Enigma intercepts that a torpedo from *U251* and not a German bomber sank the *Jutland*. Korvettenkapitän Heinrich Timm, in command of *U251,* had first made contact with PQ15 at 2200 hours and later attacked it claiming one hit.[61] He could not confirm success because *U251* had then been attacked and driven off. However, *U703,* which was in the same area, surfaced among a large area of wreckage at 0400 hours on the 3 May, and salvaged one of the *Jutland*'s life-belts. The four U-boats sent to intercept PQ15 were later joined by two others that had been involved in the operation against HMS *Edinburgh*. Intermittent contact was made with the convoy up to the early morning of 4 May. In this, the pack was undoubtedly assisted by signals from the shadowing aircraft, but after midday all U-boats withdrew to the vicinity of the Kola inlet to try and pick up PQ15 as it steamed towards Murmansk[62]. Crombie's record of events also indicates that this was a coordinated attack. In his post-operation report, he wrote that the convoy had been constantly shadowed by submarines abaft of either beam from noon on the 2nd to p.m. on the 4th. In particular, just before the 3 May attack:

It had been suspected that the convoy was being shadowed from the starboard bow by a submarine but doubt arose whether the signals received were not those of aircraft who were shadowing on the reciprocal bearing on the port quarter. HMS '*Badsworth*' however, reported from the intercepted signals that the submarine was surfacing and very shortly afterwards the aircraft attacked.

Crombie also suspected that the torpedoes that forced HMS *Somali* to take evasive action during the attack had come from a U-boat. It is also significant that, shortly afterwards, an officer and a lookout in HMS *Leda* noticed what was described as a black shape on the surface. *Leda* altered course, got a contact on ASDIC and attacked with depth charges. Contact was subsequently lost, but there was no visual evidence that the attack had been successful.

The following day started dull and with occasional snow squalls. There were constant sightings of U-boats on the surface throughout the day, and a number of chases and attacks with guns and depth charges ensued but without tangible result of any success. Crombie reported that ships in the escort also resorted to keeping U-boats at bay by dropping the occasional depth charge, even though there was no direct evidence of their presence. Storheill, the captain of the *St Albans*, reported chasing off a U-boat just before an over flight of German bombers in the early hours of 4 May. The cloud base was low and the visibility poor, so there was no reconnaissance plane in the vicinity to home the bombers onto the convoy. It was assumed that this duty had now been passed to the U-boats, and there is solid evidence for this from signals intercepts of U-boats tailing convoys whilst transmitting homing signals. It was Storheill's belief that his actions and those of other escorts keeping U-boats off the surface had thwarted further aerial attacks on the convoy. Nevertheless, there was one final attack by two Junkers Ju 88s at 2030 hours on 3 May that narrowly missed the trawler *Cape Palliser*, and resulted in some minor damage to her. Crombie noted in his report that at the time the cloud base was about 2,000 feet [615m], and that the attackers, of which he estimated 4-6, seemed frightened to come through. Again, we know from Enigma intercepts that this was a planned attack against PQ15. Following that, no further air attacks took place, although Crombie noted as a manuscript insert in his report that one Ju 88 was shot down.

At 1024 hours on 4 May, two Russian destroyers met PQ15 and took up station on the port and starboard beams of the convoy. Later that day, the weather deteriorated and a south easterly gale sprang up, bringing heavy snow. This provided excellent cover, and the convoy safely entered the Kola Inlet at 2200 hours on 5 May where each vessel hove-to until it picked up a pilot and was guided to its anchorage at Murmansk.

The loss of life during the passage of PQ15 was greatest on the SS *Cape Corso*. From a crew of 56 including 12 DEMS gunners, only 5 crew members and one gunner survived.[63] *Jutland* lost just one member, an American passenger named Mr Weinstein who was in his cabin at the time, and probably killed by the explosion when the torpedo struck. Captain J.H. Smith reported no casualties from the *Botavon*'s complement of 73, including the Commodore, his staff of six and six gunners, most of whom had been rescued by HMS *Badsworth*. In addition to incurring no casualties, Captain Smith had the added pleasure of being reunited with his son, who was *Badsworth*'s navigator. Sadly, 21 members of *Botavon*'s crew, although having survived PQ15, later lost their lives returning from Russia in HMS *Trinidad*, an incident that will be covered later.

Crombie's final reflection on the passage of PQ15 acknowledged:

> the excellent conduct of the convoy, the majority of which were American ships unused to convoy work. Their steadiness when the torpedo attack took place and leading ships, including the Commodore and Rear-Commodores' ships were sunk, their speed of opening fire and their excellent station keeping made the task of the escorts very much easier. It was largely due to the good conduct and discipline of the convoy that twenty two ships out of the twenty five arrived at Murmansk undamaged.

It took another three years for the US authorities to recognise formally the part played by their Naval and Armed Guard personnel who fought through PQ15 with the award of a battle star. PQ15 had been code-named COMPETENT and, in spite of the unfortunate incidents experienced by the escorts in the fog of war, it had at least been a highly competent effort by the merchantmen and their crews.

# 7 MURMANSK – THE EDGE OF THE EARTH

## (6 MAY TO 27 JUNE 1942)

The snow whisper of bows through water
Asking and answer in their lift
And screw, ceremonials
Of salt and savagery
Burial of man and mermaid

I remember the thirst of Murmansk
The great eyelids of water.
Can one ever see through them?

From *Murmansk* by Alan Ross

By Russian standards, Murmansk is a relatively new city. It was founded in 1916 as Romanov-on-Murman changing its name to Murmansk during the Soviet era. Before then it was very much a frontier town of log cabins, with a few timber piers serving an Arctic fishing fleet. During the Revolution, British and American forces landed there in support of the Tsarists opposing the Bolsheviks, and remained until 1921. Such overt support of the White Russian cause inevitably made few friends among the Soviet authorities, and when the British and Americans returned during the Second World War they were not exactly welcomed with open arms. Today it is one of the largest, most economically developed regions of Northern European Russia. Towering over its harbour is the Aloysha Memorial; a 150ft [45m] concrete statue of a Russian soldier in massive Soviet brutalist style, one of the few reminders of what the city suffered during the Great Patriotic War. The port lies at the end of the Kola Inlet, and the fact that it is ice-free all year round is one of its greatest assets; both for trade, and access to the arctic fishing grounds. This, together with its proximity to the Russo-German Front in the Second World War made it a natural, albeit dangerous, terminus for the Russian convoys[1].

The strategic importance of Murmansk had not been lost on the German High Command. Between the wars, the Soviets had developed the port as a trade cum naval centre, constructing bases to house their Northern Fleet at Polyarnoe, Grasnaya and Vaenga. As the only Arctic port free of ice all year–round, Murmansk had been an important objective for the Germans in their plans for the invasion of the Soviet Union. Within a week of the launch of the invasion, codenamed Operation Barbarossa, on 22 June 1941, the Germans had begun two subsidiary operations. Operation *Platin Fuchs* (Platinum Fox) threatened Murmansk directly from the west, whilst Operation *Polar Fuchs* (Arctic Fox) aimed at severing all links running south. General Eduard Dietl, Commanding General Mountain Corps Norway, was tasked with capturing the valuable nickel mines around Petsamo, overrunning Murmansk and cutting the Kirov railway running between Murmansk and Leningrad, today's St Petersburg. This was the route that transported the materiel supplied by the Allies to support the Soviet Army on the Eastern front. The fact that it had originally been constructed by German and Austrian prisoners of war 25 years earlier made it an important political as well as military objective for the German Army. A large contingent of Finnish troops was also used during Operation *Polar Fuchs* and, although the strategic objective was never achieved, the Finns met with considerable tactical success compared to their non-Arctic trained German counterparts. In spite of Dietl's excellent credentials as a commander, he faced an increasingly uphill task. The Soviets used the terrain to great effect, especially in the blocking of roads, building strongpoints and stubbornly defending fortified positions. Unlike the poor performance of the Red Army on the main front during the initial stages of Barbarossa, the Russians fighting in the Arctic theatre conducted a well-led and highly effective fighting withdrawal that delayed the German advance, to the point where German operations failed in their strategic intent of isolating and capturing Murmansk. Instrumental in this success was the conscription of local workers into a fighting division. Formed on 5 September 1941, the 186th Polar Division of the Peoples' Militia included more than 10,000 militiamen. These were mainly shipyard workers, railwaymen, fish farmers and employees of the institutions of the city of Murmansk. The Soviets also released prisoners for duty in the Division. During the Division's first operation, it successfully blocked the route of the Wehrmacht's 3rd Infantry Division, tasked with taking Murmansk, and eventually stabilised the front line some way from the city[2].

During the ensuing stalemate, the port continued to operate – albeit under frequent and intense bombardment from *Luftwaffe* squadrons stationed at Kirkenes in Norway and Petsamo in Finland. However, with the front line a mere 20 miles [32km] from the town, there remained the continuous existential threat of a German push that could eventually engulf it. In spite of the fact that it never materialised, the population quite naturally existed throughout this time in a permanent state of fear and apprehension.

Those confined to Murmansk suffered terrible privations. Food was short and there were long queues outside communal soup kitchens; disease was prevalent, and the German bombing campaign against the town, together with those of Leningrad and Stalingrad (the latter modern-day Volgograd) was among the heaviest of the war and later recognised by the Soviet authorities in the award of 'Heroic City' status to all three. The rather primitive feel of the war-torn town and the impact of the bombing were concisely captured by Rear Admiral Boucher following his arrival there:

The houses on each side were tall. Tinny music interspersed with news and propaganda, continually blared from the tops of them out of loud-speakers. On entering... we passed beneath a wire stretched across the street from which were suspended some little tin signs. There was a motor lorry, a horse and cart, a reindeer sledge and one or two more things to indicate the classes of traffic which were allowed to use that street... Half of Murmansk consisted of wooden buildings while the other half was of stone. The walls of the wooden houses seemed to have been made of tree trunks piled one on top of the other with their ends cleverly mortised together. I was afterwards told that this was done by the use of an axe alone... The Germans had shrewdly concentrated with incendiary bombs on the wooden part of the town, reserving their high explosives for the part built of stone... Blackout precautions were simple and economical. If a light showed from any window, some soldier, passing by, fired one or two bullets into it – just as a sort of hint."[3]

Shortly after midnight on 6 May 1942, SS *Capira* dropped anchor in the Kola Inlet just off Murmansk. It had been intended to discharge her cargo at Archangel, but the prevailing ice conditions had prevented that; however, the two icebreakers *Krassin* and *Montcalm* in PQ15 were escorted there and arrived on 21 June. From the time *Capira* commenced discharging until she stood out to sea again 53 days later, the crew experienced 125 alerts resulting in 66 air raids. Ensign Combs noted: 'The target for these raids was practically always ships at anchor in the harbour or those discharging alongside a pier.' He went on:

> On May 31, 1942, we finished discharging and loading ballast; and during this period of twenty eight days which followed we lay at anchor about ten miles from the city. From this distance we could see the anti-aircraft fire of Murmansk's defences but could seldom distinguish the attacking planes. In spite of this fact I actually counted two hundred and fifty enemy planes which attacked the city... During the stay there I was forced to instruct all my gunners to hold their fire unless we were attacked, or the planes came close enough to distinguish enemy markings. This action was taken because of the great quantity of targets, and the great scarcity of ammunition.[4]

Combs' observation on the scarcity of ammunition due to the incessant attacks from the air was borne out by others, who noted that some natures of anti-aircraft ammunition simply ran out even before they had reached port[5]. The raids on Murmansk were in the main carried out by Junkers JU 88 dive-bombers, although Messerschmidt ME110 fighter bombers and JU 87 Stukas were also seen on occasion. They were invariably accompanied by ME109 fighter cover. Attacks emanated from the north at high level, or relatively low level from the south, the aggressors using the surrounding mountains to cover their attack. The German planes were painted silver underneath, and a dark colour on top, and as a result were difficult to pick out at any great altitude. Dive bombing was the favoured method of attack, although strafing attacks were also made on ships. Nevertheless, the accuracy of the German bombing appeared to be very poor, and Combs only observed two ships sunk and two damaged by near misses during the time

*Capira* lay at anchor. However, Murmansk itself took a pounding during that time, as witnessed by the smoke and fires that could be seen from the ship. Combs reported that the Soviet Air Force response, in the shape of British Hurricanes, United States P 40s and a few Russian-built fighters, seldom appeared until the enemy had delivered their payload.

Walter Hesse's experiences were much the same[6]. His ship the *Mormacrey* could not berth straight away due to extensive bomb damage in the port area, where several ships that had been hit by the *Luftwaffe* lay half submerged in the water. It took a full ten days to unload, with women playing prominent roles, including fuelling and driving tanks and jeeps off the dockside. *Mormacrey* was also attacked whilst at anchor, and narrowly missed being sunk. In spite of the danger, Hesse observed that air raid warnings were so frequent that, after a time, they began to be treated with some nonchalance. Once unloaded, the *Mormacrey* was ballasted with fifteen hundred tons of rock. Ships were also loaded with military and other sundry items of scrap, that were to be taken back to the States and reconstituted back into war materiel.

The SS *Deer Lodge*, another ex PQ15 vessel, was not as fortunate as the *Mormacrey*. On 18 May, she was attacked whilst at anchor in the Kola Inlet, awaiting a homeward bound convoy. A flight of six enemy bombers went for her, and one near miss lifted the ship's stern bodily out of the water. The explosion blew in several plates and frames, and her stern immediately settled on the bottom. The Chief Engineer rushed below and closed the shaft alley watertight door, which prevented the flooding of the engine room and boiler room, whilst the Master ordered flooding of the No. 1 hold. This action put the ship down by the head and raised her stern off the bottom. She was then beached stern-to by her crew on a nearby mud flat, and wire hawsers made fast to huge boulders ashore. The ship was then hove ashore on top of high water by her own deck machinery. For two months, the crew carried out temporary repairs between tides which enabled the ship, eventually, to shift to dry dock where she was again made seaworthy for active service. Both the Master, Alexander Henry, and the Chief Engineer, Frank Townshend were awarded the US Distinguished Service Medal for their quick thinking and courage that day[7].

Rear Admiral Bevan, the Senior British Naval Officer (SBNO) North

Russia, based with his small staff at Murmansk, also remarked[8] on the frequent attacks endured by the thirty or so ships at anchor in the Kola Inlet. As the nearest German airfield was a mere 30 miles [48km] distant and the *Luftwaffe* aided by continuous daylight and clear weather, it was little wonder that Murmansk was by this time largely in ruins. Walter Hesse took time off to walk its streets and found them littered with debris. Many of the high-rise blocks in the centre had been damaged or destroyed, and the surrounding dwellings made of wood raised to the ground; only the brick chimney stacks were left standing. There was no plumbing, and the population had been reduced to pumping their water from hydrants in the street. In this respect, it was little better on the ships anchored in the Kola Inlet, for a shortage of water-boats constantly delayed the supply of fresh water to them.

This was only one of the many daily frustrations endured by Rear Admiral Bevan. When dealing with the Soviet authorities, requests were subject to the Soviet chain of command and decisions were usually taken at the highest level. As a consequence, Bevan's efforts to negotiate the provisioning of ships with even the most basic of commodities such as fresh drinking water were subject to considerable delay. Given the adverse military situation at that time, Bevan was also constantly worried that continued use of the facilities at Murmansk during the summer months would result in all ships entering the port being either damaged or sunk. He was also concerned over the timing of convoys leaving the Kola Inlet. Sailings of QP convoys were timed to coincide with PQ sailings from Iceland. This was done to ensure the most economic and effective use of the Covering Force, but if detected sent a clear signal to the Germans that a fully-ladened convoy would shortly be on its way to one or other of the two North Russian ports. If sailings from the Inlet could be made in poor weather, the chances of detection by the enemy and hence their gaining intelligence regarding inward-bound convoys would be limited. German air activity would also be limited, and the early stages of the voyage in close proximity to enemy air bases could be negotiated, hopefully without undue interference.

Bevan's diplomatic skills were also exercised over the insistence by the Russian Trade Department that Archangel could be used by convoys during the winter months. Compliance with such pressure from the Soviet authorities had resulted in six ships being stranded ice- bound in the port for some time. Nevertheless, the precarious military situation and uncertainty over the future of Murmansk in May/June 1942 presented the possibility of a forced move to Archangel in any case. Hospital staffs were already considering evacuating the wounded to Archangel, anticipating big battles ahead. German planes had recently dropped leaflets that boasted of '... destroying Murmansk by 1 July and then coming to bury the dead.' Reports had also been received of an all-arms division sighted on the Rovaniemi/ Murmansk road on 3 June, and 100 small craft collected at Vadso for a possible landing on the Ribachi Peninsular. In the opinion of the Soviet Commander in Chief, Northern Fleet, this added up to an attempt by the enemy to seize and occupy the Ribachi Peninsular, and bitter fighting around Murmansk for the next three months was anticipated. Frequent air raids and the gradual destruction of the town itself had forced Bevan to move the entire British Headquarters, including its communications centre, to the outskirts of Murmansk. He reported subsequently, and not without understatement, that the entire staff at Murmansk was going through a very unpleasant experience but continued to function, in spite of the difficulties. Nevertheless, essential priorities were being maintained, and he praised the great efforts that had been made by the Russians to improve the football pitch which was now in constant use, albeit a little dusty!

It is little wonder, therefore, that Murmansk itself held little attraction for crewmen if and when they could get ashore. Captain Barnetson, master of the *Cape Race*, whilst remarking that his ship's company were a happy crowd and adept at entertaining themselves, complained that the conditions in Murmansk left a lot to be desired from the point of view of recreation for the men. There was no canteen or place where they could purchase food or drink at reasonable prices. Although Walter Hesse of the *Mormacrey* confirmed that he could find no stores, bars or amenities of any sort, he did manage to track down a hotel that was still operating and serving tea. He also managed to locate a place showing patriotic Russian movies and, on another occasion, attended a concert given by Red Army personnel.

Even so, for the ordinary Russian living in Murmansk things were much worse. One of the most meticulously recorded accounts of this period was made by Vladimir Loktev, a 15-year- old boy who charted, in very fine detail, the daily German air raids on the city between 13 August 1941 and

30 October 1942, as well as detailing the reports he picked up from the radio and what he heard on the street. All these he recorded in his diary[9]. Like any schoolboy he was passionate about sport but was also adept at languages and was also technically creative. Sadly, he didn't survive the war. Having been called up in 1943 he was posted to the front and was killed in Poland shortly before the final victory in May 1945. In letters to friends and relatives, he wrote about how he missed his native Murmansk and dreamed of returning one day to his city; but sadly, it was not to be.

Also keeping a diary at this time was Tom Chilvers, a merchant seaman in the SS *Empire Baffin*, which had arrived in the port on 30 May having survived the German onslaught on PQ16. Chilvers supported the Republican cause during the Spanish Civil War, and had fought in Spain against the Fascists. He was therefore sympathetic to the Soviets and in company with many other merchant seamen was a committed communist himself. The following extracts from both his[10] and Vladimir's[11] diaries give a flavour of the hazards of life in Murmansk at this time:

Sunday 31 May: They tell us six planes were shot down the day before we arrived and two the same day we arrived. Witnessed a dog fight yesterday (of a few seconds duration) Soviet fighters are certainly sharp on the scene. Workers work the whole clock round – women too. Red Army men impress me in spite of all I've heard about them. Across from us they are working loading barges for the front. (They are on leave) I wonder how our boys would take it if they were asked to work in their leave. Survivors come aboard from some of the other ships – there are 1500 ashore – survivors from different convoys.

Monday 1 June: Lovely hot day. Sirens went again this morning – again the sky was full of fighters in no time. Terrific barrage put up as usual and resulted in blowing four planes completely out of the sky - saw one parachute falling out, must have been killed.

Tuesday 2 June: Four air raids in clear blue sky. In the afternoon raid one bomb landed on the quay and damaged it. Amazing escape of a young girl tally clerk who covered with straw from the bomb blast calmly smoother

her hair and laughed. The spirit of these people is truly remarkable – we also had a narrow escape ashore bombs whistled down both sides of us – we lay down behind some timber – one set of bombs sank a small schooner. Siren went again followed a crowd to a shelter – below we heard the thud of bombs landing and when we came up that a block of flats was on fire 200 yards [180m] from the shelter entrance. Watched… the heroic efforts of Murmansk firemen. Whistle went again while watching and again we went down the shelter. This time went into a big reinforced concrete hall 'in the shelter' and sat down in comfortable chair – banners and photos of Lenin, Stalin and Kalinin and raised platform at end for meetings and what I suppose was radio gramophone. Workmen are still working at this shelter – must hold thousands – hewn out of solid rock.

Thursday 18 June: The enemy threw everything at the city again. The last alarm was at 1848… this time they bombed our house. The bomb went through the kitchen hit the stove and exploded. Our room was devastated and the one next to it had a wall blown down. There was nothing left of the kitchen or my aunt's room…. I was standing on the porch at the time and there were some others with me but we were unhurt… I had gone to the kitchen and looked out of the window. The anti-aircraft guns had opened up and so I went out on the porch again. Then I saw bombs falling and detonating and I shouted lie down. Suddenly there was a loud explosion, my ears rang and it became dark as night from the dust and rubble. We were going to try and go upstairs but I ripped the door open and went out onto the porch. To my surprise I saw that the bomb had hit our house. There were logs scattered all around and a huge log had fallen on the porch… It was a wonder that we had survived. It was fortunate that the bomb had hit the stove where it had stuck… If it hadn't hit the stove then it would have gone through to the lower floor and all of us would have perished. But, thank God, we survived!

Friday 19 June: … after we had thought it about all clear Alfie spotted twenty planes in a bank of clouds overhead – and then Soviet fighters attacked them and I jumped back into the shelter knowing that if they let go they would land pretty near – everybody crouched and lay in the shelter as the bombs came whistling down both windows of one shelter were blown 'out' by the blast. I thought or I should (say) 'we' thought our end had come. When the smoke cleared we found that one house was blown sky high and two more on fire. There was other serious damage further over – must have been two raids together because smoke was coming over the hills across the fiord – firemen was ashore at the time and told me a horrible story of the raid – which I ignore here because I don't want to dwell on these things.

In spite of this almost constant bombardment, Chilvers managed to find some shops and postal facilities still operating in Murmansk. He also went to the Interclub (short for the International Club) where he met fellow veterans from the Spanish Civil War International Brigade. The Interclub had a library and smoking room, he was also able to order books from there. Chilvers was intensely interested in and sympathetic towards the Russians, and he mixed with them quite freely during his frequent spells ashore; often taking his guitar along with him for impromptu sing-songs. So, for those with the interest and motivation to go ashore, there was the occasional (albeit fleeting) semblance of normality to be had amongst the daily carnage. Nevertheless, the discharge of cargo under such conditions was a precarious affair not made any easier, or indeed safer, by the Russian stevedores not used to handling military equipment. Rear Admiral Boucher witnessed the following incidents at the dockside:[12]

The whole area was a huge, dark, snow-covered shambles. Many millions of pounds worth of cargoes were littered everywhere. Huge cases marked 'DELICATE INSTRUMENTS WITH GREAT CARE' 'THIS SIDE UP' 'KEEP DRY' were all higgledy-piggledy with feet of snow on top of them... The first tank hoisted out from the *Fort Kullyspell* went straight down through the wharf, breaking the woodwork and into the water until it was stopped and hoisted back into the ship. Soon afterwards Russians repaired the wharf with huge baulks of timber and the discharging of the cargo was continued... British tank officers arrived to hand over to the Russians the tanks we had brought up for their army. The Russians were delighted. The tanks were exactly what they had been longing for. The moment they had learnt how to drive them, they used them to charge the cases which were lying about the wharf. They pushed each case which would move, inland until the heap of snow which piled up in front of it prevented it from moving any more. Then they roared back and joyfully rammed the next one. A mammoth game of 'shove halfpenny'

On another occasion, Boucher observed a crane borne on a train rigged to a huge case some distance away. The great distance of the crane from the load did not seem to concern those who had been ordered to shift it. They proceeded to operate the gears, but to little avail as the case would not shift. Nevertheless, they persisted in their efforts. They had been given their orders to wind. It was that or punishment – therefore they wound. The case stubbornly refused to move, so the inevitable happened and the crane plus train was pulled over onto its side and remained there in the snow for some days.

Captain Leslie Saunders RN, the Commanding Officer of the ill-fated HMS *Trinidad* undergoing repairs in the Kola Inlet (after one of its torpedoes had gone rogue and hit her) added: 'The local people seemed anxious to be friendly, but always with an eye on their Commissars, who were suspicious of too much fraternising and were sometimes troublesome. There were one or two cases that I had to take up with the Authorities, but on the whole, our Russian allies did their best to help us.'[13] One of the cases that Saunders had to take up with the Soviet Authorities was that of the ship's chaplain, Graham. He was a young man who had insisted on joining the Navy, in spite of objections from Eton College where he was a junior master. He was very keen, but somewhat inexperienced. He had cultivated a full set, no doubt to appear more sailor-like, and to disguise his relative youth. However, this got him into trouble with the local police when he was asked to produce his passport, as the accompanying photograph of a clean-shaven individual took some explaining. Graham was also taken to task by his commanding officer for being too strict in his subsidiary role as ship's censor. In his defence, Graham insisted that the crew were up to all sorts of dodges to indicate where they were serving. Challenged to give an example he offered SWALK. The captain dismissed this as 'Sealed With A Loving Kiss' and told him to let it pass. After a few more acronyms were dismissed as innocuous Graham was asked if there were any more. Rather sheepishly he replied that there was one but that he was too embarrassed to mention it. When ordered to do so by the captain he blurted out BOTLOP. The meaning of this particular acronym was unknown to the captain, and Graham was asked to explain. Rather embarrassed, he replied: 'I think it means "Better Between The Legs Than on Paper."' In spite of his relative inexperience he had obviously come a long way since leaving Eton for the licentious world of Jolly Jack Tar.

Of more serious concern to Saunders was the state of the medical facilities provided by the Soviets in Murmansk, and he arranged for the medical officer to visit the local hospital and assess the conditions. On returning, the MO reported that it was a dismal place with loud-speakers blaring propaganda incessantly. He added that they thought little of taking a man's leg off without anaesthetic, and wondered if the Slav did not feel pain as much as in, as he rather disparagingly put it, the more civilised countries. Mr Waddingham, the Second Engineer from the ill-fated *Cape Corso,* also found himself in hospital in Murmansk, being treated for his burns. He reported the food and treatment there as pretty grim; the medical supplies were very short and the meals consisted of soup, black bread, barley and occasionally a piece of raw fat pork. His burns were treated with tannic acid jelly, a particularly painful experience[14]. Bill Short, the 4th Engineer on the SS *Induna,* realised that the hospital in Murmansk was a school that had been converted to a frontline casualty-clearing hospital, serving the battlefront only a few miles distant. He described the ward as a large gymnasium with a large platform at one end, and row upon row of beds with the minimum of space between them. They were full of amputation cases and there was no time to do any cosmetic surgery. He described the scene with limbs literally chopped off, and open wounds dripping gangrenous infection. 'Imagine the stench,' he wrote, 'all the windows were boarded up and Murmansk was being bombed every hour on the hour.'[15] The observations on the medical facilities in Murmansk were no different from those further from the front line. A coxswain in Archangel testified that the hospital there was filthy and that there had been no anaesthetic available for the amputation of frost-bitten limbs and very few medicines of any kind.[16] However bad the conditions were, and however primitive the treatments, the care shown by the local population was second to none as Jim Campbell, steward's boy on the ill-fated SS *Induna* who had just had his leg amputated, testified: 'I must at this time say that the Russian people were really marvellous. They had very little of anything, yet they had no hesitation in giving what they had to us.'[17]

The SBNO was well aware of the poor condition of the medical facilities provided by the Soviets, especially at the Polyarnoe Naval Hospital, but he was more understanding in his judgement, especially of the care provided by the hospital staff, than some of his naval counterparts:

Unsatisfactory and distressing as their treatment may be according to our standards, I am convinced by personal investigation and many visits that there is no want of kindness or consideration; the Russian medical staff treat our men as they treat their own, perhaps with even more consideration... During the time spent in Murmansk hospital it became obvious to all who suffered from exposure, that we were very lucky to be under the care of doctors and ward nurses who were experts in the handling and treatment of frostbite and exposure cases...[18]

Nevertheless, the parlous state of the medical facilities in Murmansk prompted the SBNO to lobby the Admiralty. On 1 June[19] he signalled that if convoys to Northern Russia were to be continued at their current rate and scale, then the number of hospital casualties must be expected to increase well beyond the present (high) level. Although he agreed that the Russian authorities were doing all that they could, given the circumstances, he was aware that their methods were below British standards and that our sailors were enduring unnecessary suffering as a result. He went on to request a 100-bed hospital ship as an 'unostentatious necessity' and that, if this could not be arranged, then a British or US field hospital of similar capacity be established ashore. He also pointed out the difficulty in obtaining even basic medical supplies such as plaster of Paris, antiseptics and all forms of anaesthetic. However, little resulted from his requests and suggestions at that time.

In addition to the prospect of physical injury, all seamen on Arctic duties were subject to high and constant levels of stress that could also render men totally ineffective. This had been identified earlier in the war, when the potential for mental stress had been recognised and measures put in place to deal with it. As an example, the crew of HMS *Hebe* had to be rested during the Dunkirk evacuations to avoid the onset of mental breakdown; the crew of HMS *Hussar* was replaced for the same reason, following constant attacks whilst escorting East Coast convoys[20]. With specific reference to service in Arctic waters, the Medical Officer on HMS *Leda* wrote:

> It has been rather interesting to observe the reactions of people to the abnormal stress and strain which action in this climate has imposed upon them. The immediate effect of air attack is one of nervous stimulation, coupled with fear or acute apprehension. This apprehension is minimised for those whose minds are occupied with a particular job. But for those whose task it is to watch and wait, it is at a maximum. When a particular incident is over a variety of reactions are seen. Some men laugh hilariously and hurl illustrated epithets after the departing enemy. By contrast, other men reflect despondency. Following a prolonged period of attacks, there may be a period during which everyone outwardly appears normal apart from obvious weariness from lack of sleep. Then the glimmerings of psychoneurosis begin to appear.[21]

The MO concluded that no-one, except those who desire to stay, should remain in ships especially small vessels such as Flower Class Corvettes, under the conditions prevailing in the Arctic convoys for longer than 18 months. Senior officers appear to have been at particular risk. At the end of a year's service in Arctic waters, for example, nine officers, all with good records, were invalided from a single warship. By 1943, it was recognised that for a number of destroyers and smaller vessels, captains had been left in command beyond the point at which they were effective leaders. Mid-way through the conflict, the Navy accepted that even experienced sailors had a breaking point, and introduced the term 'fatigue' for those who earlier in the war might have been diagnosed as suffering from an anxiety state eventually leading to mental breakdown. This was designed to avoid any stigmatizing label and to encourage natural recovery[22].

Merchant seamen were subject to the same stresses, especially those exposed to attack from the air. Tom Chilvers' diary entry for 28 May, when PQ16 was nearing the Kola Inlet, reflected precisely the behaviour described by RN psychiatrists above:

Everyone's nerves rattled and nobody is sleeping below – (if anyone is sleeping at all.) As it's my 4/8 I tried to get some sleep. About 12 of us tried to get some rest in the mess-room but everyone was dreaming the same nightmare, dive bombers and more dive bombers. I couldn't sleep: sometimes nearly fell off but would be awakened by the snores of 'Dunkirk' each snore being a Stuka. (Later) Found that we have 4 Soviet destroyers with us – everybody is relieved – you can feel it in the air – sailors and gunners laugh as they talk.[23]

Extreme stress could also result in bizarre behaviour:

One of the American seamen whom we took onboard was sent to us straight from a mental hospital, where he had been kept since he was put ashore in Russia. The poor chap had lost his reason during the latter part of his trip out. As soon as he stepped on to the deck of the *Northern Gem*, he made several attempts to throw himself over the side and had to be physically restrained from doing so each time. Eventually with the help of some of the crew, I managed to get him into a bunk in the forward mess-deck, but from then on he would take nothing to eat or drink, saying that we were trying to poison him. It was tragic to see a man like this; his nerve had completely gone. Nothing we did would pacify him, and it became evident to me that we could not keep him onboard.[24]

Others spoke of sailors who, having survived the passage to northern Russia, could not bring themselves to venture onto hostile waters again. One such severely afflicted crew member was put on a plane to return to the States by stages. Ironically, it never reached its destination having been lost somewhere over the Atlantic.[25]

For other aspects of life in the North Russian ports that directly affected those awaiting passages back to the UK or USA, we need to turn primarily to Rear Admiral Bevan's reports.[26] Most of the issues of major concern to him impinged directly of the wellbeing and safety of both Royal and Merchant Navy personnel anchored in the Kola Inlet or ashore at Murmansk and Archangel. Even after a year into his North Russian posting, he reflected that one could not pretend to know the conditions or even the general outlook of the population. He was not reticent, however, in stating his professional opinions on matters of his direct concern. His criticisms of the Soviet Hierarchy in Murmansk were well-founded and robustly expounded in his reports.

Bevan had already had ample experience of the Soviet's intransigence. Once inside the Kola Inlet, no vessel no matter how big or small could move without the express approval of the Soviet duty officer. Without such approval, the boom would not be opened for the vessel to exit. British boats had been arrested and their coxswains detained when coming to the jetty at night to take officers back to their ship. Soviet sentries had threatened to open fire on a British officer taking soundings astern of his ship in Polyarnoe harbour. The whole atmosphere, Bevan commented, was one of ignorant suspicion or rigid adherence to the letter of the law. Nevertheless, when the Soviet authorities decided that something had to be done, no matter how difficult, it was. As an example, Bevan cited an incident where some heavy machinery had to be removed from the hold of a merchantman. Unfortunately, the weight of the load was far in excess of the capabilities of the lifting gear available. Undaunted, the Russians proceeded to lift each end of the machinery alternately, placing logs, wedges and planks underneath as space became available. In such manner, the machinery was brought level with the deck and then slid down a ramp onto the jetty. Sixty truckloads of timber were then unloaded from the hold. During this process, the ship's foremast had gone over the side – but the Russians made no attempt to recover it.

Bevan also commented favourably on the speed with which dock facilities were repaired following air raids. Work continued in shifts day and night even in the coldest weather, and he reserved especial praise for the efforts of Russian women who were frequently employed as winchmen on the wharves. In Archangel, all timber-loading was carried out by women working in gangs of eight in each hold on 12-hour shifts. However, Bevan was less enamoured with Russian timekeeping. There was a general indifference to punctuality; consequently, all Russians waited patiently and expected to do so. Appointments were also very difficult to fix except when dealing with very senior officers. One event where there was no difficulty in bringing British and Russian personnel together at the same time, however, was during the showing of films provided by the Royal Naval Film Corporation. These were much appreciated by the Russians as well as their British counterparts; the Russians having a particular liking for movies such as *Robin Hood* and *Snow White*. Apparently, Admiral Golovko frequently requested films for a private viewing, demonstrating that the products of Hollywood were not considered decadent by Russians requiring some light relief during Murmansk's darkest days.

Other forms of recreation reported by the SBNO included pulling and sailing races on Sunday afternoons, football matches attended by a band that played during the match but not at half-time, and a home-grown form of volleyball. Some gymnastic equipment was also provided and in the winter skiing was popular. Swimming, however, was rarely indulged in even on the warmest days; whether this was due to the temperature of the water or the pollution attendant on most ports is not recorded. Most of these activities were primarily indulged in by those personnel based in Murmansk, although individuals from visiting ships would avail themselves of these facilities given the opportunity.

Commenting on the perilous situation of the ordinary Russian, Bevan was much concerned by the general shortage of food prevalent in North Russia during his tour of duty. Eggs, potatoes, green vegetables and sugar were at best in short supply, or unobtainable. In addition to chocolate, cigarettes could not be bought without a special permit, forcing Russian sailors and dock workers to roll their own using poor tobacco and any piece of newspaper that was handy. In such circumstances, currency was of little value or indeed utility and a barter economy ensued. A tin of condensed milk or loaf of bread could be exchanged for a bottle of vodka or, bizarrely, a guitar. Wild strawberries brought from the country to the railway station by young children were not sold but bartered for other foodstuffs. Small wonder therefore, Bevan reported, if British provisions sometimes find their way ashore in spite of all precautions. Where cash transactions were attempted, prices were often vastly inflated, and Bevan relates an incident where a young apprentice sitting in the public gardens in Archangel was offered 100 roubles for his socks. The official exchange rate at that time was less than 50 roubles to a pound sterling. £2 for a pair of second-hand socks at 1942 prices was indeed inflationary, but a means to easy money for those with socks to spare.

Apart from occasional sorties into the black market and other minor infringements, there is little evidence of any major disciplinary issues coming to the attention of the authorities. However, during his tenure as SBNO, Admiral Bevan requested that he be given powers to convene Naval courts under s. 480 of the Merchant Shipping Act[27]. Apparently there had been a Merchant Seaman on a heavy lift ship deployed in Murmansk who had been causing some disciplinary problems. This generated considerable correspondence on the issues arising. For example, was there a possibility of merchant seamen being imprisoned and if so where? Would requests be made to the Russians for prison facilities? As an alternative, could miscreants be escorted to British sovereign territory or to somewhere where a British consul was in residence and tried there? Could the SBNO, as a flag officer and against Naval tradition, be made a CO of a small British ship for the purposes of administering summary justice? If so, what sort of ship could be deployed? Etc., etc. Legal advice was sought by the Second Sea Lord, which inevitably gave no concrete opinion, but did go through all the possible scenarios of who could have jurisdiction. This included the Russians and the possibility of British merchant seamen being tried in their courts and held in their gaols; to which one of the Navy's personnel branches commented:

'… it would be politically and psychologically unfortunate to proceed with the idea of imprisoning British merchant seamen in North Russian prisons. It is bad enough for our merchant seamen to have to put up with Russian hospital accommodation.' The Foreign Office most strongly endorse this view, and oppose the holding of Naval courts in Russia other than on board one of HM Ships.

The issue eventually fizzled out in the Spring of 1942 when SBNO was denied his request.

Those survivors, wounded or otherwise, who had been unfortunate enough to have their ships sunk under them, were understandably keen to get back home as soon as possible. The SBNO was also concerned about the build-up of survivors, and was equally keen to see them sent back on whatever transport was available. Even so, survivors could prove a little picky over the ships they were assigned to. For example, a number of Americans assigned to HMS *Northern Gem*[28], a coal-burning ASW trawler, were not very happy about the size of the vessel. However, after giving a little trouble, they knuckled down and gave a great deal of help in the stoke-hold. No doubt the energy expended in shovelling coal dissipated any further concerns that they had about their somewhat tight accommodation. The fact that they had raised any objections at all is surprising, given the conditions that they had endured in Northern Russia, and were recorded by the *Northern Gem*'s coxswain as they settled in for the passage home:

> from these survivors… we heard how they and some of the wounded and frost-bitten men had been treated; they had suffered a rough time compared to what we'd had to put up with. They had been herded into wooden huts, with only sacking at the windows to keep out the bitterly cold Arctic winds and the nightly frosts. They slept on bug-ridden straw mattresses, if they were lucky that is; others had to sleep on bare boards and even the cold frozen earth. On most days they had to make do with one meal a day of what was laughingly called by their providers, vegetable stew… Those who had been able to move were shared out between all the ships that were to make up this convoy, and they were more pleased than we were, if that was possible, to be on the way home at last, and like us were prepared to take any risk to get away from North Russia. They vowed that never again would they sign on a vessel bound for that area of war, but I have no doubt that many of them did just that, and in my opinion all who sailed in merchant ships during the war years were very brave men doing a dangerous but necessary job of work.[29]

Such primitive conditions and the constant threat of death and destruction made it imperative that survivors of ships sunk during the passage up to Russia were returned home as soon as possible. However, the experience of the survivors of SS *Botavon* demonstrated how much of a lottery this could be. Following their rescue, survivors from the *Botavon* proceeded on board HMS *Badsworth* to Murmansk, where they were disembarked and accommodated in Russian barracks on 6 May. They remained there for five days in unsanitary conditions, surviving on a plate of rice three times a day. Thereafter they were moved to Murmansk itself. Forty *Botavon* survivors were selected to go home on 13 May in the cruiser HMS *Trinidad. Trinidad* had been in Murmansk being patched up after sustaining a hit from a rogue torpedo that she had fired during an engagement with German destroyers whilst escorting PQ13. As a consequence, her speed was reduced to 20 knots [37km/hr]. Two days out of Murmansk, she was attacked by more than twenty JU 88 bombers. A single bomb struck the ship, exacerbating previous damage and starting a fire. Sixty-three men were lost. Among them were 20 survivors from HMS *Edinburgh* and 21 survivors from SS *Botavon*, including Alan Robinson the galley boy. The decision was taken to scuttle her and she was torpedoed by HMS *Matchless* and went to the bottom off the North Cape. The remaining survivors, including Captain Smith the Master of the *Botavon*, left Murmansk in HMS *Badsworth* on 21 May, finally arriving safely in Londonderry on 30 May.

As a postscript to the sinking of the *Trinidad,* her captain later wrote that he had been approached by Rear Admiral Stuart Bonham-Carter[30], who had raised his flag in the ill-fated *Edinburgh* before she was attacked and sunk, and told that he intended to return to the UK in the *Trinidad*. Saunders was not enthusiastic, observing that Bonham-Carter had also been aboard HMS *Sheffield* when she was mined. These things have a habit of going in threes – and, as it transpired, they did.

Those returning home no doubt took with them mixed feelings about their time in North Russia. Some, like Tom Chilvers, were impressed especially by the spirit of the ordinary Russian coping with both daily hardships and the threat of sudden death. Others were grateful for the sacrifices made by those endeavouring to relieve their suffering; but the majority left without a backward glance or thought and were pleased to be on their way far from such a depressing and dangerous environment. Senior officers, like Saunders, were vocal in their criticism of the system and its people, whom he described as:

...a hardy but crude race, industrious, brutal and under constant supervision by the 'Party', with dire penalties for misbehaviour... They were not to be trusted as far as carrying out to the full any undertaken (sic) that they had (been) given, as was evidenced by the Naval and Air support which they were supposed to give us; it always fizzled out. All their educated and upper classes had, of course, been eliminated by the Revolution.

Setting aside their assumptions and bias about Russians in general and the Soviet system in particular, criticisms by senior officers such as Saunders, Hamilton, Bevan and Boucher were not endorsed by ordinary seamen who engaged with a terrorised Russian community desperately attempting to survive and return to some semblance of normality. In doing so many experienced the kindness of strangers. However, the various eyewitness accounts do provide an accurate picture of the state of the war and conditions in Murmansk at that time.

Conditions for Allied ships and their crews were only slightly better at the other Soviet port of Archangel in the White Sea, largely due to it being more remote from the German front line. But for the ordinary Russian, the privations brought about by the war, exacerbated by Stalin's economic policies, made matters much worse. The old and infirm, dwelling outside the towns and cities and remote from any assistance were especially at risk, as Austin Byrne witnessed when he returned to Russia in convoy JW57. This time his ship, SS *Fort McMurray*, had discharged its cargo at Archangel and had then been towed by a Russian icebreaker down river and into the White Sea, where it was left overnight in the pack ice.

It was morning 8 am, we had just changed watches, the other watch had had breakfast and were cleaning the mess, they came on deck and emptied the slops bucket over the side onto the ice. It was cold tea, cigarette ends, cigarette ash, burnt bits of toast, bacon rind, old chop bones, cold potatoes, bits of everything that had not been eaten or chewed and spit out and the deck sweepings from the mess... When we looked over the side we saw this scrawny, very thin scarecrow of an old woman dressed in dirty thin, old rags. They were just hanging from her... She knelt down on the ice, in a biting wind, picking up tea leaves and anything else she could and wrapped them in dirty cloths. Someone threw her a lump of bread, she joined her hands in a thank you prayer, then with a wave she started to walk across the ice... The next thing was her screaming, three lads were mugging her for the slops that she had just picked up... All three kept kicking her until they got their bits of salvage and off they ran with their ill-gotten loot. The old dear was left on her back screaming. The cook said call her back... Then the lads came up with some more bits, the cook gave her some left-over food and the Chief Steward gave her a loaf. She was all smiles, she knelt on the ice, joined her hands and made the sign of the cross... As she walked away she turned, kissed her hands and waved a thank you again.

By now, the middle of May, twelve of the merchantmen in PQ15 had been unloaded and were ready to join QP12 returning to Iceland. QP12 left the Kola Inlet on 21 May and arrived without loss at Reykjavik on 29 May. *Capira*, having finished discharging on 31 May, had to remain in company with other merchantmen in the Kola Inlet for a further month, waiting for the next convoy to form up before she could return. The delay occasioned further casualties and on 21 June the SS *Alcoa Cadet* was mined and sank, bringing the total losses from PQ15 to four.

As *Capira*'s stay in Murmansk reached its end, it is worth reflecting that during this period on the other side of the globe, in the middle of the Pacific, the Battle of Midway was fought. The destruction of four Japanese carriers and a large proportion of their naval air capability marked the high watermark of the Japanese advance in the Pacific. Had events gone the other way, the west coast of the USA would have been increasingly exposed to Japanese attack, and the Allied agreement to deal with Germany first could have been put at risk. One can only surmise what the reduction or total withdrawal of US support in the North Atlantic would have meant for the Arctic convoys, or the outcome of the Battle of the Atlantic itself. What is not in doubt, however, is that this was the critical point in the Second World War, from which events could have moved in favour of the Axis powers. As far as the Arctic convoys were concerned, however, the Allies were about to reach their lowest point with devastating losses to PQ17 and returning convoy QP13; the latter to which we now turn.

# 8 UNLUCKY QP13

## (27 JUNE TO 26 JULY 1942)

On what slender threads do life and fortune hang… !

*The Count of Monte Christo,* Alexander Dumas

Four weeks after she had unloaded her precious cargo, *Capria* weighed anchor and, in the early evening of Saturday 27 June, sailed out of the Kola Inlet under pilotage. By now the Arctic was in perpetual daylight, but the weather could still reduce visibility to very low levels, casting a twilight gloom over proceedings. The Murmansk element of QP13 comprised 23 ships as shown in Appendix III[1]. The warlike stores carried up to Russia were replaced by scrap and ballast in their holds, with returning survivors from previous convoy actions occupying any other place that would serve as temporary accommodation. The SBNO reported that there were 800 survivors[2] dispersed among the ships of QP13. This would have included the naval escorts that were to accompany the convoy to Scotland or the USA.

QP13 formed up under Commodore N.H. Gale DSO, RD, RNR, who raised his pennant in the SS *Empire Selwyn*. Gale was one of that small band of highly experienced retired senior Royal Naval officers who volunteered for convoy duties following the outbreak of war. He had successfully brought PQ16 to Russia against severe enemy opposition, and had just been awarded the DSO for his leadership during that convoy operation[3]. The local escort out of Murmansk comprised three Russian destroyers and four British minesweepers. These remained with the convoy for the first two days only. The local escort was accompanied by the ocean escort comprising a further five destroyers, two minesweepers, four corvettes, two anti-submarine trawlers and, until 1 July, a submarine, HMS *Trident*. A not-inconsiderable force, but totally lacking in air cover; not even a CAM ship like those that had accompanied PQ15 and PQ16 on their passage to Russia. To compensate in some small way for the lack of air cover, the anti-aircraft ship HMS *Alynbank* was placed near the centre of the convoy at

#63[4]. The escort senior officer was Commander A.J. Cubison DSC & Bar, RN in the Halcyon class minesweeper HMS *Niger*. Like Commodore Gale, Cubison was an experienced pre-war sailor who had re-joined the navy on the outbreak of hostilities.

Admiral Tovey's Covering Force was also at sea patrolling east of Iceland. It comprised the battleships HMS *Duke of York* and USS *Washington*, the carrier HMS *Victorious*, the cruisers HMSs *Cumberland* and *Nigeria,* plus ten destroyers. Nine British submarines were also deployed off the Norwegian coast, covering the anticipated breakout of German capital ships from their protective fjords. The escort order of battle is given in Appendix IV. QP13 therefore appeared to be in highly experienced hands and, with the possible exception of air cover, was as well protected as could be expected given the naval assets available at that time.

At 2100 hours, QP13 began its passage under an overcast sky in light rain, ideal conditions in which to slip away unnoticed by the *Luftwaffe*. Even so, the close proximity of German airfields made the passage risky at the best of times, therefore the Armed Guard detachment on the *Capira* remained at high alert with lookouts posted by the .50 calibre machine guns and in the anti-aircraft pill box. The following day, 12 ships from Archangel joined the convoy, swelling its number to 35. The convoy was now formed up in nine columns. The inclusion of HMS *Alynbank* in the body of the convoy meant that there were exactly four ships in each column. The convoy proceeded on a frontage of roughly four nautical miles [7.4km] and a depth of one and a half nautical miles [2.7km]. There was no enemy activity that day in spite of an air-raid alarm and a number of depth charges being dropped on the port side of the convoy. However, on the following evening of 30 June, a single FW 200 Condor[5] appeared and shadowed the convoy for about an hour; flying low but, as was its custom, keeping well out of range. Soon after its appearance, however, heavy fog set in and lasted for the next 30 hours, covering QP13's movements from the air and allowing it to slip away unmolested by the enemy. On Thursday 2 July, the convoy passed Jan Mayen Island. Scattered fog banks continued to interrupt visibility, but QP13 was picked up during the morning by two enemy BV138 flying boats. These too kept low and out of range, although one flew out of a fog bank close to the convoy and was engaged by the escorts but to no effect.

It was standard procedure for the escorts to monitor and record enemy transmissions. Such signal intercepts provided intelligence on convoy sightings that were being sent back to German bases, and also revealed the transmission of homing signals from shadowers to prospective attackers. These could be anything from bombers through U-boats to enemy surface ships. Analysis of call signs, frequencies and other signals intelligence gathered by the convoy escort added to that provided by the Admiralty and other agencies, including the SBNO in Murmansk, enabled the escort to make an informed judgement on enemy intentions and take appropriate action. HMS *Inglefield*, under conditions of strict radio silence, had by this time picked up the signals transmitted by the enemy shadowing aircraft[6]. On the first occasion when the shadower appeared over QP13, no homing signals were detected but analysis of signals traffic on the second occasion indicated that the shadowers were transmitting homing signals, together with the speed and bearing of the convoy. Homing signals from a U-boat to the north were also detected by *Inglefield*. The escorts were therefore in a high state of alert, expecting multiple attacks from U-boats. Subsequently, a number of sonar contacts were made, prompting the dropping of several patterns of depth charges by the escorts, but in all cases the targets detected were shoals of fish. Fortunately for the convoy, no U-boat attack materialised – but unfortunately for the escorts, they could not tarry to recover the largesse of fresh rations from their depth charging efforts. This was somewhat in contrast to a fortnight previously, when Lieutenant T.B. Johnston RNVR in HMS *Niger* wrote home:

We are just returning after a spell at sea and have had fun and games of a pleasant type. Conditions being pretty unfavourable for enemy interest in our proceedings we dropped a depth charge amongst a shoal of fish and we were rewarded with a real harvest. Great fun and games recovering them as they floated on the surface – they're all stunned or concussed. We didn't have any nets suitable for the job so we sent a whaler away to collect some of them whilst various products of ingenuity were used for recovering from the ship. The favourite being a waste paper basket on the end of a boat hook or dan-buoy pole, but buckets and small cooking nets were also in play and after a short while everyone was most proficient.

One of our flotilla mates had a whaler down and one bloke fell out of it to provide a bit of extra amusement. Our total catch was 27 stone, mainly haddock but including a dozen or so fair-sized cod.[7]

From about midday onwards, air activity over QP13 ceased and Force Q rendezvoused with the convoy. On this occasion Force Q comprised only two vessels, the by now ice-damaged oiler *Gray Ranger* and her destroyer escort HMS *Douglas*. Their presence, unimpeded by the *Luftwaffe,* allowed the escort destroyers to refuel whilst maintaining watch over the merchant vessels. Once the refuelling was complete, the convoy had to make a bold alteration of course to avoid ice extending 40 miles to the south eastward of Jan Mayen Island. Visibility was low at this time and there was a considerable amount of small floe ice, through which the convoy passed. Enigma intercepts of U-boat communications[8] detailed below indicated that the Germans were also aware of the difficult ice conditions around Jan Mayen Island and the effect it would have on the passage of convoys to and from Russia, thus further reducing their search and possible intercept areas. At 2315 hours on 30 June *U376.* which was moving north eastward from its previous operational area north of Iceland, reported that the route north and west of Jan Mayen Island could not be used by convoys. *U251* also reported difficulties with the ice 15 miles south east of Jan Mayen. As a result, *U251* and another U- boat were ordered to patrol positions ENE and ESE of Jan Mayen, thus covering the area where the latest eastbound convoy, PQ17, and westbound QP13 were anticipated to arrive on 2 July.

As previously noted, one of the necessary weaknesses in the Arctic convoy system was the coordination of departure times from Iceland and Murmansk for PQ eastbound and QP westbound convoys respectively. This was done deliberately by the Admiralty at Admiral Tovey's request[9] to make best use of the covering force in the area between Bear and Jan Mayen Islands, where the risk of attack by surface ships such as the *Tirpitz* were deemed to be most severe. However, it gave the enemy the advantage of predicting roughly where a ladened PQ convoy would be, having detected the departure of a returning QP convoy. Thus having detected QP13 the enemy, knowing the prevailing ice conditions, would be relatively confident in detecting PQ17. This was indeed the case. Following the refuelling of the escort destroyers on 2 July, Ensign Combs commanding the Armed Guard detachment on the *Capira* noted that the *Luftwaffe* seemed to be abandoning QP13 in favour of an eastbound convoy that could be seen far down on the horizon. Combs' observation was confirmed, as the following intercepts of contemporaneous German Enigma naval signals traffic show: 'On the evening of 30/6, following an aircraft report on QP13 at 1650 hours in position 150 miles north of North Cape, it was appreciated that convoy PQ17 could therefore be expected to pass Jan Mayen Island "at any time now".'[10] A long distance flying boat was in contact with PQ17 at 1232 hours (1 July) in bad visibility, and was unable to hold contact. U-boats were directed that PQ17 was their main objective and that QP13, 'expected in the U-boat operational area p.m. 2/7, was to be allowed to proceed.'[11]

The Germans had therefore opted to concentrate their destructive effort on the heavily-ladened PQ17 leaving QP13 to proceed unmolested on its lawful occasions. Only 11 of PQ17's 33 merchantmen would eventually reach port; the rest were sunk by aircraft or U-boats following the Admiralty order to scatter late on 4 July. It was thought that the convoy was about to be attacked by the *Tirpitz;* however, this was flawed intelligence and led to the virtual destruction of the convoy. After both convoys had passed each other and put about a thousand miles between them, the escorts in QP13 began to pick up distress signals from the beleaguered merchantmen in PQ17. There was absolutely nothing they could do about it, but it did reinforce the assumption that heavy German surface ships were at sea, and increased the perception among the escorts that a major fleet action was imminent[12]. This perception also permeated US Patrol Squadron 73 with its 11 PBY 5A Catalinas based in Iceland. From early on the morning of 4 July, the squadron had aircraft aloft searching for the enemy. By 1630 hours, the squadron had 4 aircraft equipped with torpedoes standing by to strike against German surface vessels reported loose in the north Atlantic. A further 5 aircraft were likewise equipped as soon as they returned from patrol. These 9 planes remained on standby throughout the following two days[13].

A celestial fix was taken by the escort commander in the early evening of 2 July. Because of the poor visibility and bad weather that followed, this was the last fix that was taken during the passage to Iceland, and therefore the uncertainty of the convoy's position gradually increased as QP13 continued its passage in poor visibility but without further incident. At 1550 hours on 3 July, the convoy divided in two in response to a signal from the Admiralty received late on 2 July[14]. This was an unexpected change of plan that required sixteen ships re-designated as QP13U under Commodore Gale to make directly for Loch Ewe in Scotland, instead of staging via Iceland. Meanwhile the other nineteen, sailing under Captain J. Hiss as the newly-appointed commodore in SS *American Robin,* would continue to Iceland and then to New York, joining one of the ON Atlantic convoys en route. The problem that this change of plan presented to Commodores Gale and Hiss should not be underestimated. Although the bulk of the ships destined for Loch Ewe were at the rear, and could therefore be detached relatively easily, others were dispersed among the remainder of the convoy. Once these had been successfully detached, Hiss had to reorganise his remaining nineteen merchantmen from nine columns into five to complete the passage to Iceland. The prevailing weather conditions and need to maintain radio silence would have undoubtedly added to his difficulties. However, this complex manoeuvre was carried out successfully and the Iceland bound component's close escort moved into its protective pattern around the convoy. It comprised two destroyers, a corvette, two minesweepers, including HMS *Niger,* and two ASW trawlers[15] and escorted the convoy until the morning of 5 July when the destroyers parted company with Commander Cubison's by now much-depleted force.

Cubison had gained his first DSC as a gunnery officer in the First World War, and his second at Dunkirk, where he had commanded a flotilla of minesweeping East Coast herring drifters evacuating men of the BEF from the harbour. At his own request he had retired from the Navy in 1934 but re-joined the Royal Naval Patrol Service (RNPS) on the outbreak of war. The RNPS was formed mainly from trawlers called up for the duration of the war, complete with their RNR crews. These were tough, independently minded, professional sailors hardened through many years of plying their trade around the coasts of Great Britain. The finer points of naval discipline were not particularly high on their agenda, and although a leaven of RN senior rates was introduced into their ranks, these were used largely to provide technical expertise. The RNPS was employed in a range of duties most suited to smaller vessels such as anti-submarine warfare, general patrolling and minesweeping. It was this latter activity that Cubison had specialised in. Now aged 46, he had been in command of HMS *Niger* for 6 months, and since mid-February had been detached on escort and minesweeping duties in the Barents Sea. Cubison had made the voyage to Russia between 14 and 22 February as the escort senior officer in *Niger* protecting PQ11. Because of winter ice, this convoy had been routed south of Iceland rather than through the Denmark Strait. For the next five months *Niger* had been employed keeping the approaches to the Kola Inlet and Murmansk itself clear of enemy mines as well as taking on anti-submarine and local escort duties; the latter usually involving close escort 300 miles out into the Barents Sea from the Kola Inlet. In both roles *Niger*, in company with other Halcyon class minesweepers, had gained the respect and praise of those relying on their support, regardless of the conditions, as the following extract from the SBNO's March report records:

> I wish to pay tribute to the recent work of the Minesweeping Flotilla, consisting of HMS *Harrier* (Senior Officer), *Niger*, *Gossamer*, *Speedwell* and *Hussar*, under the command of Commander E P Hinton, DSO, MVO, Senior Officer, 6th Minesweeping Flotilla. These ships have been escorting QP and PQ Convoys in most severe weather conditions and expected every form of attack by the enemy at distances up to 300 miles [555km] from the base. They have little rest except when cleaning boilers, and can seldom berth alongside or obtain relaxation. Their work, especially when meeting convoy PQ13, has been extremely well done and reflects credit on all concerned.[16]

Cubison's command, HMS *Niger*, was a relatively modern vessel launched in 1936. She had been fitted with a Type 271 radar during her refit prior to her deployment in mid-February. The Type 271, which was also fitted to the other minesweeper in the escort HMS *Hussar*, was the first microwave radar to be fitted to ships of the Royal Navy and had been designed primarily for detecting submarines on the surface in darkness or poor visibility. When operating correctly, a Type 271 was capable of picking up a relatively small objects, such as a periscope, at about 900 yards [830m]. A larger object such as a battleship could be detected at around 13 nautical miles [24km], and land echoes much further. These early radars were capable of giving both bearing and range information on a target or other object, and were therefore a great asset when shepherding merchantmen in convoy. Trials conducted during the summer of 1941[17] impressed one captain so much that he wrote 'After being in a ship fitted with T271, night navigation in one without will seem a perilous business.' However, the early technology on which they were based did not permit all-round surveillance, and they were limited to sweeping an arc of only 200 degrees. A comprehensive 360 degree sweep took about five minutes. Unlike later surveillance radar displays[18] that gave an all-round schematic of the local environment, the Type 271 utilised a simple 'A' scope, where targets were displayed as electronic pulses emanating from the background noise. A well-trained operator was therefore essential to interpret the results. However, like all new technology, the Type 271 was not all that reliable – especially when subjected to the rigours of an Arctic passage. For example, both HMS *Bulldog* and HMS *Amazon* reported their Type 271s out of action prior to their engaging German destroyers during the passage of QP11 in early May 1942[19]. So provided *Niger's* and *Hussar's* radars were working and operating correctly, which is doubtful after so long a deployment in Arctic waters, they would have been a navigational asset as the rump of QP13 approached the northern coast of Iceland and the heavily mined Denmark Strait, which neither captain had negotiated thus far in this war under any conditions, let alone those of bad visibility and navigational uncertainty that now prevailed.

As a minesweeping specialist, Cubison would have been well aware of the threat that mines presented to convoys. He would also have appreciated that the effort put into mine-laying by the Royal Navy was more than matched by the effort put into minesweeping. In both the First World War and this conflict, the Royal Navy had invested considerable resources in laying mine barrages to impede German shipping in the North Sea and beyond. No less than 110,000 mines were laid during the first three years of the war in what became known as the Northern Barrage. Codenamed SN by the Navy, this extended north of Orkney and Shetland covering the Iceland/Faeroes Gap and, crucially, the Denmark Strait between Iceland and the ice off the Greenland coast that QP13 was now steadily approaching. Mines were laid in rows and anchored at various depths to impede the passage of U-boats as well as surface ships. These minefields were marked on British charts together with safe passages through them. The mines themselves were of varying sophistication, depending on the state of mine warfare technology at the time they were laid. Contact, magnetic and acoustically-triggered mines were sown in the Northern Barrage during its construction and follow-on maintenance, which kept a flotilla of five ships fully occupied from the outbreak of war until 1943, when further effort on the development of the barrage ceased. Maintenance alone was a major task, especially in Arctic latitudes, where pack ice and icebergs provided a major source of disruption to the minefield and danger to shipping when mines broke free from their moorings and strayed into safe lanes.

In spite of the effort expended, there was increasing concern during the war as to the effectiveness of the barrage itself, and it was eventually admitted that the large defensive minefields had failed to justify their existence and been more dangerous to our own forces than to the enemy.[20] Particular concern was expressed over the deterrent effect of the minefield north west of Iceland, and the passage of allied shipping around it. Such concerns were set out in the spring of 1941 by Captain A.J.L. Phillips RN, captain of the heavy cruiser HMS *Norfolk*. At this time, mid-March to mid-April, *Norfolk* was supporting the Denmark Strait patrol in its efforts to intercept German raiders and blockade runners[21]. Phillips emphasised the need for regular air reconnaissance to ascertain the state of the ice, and passages around the minefield and the critical need for accurate navigation to fix a ship's position relative to the minefield itself. In bad weather, this could only be accomplished by means of soundings and D/F bearings. And it was the woeful state of these two aspects that he criticised most trenchantly:

Chart is hopelessly inaccurate. Soundings... must be collected and published and gaps filled in. To use these soundings ships must have efficient echo sounding gear up to 500 fathoms [923m]. Present position as regards echo sounding very unsatisfactory and the department concerned wants a shake-up. Corvettes either have no echo sounding or it only goes up to 150 fathoms [277m].

And on the subject of D/F, Phillips wrote:

Station must be close so as to give accurate bearings... Set need only transmit and could be automatic. Young R.A.F. officer dealing with R.A.F. D/F stations when asked if they could give bearings to ships replied, somewhat indignantly, 'No we're fighting the Battle of the Atlantic'. Corvettes should have D/F.

He went on to propose establishing an RDF station (essentially a radar beacon) at the location where a coast watcher had already been installed, but pointed out the fact that the coast watcher's radio set was currently out of action due to the absence of spare parts. Phillips was also convinced that the minefield itself was being treated with impunity by the Germans, who he suspected of passing fast ships in and out of the inshore minefield gap when they liked. His suspicions were of course confirmed on 23 May 1941, when the *Bismarck* accompanied by *Prinz Eugen* steamed through the Denmark Strait at high water, engaging HMS *Norfolk* as they broke out into the Atlantic. Fourteen months on as QP13 approached the Denmark Strait, little appeared to have changed, although an RDF facility had been installed at Adalvik Bay on the northwest coast of Iceland close to Straumnes, which could have provided a beacon for ships tuned to its frequency.

It is a supreme irony that, having escaped the certitude of a severe mauling at the hands of German planes and U-boats, the Iceland-bound portion of QP13 was to suffer a devastating blow as it neared the end of its passage. Walter Hesse in the *Mormacrey* recalled the moment:

> The evening prior to reaching port, we crossed the Arctic Circle and were sailing south along the west coast of Iceland. The wind was up and the sea was choppy. As I was cleaning up after coming off watch, I heard someone running along the deck shouting, 'They're sinking around us!' In less than a minute I was dressed and rush out on deck in time to see the ship behind us up-ended and going down. A wolf pack...Four more ships went to the bottom. The ships at the head of the convoy sped up when they saw ships to the rear sinking. The convoy is in disarray. It is every man for himself.

Some ships crews thought that a German raider had broken out and was now shelling the convoy, and as a result there was much indiscriminate firing by the merchant ships against an assumed raider. Others, however, confirmed that they had seen torpedo tracks. The captain of the *Lady Madeleine,* recalling the incident some years later, wrote:

> Looking aft, I saw what I took to be the track and bubble wake of two torpedoes. I had seen plenty of torpedoes one way and another, and I remember noting that these two were rolling and burrowing their way through the waves, which meant they had been fired at long range and were slowing down.[22]

Those merchant seamen in the *Capira* were also initially convinced that they had been ambushed by U-boats or perhaps a German battleship, but Ensign Combs thought, correctly as it transpired, that the convoy had run into a minefield. His report written two days later recorded:

> On Sunday at 2115 a ship ahead was heard to explode. Immediately thereafter others were hit all around us. The convoy had, from all appearances, ran (sic) into a minefield; lookouts reported seeing several mines on either side of the ship. Ships close by were hit almost simultaneously; one on the port side, one on the starboard side, and another appeared to have been hit on both sides amidships. Five were observed to have been hit after the first explosion, and later we passed close abeam of an escort vessel which had only it's (sic) bow yet above the water. No warning signals of any sort were given till three or four ships had been hit, at which time one ship was seen to fire one red flare in coincidence with receiving its second explosion. This was the only signal, of any sort, which was seen or heard. Of seven ships visible to us at the time of the first explosion, only one other ship escaped. The last explosion was heard before 2130, at least ten (10) explosions occurred, some of the ships were seen to have been struck twice. At 2150 three persons reported sighting submarine close abeam on the starboard side. All reports varied greatly as to size, distance to, and appearance of the submarine; in view of which the report was discredited by the captain and myself, as neither of us or the mate on watch could see any such vessel.

It would appear that the *Capira* was very fortunate not to have been hit, for the majority of ships in closest company with her were sunk. The stricken escort vessel observed by Combs was HMS *Niger*. *Niger* had gone on ahead of the convoy in order to sight the Icelandic coast. It should be recalled that the last celestial fix had been made three days previously, and the convoy had sailed by dead reckoning during the intervening period. Cubison was aware of the presence of a British minefield in the Denmark Strait, and therefore keen to fix his position so as to guide the convoy between it and the coast of Iceland. At 1710 hours he signalled *Niger*'s estimated position taken by sounding to the convoy commodore[23]. A few minutes later the Commodore advised *Niger* that his echo sounder was out of action, and requested advice on his position at intervals. As far as we are aware, Cubison and indeed Lieutenant R.C. Biggs DSC, RN, captain of the other escorting minesweeper, HMS *Hussar,* had not navigated these waters before; unlike the captains of the other three escorting vessels the Free French corvette FFL *Roselys* and the A/S trawlers *Lady Madeleine* and *St Elstan,* who had passed through the Denmark Strait on the way up to Russia in PQ16. As a preparatory measure before negotiating the passage between the minefield and the Icelandic coast, Cubison had suggested to Captain Hiss that the convoy reform from five to two columns; an involved and lengthy manoeuvre even in benign conditions. However. the manoeuvre was largely completed by about 2000 hours, and whilst it was in progress *Niger* signalled an alteration of course to 222 degrees true for Straumnes. This was the first indication that Hiss had that there was a minefield off the coast. The instruction in his sailing orders to pass 3 miles [5.6km] from Straumnes at the entrance to the Denmark Strait he had interpreted as an ordinary navigational precaution to avoid unduly closing with the land.

As QP13 approached the northwest corner of Iceland, the weather was overcast and visibility about one mile [1.8km]; the wind was force 8 from the north east and the sea was rough. At 1946 hours, *Niger* ordered the other minesweeper in the escort, HMS *Hussar,* to maintain a visual link between her and the convoy. Thereupon *Niger* steamed off to locate the Icelandic coast. About fifteen minutes later her lookout reported what he thought was land about a mile away. As a consequence, a course alteration to 270 degrees was ordered. There is no mention in the account of any radio contacts being received from the station at Adalvik or Type 271 radar echoes received from the land to confirm landfall around Straumnes. It seems unlikely that an experienced captain like Cubison would not have used all the navigational aids at his disposal, especially when in heavy weather, so it is highly probable that the radars in *Niger* and *Hussar*, like the *American Robin*'s echo sounder, were out of action. Unfortunately, the land sighted was an iceberg; the convoy was not where Cubison thought it was, and the bearing he had given to Captain Hiss had set QP13 on a course directly into the minefield. Too late, Cubison realised the mistake and at 2040 hours *Niger* was fatally struck by a mine, but before going down managed to signal *American Robin* 'Land we sighted was a large iceberg. Suggest you alter back to 222 degrees true.' The Commodore accordingly hoisted the new course signal. Other detonations followed in quick succession. *Heffron, Hybert, Rodina* and *Massmar* were hit and sank whilst *John Randolph* was severely damaged and *Exterminator,* although damaged, was still able to steam.

*Lady Madeleine*, captained by T/Lieutenant W.G. Ogden BA RNVR, was the escort vessel closest to *Niger*. She was on the port beam of the port column of the convoy and went to her aid immediately. *Niger* had been crossing *Lady Madeleine*'s bows from port to starboard about five cables [1km] distant, and was swinging around so as to take up her position ahead, when she struck a mine on her port side abaft amidships. Immediately after the explosion she listed to port and then rolled to starboard, rolling back to port again and then turning over completely. She then floated bottom up, with the after part of the vessel submerged for about one third of her length or more, the stem rising clear of the water. She hung in this position for about five minutes and then sank still further, the stem rising perpendicularly out of the water, remaining visible for nearly an hour[24]. Seeing the stricken *Niger* in this position, Lieutenant Ogden assumed that an acoustic torpedo had blown her stern off, convincing him that the convoy had been under attack from U-boats[25]. Ogden's account of the subsequent attempts to rescue members of *Niger*'s crew is contained in his book *My Sea Lady*. Part written in 1943 using diaries that he had kept during the events related, the book was eventually finished and published in 1963. Ogden freely admitted that his impressions, gathered seventeen years previously, may have easily been out of focus and also incorrect; and in a few instances, it is difficult to reconcile his recollection of specific details with contemporary reports and primary sources. Nevertheless, *My Sea Lady* paints a vivid picture of the confusion in the immediate aftermath of the sinking of the Niger and the events of the next few hours. His account of the difficulties encountered attempting to rescue members of *Niger*'s crew in the north easterly blowing at that time is particularly poignant:

> The heavy sea made it necessary to get to windward, thus making a lee and drifting on to the raft. (A ship beam to wind will drift much faster than a waterlogged raft.) *Lady M*'s stern just missed the raft, but a heaving line was grabbed by the men hanging on to it and now began the struggle to get these men aboard. In those days we did not carry scrambling nets to help survivors climb inboard, and the task of rescuing those oil-covered sailors from the raft as it rose and fell in the heavy seas was heart-breaking. I .... went aft to help get *Niger*'s men aboard and actually had my arm round her oil-covered Australian first lieutenant when a wave swept him away never to be seen again.[26]

Unbeknown to Ogden, the Australian First Lieutenant, P. Wishaw, survived this ordeal and was subsequently picked up, probably by *Roselys*.[27] Ogden was also acutely conscious of the precarious position he now faced, stationary in an area where he was convinced a U-boat attack had just taken place. He was also careful not to close with the wreck of the *Niger* for fear of her ready-use depth charges exploding as she sank further into the depths, thus avoiding the damage that HMS *King George* V sustained after she had cut the *Punjabi* in half whilst covering PQ15. As *Lady Madeleine* manoeuvred towards a second raft, someone aft yelled, 'Torpedoes running starboard quarter.' Ogden looked aft and confirmed in his own mind what he had just heard. He therefore broke off immediate attempts to rescue survivors and made an anti-submarine sweep, describing a giant circle around the ships that had been hit. Having picked up some strong ASDIC contacts *Lady Madeleine* made several quick attacks with the aim of deterring any U-boats that may have been loitering in the vicinity from further attacks. Thereafter she returned to the centre of the wreckage, and for the next four hours continued to pick up survivors. Among those she rescued was Captain Dalton, the master of the SS *Hybert*. Ogden recalled that Dalton told him that his ship had been hit by heavy calibre shells. In the Admiral Commanding Iceland Command (ACIC) report[28] dated 12 July, Dalton and his second officer were reported as being convinced that their ship had first been hit by a large shell and then torpedoed. It is not beyond the bounds of possibility that the *Hybert* was hit by a stray shell, given the panic firing that had emanated from the merchantmen in the convoy. However, the distinction between hitting a mine and being hit by a torpedo is a fine one. and in the evident confusion Dalton and his second officer were undoubtedly mistaken. Nevertheless, Ogden was still inclined to believe that *Hybert* and the ships close by, having been hit simultaneously, were the victims of a torpedo salvo rather than shells or mines. Ogden had received a signal from ACIC timed at 0048 hours on 6 July which was much nearer the truth: 'You appear to be in a minefield. Tug being sent. Report situation.'[29] However, he still maintained his conviction when he wrote *My Sea Lady,* rejecting the likelihood that QP 13 had run into a minefield.

*Lady Madeleine,* having been joined by *St Elstan* earlier on, continued to search the area until 0200 hours the following day, when the heavy cruiser HMS *Kent* appeared out of the gloom. She had been patrolling the area at the time, and picking up the convoy's frantic signals had attempted to locate the reported raider but to no avail. Ironically, Ogden at first mistook *Kent* for a German raider and was expecting the worst before she signalled her identity. Ogden was unsure of his position by this time, having spent the last five hours in frantic activity and constant fear of another attack. After enquiring about the presence of German raiders, *Kent*'s CO, Captain Cunninghame Graham, gave Ogden his current position and then sent *Lady Madeleine*, *St Elstan* and an Icelandic trawler, the *Negafel*,[30] to search for stragglers. It is clear that Cunninghame Graham believed some of the merchantmen had been mined; however, he had not ruled out the possibility that there was a German raider in the vicinity and signalled ACIC and HMS *Renown*[31] at 0315: 'Situation probably as follows: Part of convoy ran into minefield in thick fog. Gunfire may have been from ships in convoy. No ships appear to have sighted U-Boats or enemy surface vessels... Am searching to westward and providing cover for convoy. Request air R/C for possible raider.'

ACIC had already despatched an aircraft to cover QP13 on 5 July, but it had returned at 2020 hours because of bad weather. Following Cunninghame Graham's request for air reconnaissance, further sorties were flown over the area on 6 July between 0910 and 2000 hours, when bad weather again forced a return to base, no enemy surface ships having been sighted.

HMS *Hussar*, the other Halcyon class minesweeper in the convoy, was on the other side from *Lady Madeleine,* positioned 2 cables [400m] on the starboard bow of the lead ship of the starboard column. She had last seen *Niger* at 2010 hours as she attempted to close with the shoreline. Under Cubison's orders, *Hussar*'s captain, Lieutenant Biggs, had been attempting to maintain contact with *Niger* and was now (at 2045) unaware of the mayhem erupting aft within the convoy, until he observed the *American Robin* alter course and the Commodore, Captain Hiss, signal that he had heard gunfire and seen two ships sink. Fearing the presence of a German raider, Biggs ordered him to proceed at maximum speed to Isafjiord. Isafjiord was to the south of Straumnes, and was in the lee of the unabated north easterly. Presumably Biggs assumed that it might also provide more protection for the convoy from a raider than being exposed in the Denmark Strait. The Commodore replied by requesting a positional fix and asking *Hussar* to lead the convoy to Isafjiord. At this time there were only five merchantmen in company, but Biggs was successful in leading them out of the immediate danger area, and at 2305 hours was able to fix his position accurately by means of a shore bearing. The visibility had improved markedly to five miles, and shortly afterwards five more ships were sighted. By 2350 hours, visibility had deteriorated again but by now ten ships from QP13, including the damaged *Exterminator*, had reformed under *Hussar* in the mouth of Isafjiord and were set on a course for Reykjavik at a speed of 8 Kts[32] [15km/hr]. Biggs must have felt vulnerable at this point as none of the other escorts were in sight (They were fully engaged in the rescue effort) and there was the possibility of a German raider at large in the Denmark Strait.

The other ASW trawler in the escort, HMT *St Elstan,* captained by T/Lieutenant G. Butcher RNVR, was at the very rear of the convoy when the incident occurred. She was astern of the rear ship in the starboard column, endeavouring to close up the rear three ships in the port column to complete the reorganisation of the convoy from five into two columns. Butcher was the first to see the Russian merchantman *Rodina* going down; his subsequent thoughts were in line with Ogden's, and he immediately carried out an anti-submarine sweep around the wreckage. As *St Elstan* proceeded, two other ships were seen to be sinking and she signalled at 2120 hours that three ships had been mined or torpedoed, giving their estimated position north of Straumnes about ten miles off the coast. She then proceeded to pick up survivors from the *Rodina*. This was not an easy task, as many were scattered among the wreckage and others were in boats. Among those rescued by *St Elstan* were three women including M. Stukhalov, the wife of the Russian Naval Attaché in London. Also rescued were the 1st and 3rd Mates, both of whom stated that they had seen torpedoes strike their ship. *St Elstan* continued to sweep for U-boats, and at 2242 hours attacked what she perceived to be a firm contact – but it is possible this was the remains of one of the QP13 ships that had already been sent to the bottom. Just under an hour later, she broke off the search and joined *Lady Madeleine*.

FFL *Roselys*, a Free French-manned Flower class corvette, captained by Lieutenant de Vaisseau A. Bergeret, was also seaming towards the rear of the convoy six cables [1.2km] on the starboard beam of the sixth ship in column when *Niger* and the merchantmen were mined. On hearing the explosions, Bergeret, unlike Butcher and Ogden, rapidly came to the conclusion that the convoy was too far to the west and in the minefield. Regardless of her own safety *Roselys* spent the next six hours in the minefield picking up survivors[33]. There were only 3 survivors from HMS *Niger* but, according to ACIC, a further 175 were rescued from the four American merchantmen. Not only had there been a massive loss of life on the *Niger*, but the *Massmar* also suffered dreadfully, losing 48 crew and passengers; some of whom were ex SS *Alamar* survivors who had previously been sunk whilst sailing in PQ16. One of the surviving Armed Guard detachment members, Charles Hayes, later described his second ordeal as the *Massmar* was hit:

I had just laid down when there was a horrendous explosion that shook the ship... I hit the deck and started for the hatch when another powerful explosion sounded. When I reached the main deck it was already only three or four feet above the water. I looked down midships and saw a crew member trying to get a lifeboat free. The water was coming up so quickly the boat was already floating in the water before they had time to unhook

HMS *King George V* showing damage to her bows after the collision with
HMS *Punjabi* on 1 May 1942

(© IWM A9943)

The ceremony to rename US S-class submarine as Polish submarine ORP Jastrz b.
Lt.Cmdr. Boleslaw Romanowski waits for officials in front of the crew
(Unknown author)

Austin Byrne was called up as a
DEMS gunner on the ill-fated
SS *Induna*
(By kind permission of Paul Byrne)

Tom Heley when called up was
trained as a radar mechanic and
served on HMS *Nigeria*
(By kind permission of Jill Britton)

Tom Chilvers was a veteran of the Spanish
Civil War and served as a merchant
seaman on SS *Empire Lawrence* in
Convoy PQ16
(By kind permission of Stuart Chilvers)

177/6

C'AM· Empire Lawrence
fires off her Hurricane
Monday. 25th May

SS *Empire Lawrence* fires off her Hurricane 25 May 1942.
Sketched by Tom Chilvers as it happened

'As I saw it when at the wheel'
The ariel torpedo attack on PQ16. Tom Chilvers' sketch
(© NMM MSS-87-090 Tom Chilver's Diary)

Murmansk – Blast shelters on wharves, usually between railway lines.
Tom Chilvers' sketch

Murmansk – Large air-raid shelters, caverns inside the hills containing meeting halls.

Tom Chilvers' sketch

(© NMM MSS-87-090 Tom Chilver's Diary)

John Chuter merchant seaman on the
SS *Capira* throughout her last voyage
(Author's collection)

the davits. When I next looked over the side just in front of me, the deck was only a few inches above the surface. There was someone standing next to me .... and we both stepped over the side into the water... All of a sudden, an overturned lifeboat came over the top of a wave, directly at me. There was a merchant seaman clinging to it and I noticed a line wrapped around the upturned bottom. The merchant sailor tried to reach me, but he was exhausted and wasn't able to pull me out of the water. I was able to grab the line that was wrapped around the boat and with some help from him I was finally able to climb onto the boat. We were both able to secure our arms under the taut line and this kept us from falling off. Then as happened when the *Alamar* went down, I fell asleep from the cold.

Hayes regained consciousness after arriving at Reykjavik and had no recollection of the time that had passed between the lifeboat and the hospital where he now found himself. However, he later learnt the full scale of the tragedy and that he had been rescued by a Free French corvette. Reflecting on this many years later, he admitted that given the prevailing conditions he could understand the mistakes the *Niger* made and sympathise with the crew's loved ones over their loss; and that he could never repay the courage of the crew of the French ship *Roselys*, who had so bravely saved so many lives at great risk to their own."[34] To this one might add both *Lady Madeleine* and *St Elstan,* whose captains and crews displayed unselfish courage in remaining in the minefield for so long, attempting to locate and pick up survivors. Eventually the likelihood of locating any more survivors grew remote; *Roselys* ceased searching at 0330 hours, and at some time during the next 2½ hours joined *Lady Madeleine* and *St Elstan.* At 0600 hours she signalled ACIC as follows:

Unless otherwise ordered *Roselys* and *Lady Madeleine* intend to proceed independently to Reykjevik at maximum speed to land cot case survivors from *Rodina, Hybert, Massmar, Heffron, John Randolf* and HMS *Niger.* Survivors are distributed as follows:- *Roselys*120 including 5 cot cases, *St Elstan* 23 with no cot cases, *Lady Madeleine* 40, including one cot case. Medical treatment required by other survivors. E.T.A. *Roselys* 1630 G.M.T. E.T.A. *Lady Madeleine* 2130 G.M.T. Contact with convoy lost during rescue operation. The last survivors I picked up at 0200 G.M.T. were in 315° 12 miles [22km] from Straumnes.[35]

Given *Roselys'* top speed and her ETA at Reykjavik, she was most likely in the area of Isafjiord, in company with the escort trawlers and maybe other ships, at the time the signal was sent. If this is correct there would have been an opportunity to transfer casualties and survivors picked up by the escorts before setting out for Reykjavik. This subject will be covered later. Meanwhile, HMS *Hussar* was making steady progress towards Reykjavik and at 1625 hours signalled ACIC: 'QP13. ETA with Lady M and St E 2115, 12 or 13 merchant ships in company.' In fact, there were only 12 merchantmen in company with *Hussar* including the damaged *Exterminator*. They arrived around midnight on 6 July.[36] Three other merchantmen were reported adrift NE of Akureyri in the early hours of the 6 July by ACIC. These were the *Hegira* and *American Press* from QP13 and the *Alcoa Banner,* which had been in PQ16 earlier in the year and is known to have returned in QP14 in September. The bow section of the crippled *John Randolph* was recovered later. *Hegira* and *American Press* eventually reached Reykjavik on 9 July.

There is little doubt that as the reports came into ACIC he, Rear Admiral Dalrymple-Hamilton, was convinced that the tragedy of QP13 was solely due to its straying into the British minefield protecting the Denmark Strait. *St Elstan* reported that three ships had been mined or torpedoed at 2120 hours, giving their position about ten miles [18km] off Straumnes. This was the first indication that ACIC received of the unfolding tragedy and prompted the despatch of the rescue tug *Adherent* to the area, in case any ships required assistance. A signal timed at 2130 hours from the station at Adalvik Bay reported six fast ships fifteen miles [27km] off the coast. The position of these six ships and their direction of travel towards the southwest given by Adalvik tallies with *Hussar* leading part of the convoy out of the minefield. HMS *Kent* was sent to investigate and subsequently encountered *Lady Madeleine* after she had completed her rescue and anti-submarine sweeps. *Kent*'s commanding officer was of the opinion that the damage inflicted upon QP13 was due solely to mines, as his signal cited above shows. Therefore at 1020 hours on 6 July, ACIC signalled the Admiralty: 'QP 13. My appreciation of the situation is that the convoy ran into minefield. This is supported by reports from Seabol I. There is no direct evidence of raider or S/M and position of occurrences, combined with very low visibility, make it unlikely that a successful attack could have been made on so large a scale...'

*Adherent* was followed at 1200 hours on 6 July by the tugs *Empire Larch* and *Empire Bascobel* bound for Isafjiord, and at 1300 hours HMS *Namsos*, an auxiliary patrol vessel, was sent to Adalvik. The purpose of the tugs was to assist *Exterminator* and recover what could be salvaged of the *John Randolph*. The latter had been spotted by air reconnaissance at 1050 hours. Whilst in the minefield she had fouled two mines and broke in two; the bow section remained afloat but the stern sank. Five members of the crew died in the incident, but none of the 12 passengers or the 12 men of the Armed Guard were lost and were picked up later.[37] The bow was eventually recovered and towed to Reykjavik[38]. *Exterminator*, however, had managed to remain in company with the convoy but was straining in # 3 hold and was going down by the head. *Empire Bascobel* came alongside and attempted to pump her out but this was not successful and she cast off. Eventually *Empire Larch* made fast alongside *Exterminator* and took her into Reykjavik.

After the arrival of the bulk of the surviving ships in the convoy and an opportunity for ACIC to interview the escort commanders, he followed up with a further signal to the Admiralty confirming that he was satisfied that QP13 had suffered damage only from the minefield and that there were no raiders or U-boats involved in an attack.[39] Added to that, we now know that German U-boats in the Barents Sea had been concentrated much further to the northeast, in a wolf pack appropriately named *Eisteufel,* which had subsequently wreaked havoc among the merchantmen of PQ17. The 'Unfortunate Occurrence' that QP13 was subject to was certainly not due to enemy action.

## Aftermath

There is a tragic irony in a minesweeper being hoist by its own petard. Ogden's eyewitness account of HMS *Niger*'s last moments was analysed on his return to Grimsby on 30 July. In his statement, he reported that the explosion had occurred on *Niger*'s port side abaft amidships. A flash was observed, but the exact position of the explosion and any damage that had occurred could not be seen as this was on the side of the stricken ship furthest from *Lady*

*Madeleine*. The covering letter from the Admiralty's Minesweeping Division attached to Ogden's statement and addressed to DDOD(M) and DNC said that it was probable that *Niger* was sunk by the explosion of a British moored magnetic mine, but questioned if this was consistent with Ogden observing a flash. With classic understatement, the letter also observed that the rapidity with which *Niger* turned over, with consequent heavy loss of life, after successively rolling to port and starboard, was disturbing, and invited comment. DDOD(M) later confirmed that *Niger* had probably been sunk by a British moored magnetic mine with a 320 lb minol charge, laid at a depth of 25 ft below chart datum and that, in his opinion, there was no reason why a flash should not be seen.[40]

The reason why this form of attack proved so devastating to the *Niger* is that when the mine was detonated some distance underneath it, the explosion created a spherical hole in the water, and due to the difference in pressure, the sphere collapsed from the bottom creating a pillar of water capable of punching a hole straight through her, flooding adjacent compartments but limiting damage elsewhere[41]. The flash seen by Ogden may have been due to the water column itself. Pencilled notes on a copy of the covering letter stated the Admiralty's intention to compile a damage report to include all departmental remarks on the incident. In the event, this was shelved on 11 September because of a lack of further details.

One other issue remained, however; how did a minesweeper fall foul of a magnetic mine that it should have been well protected from? Had the damage report been written, there may have been some clarification on this point. Unfortunately, the Admiralty records do not address it. Halcyon class minesweepers were designed before the advent of magnetic mines. The Germans were the first to employ such weapons early in the war, and they were highly successful in sinking shipping around the coast of Britain. However, in November 1939 a German magnetic mine was dropped from an aircraft onto the mud flats of the Thames estuary during low tide. It was recovered, and following subsequent investigation measures to counter it were devised. This stroke of luck also resulted in British-designed magnetic mines being sown in the SN barrage protecting the Greenland/Iceland/Faroes Gap. Passive measures to protect ships from this form of attack were also devised. Since the triggering mechanism of the mine depended on it detecting an anomaly in the Earth's magnetic field as the ship passed over it, the obvious counter was to demagnetise, or in naval parlance 'degauss', the ship. As a temporary measure, the ship could be wiped by passing it through a magnetic field to counter its inherent magnetism. Some of the merchant ships in QP13 would have no doubt gone through this process in their home ports. However, degaussing was not a permanent solution and the ship eventually regained its magnetic signature. The permanent counter was to install degaussing coils within the ship's superstructure, such that when a current was passed through them its magnetic signature would be neutralised. The mass wiping of ships occurred just before Dunkirk in May 1940 and degaussing equipment was soon being installed in capital ships, but the equipment was expensive, especially in the amount of copper required for the coils, and therefore had to be rationed. Nevertheless, it should be recalled that the *Capira* had been fitted with degaussing coils, which was unusual for a merchant ship at this time[42] and this may have saved her in the minefield when other ships in close proximity were being hit. Some Halcyon class minesweepers began to be fitted with degaussing coils before Dunkirk but the programme lasted until well into 1943. However, there is good evidence that HMS *Niger* was fitted with her degaussing gear before July 1940[43]. It would therefore appear that *Niger's* degaussing equipment was either damaged in some way or switched off when she entered the minefield. Having been pounded by Arctic seas for the best part of six months, there is little doubt that she would have been due for some form of refit on return to home waters. During her time in the Barents Sea, she had been employed mainly on escort duties and there is little evidence of her having carried out minesweeping duties whilst there. If she had, however, then her degaussing gear must have been in working order because the threat of German magnetic mines was potent and ever-present.

In the various accounts and documents relating to this tragedy, there are considerable discrepancies between the number of casualties and survivors recorded. For example, ACIC's report of 12 July suggests that *Roselys* and *Lady Madeleine* rescued 221 survivors between them, but this total does not include those rescued from the Russian ship *Rodina* which Russian sources put at 16[44] bringing the total to 237. These were probably the numbers picked out of the water by those ships, and not the number subsequently landed by them at Reykjavik. On the other hand, the Official Chronology of the U. S. Navy in World War II-1942 gives a figure of 235 survivors from the four American merchantmen mined that day. The signal sent by *Roselys* prior to her arrival at Reykjavik quoted above accounts for only 173 survivors, but some may have been transferred to other ships despatched by ACIC the previous day. Also regarding the possible transfer of survivors at sea, it must be borne in mind that in spite of the north-easterly gale that was running at the time, the waters on the leeward side of Straumens Point, and in fact the whole Isafjord area, remained relatively calm, with no running seas, so transfers would have been possible. According to Icelandic sources[45] a small fishing boat from Isafjordur, that lay in Adalvik Bay next to Straumnes with other fishing boats that waited out the gale before rounding the North Cape, went out with the Commanding Officer of the Saebol Admiralty Experimental Station (RDF – radar) to help rescue survivors. They picked up a few dead bodies that were later transferred to the *Roselys*. The crew received a Royal Navy citation for their brave effort. Finally, the Iceland Base Command (US forces) War Diary or Record of Events states that a total of 218 survivors were received from QP13. Again, caution over the figures is called for as numerous survivors from convoys were constantly being landed at Reykjavik and the IBC operated facilities for them including hospitals, but it's possible that not all were recorded, and some may have ended up in the care of the Royal Navy. As to the casualties, the official US account gives 49 deaths from the four American ships. Add to this 147 dead in HMS *Niger*, including any ex-HMS *Edinburgh* on board at the time and 38 dead from *Rodina,* we arrive at a grand total of around 234 dead and about 240 rescued. Whatever the true figures, however, one fact remains clear; this was both the greatest maritime disaster and rescue in Iceland's history.

In his full report[46] on the incident, prepared a few days later, ACIC confirmed that the convoy had steamed into the eastern edge of the minefield. The report went on:

This was not so clear to the escorting vessels who were under the impression that a submarine attack had been made, or to the vessels in the convoy, who having no knowledge of the minefield were convinced they had seen their consorts torpedoed. Several ships in the convoy opened fire and in the general confusion it was thought that an armed raider was also in the convoy. The low visibility in no way helped to dispel these illusions and the convoy scattered.

The report concluded that it was difficult to attribute blame to any individual, but that a combination of factors had led to what it rather euphemistically referred to as an 'Unfortunate Occurrence'. Foremost among those factors was the change of plan signalled by the Admiralty on the 2 July, which took little account of Hiss' lack of knowledge of the minefield off Iceland, and the lack of a coordinated plan as a contingency against failing to locate the Icelandic coast. Other factors mentioned in the report included the thick weather that had prevented the convoy escort taking a celestial fix for three days, the decision by the escort commander to alter course to 270 degrees having mistaken an iceberg for land, the absence of any sort of navigational aid such as a D/F beacon that would have helped lead the convoy through the gap, and finally the unreliability of the RDF sets in *Niger* and *Hussar* which may have been due to a lack of sufficiently skilled personnel to maintain them in proper order[47]. There was an understandable reluctance to overly criticise Commander Cubison, a twice decorated sailor who had gone down with his ship, but the report hinted at his misplaced confidence that he could find the passage between the coast and the minefield and direct the convoy through it. This is not surprising given that he had not navigated the minefield gap before. This led to a later clarification of the respective roles of both Escort Commander and the convoy Commodore. In a letter from the Admiralty Trade Division to the Chief of Staff, Western Approaches the following redraft of the standing orders was proposed[48]:

The Senior Officer of the escort forces is responsible for the safety of the convoy from enemy action, but subject to his orders the Commodore is to take charge of the convoy as a whole. Although the Commodore is responsible for the safe navigation of the convoy the Senior Officer of the escort should not hesitate to inform the Commodore at once if in his opinion the Convoy is standing into danger whether from our own or enemy minefields or the proximity of shoal water. Decisions regarding alteration of route of the convoy, including diversions, other than those ordered by the Admiralty or the local Naval Authority, are the responsibility of the Senior Officer of the Escort, after discussion with the Commodore of the Convoy.'

After the last sentence there was a pencilled comment – *(if possible?)*.

To all of the shortcomings mentioned by ACIC, one could add Captain Phillips' criticisms over the inaccuracies in the Denmark Strait charts, lack of suitable echo sounders and his comments on the lack of RAF cooperation in providing ships with bearings whilst navigating these waters. Finally, HMS *Niger* may not have fallen foul of a British magnetic mine (if indeed that was her nemesis) if her degaussing equipment had been operating properly at the time. However, what is not mentioned in these documents is the likelihood of any change in the minefield narrowing the gap between it and the Icelandic coast during the time between the passages of PQ11 and QP13. This has been suggested in some accounts[49] and, as a consequence, it has also been suggested that no accurate charts were available to the convoy showing the minefield changes. Such a possibility cannot be dismissed, since there was a major mine laying effort south of Iceland beginning in February 1942 followed by the laying of moored magnetic mines in the Denmark Strait as soon as the weather permitted. This was designated SN 72 and designed to replace earlier losses due to ice. It took place in June 1942[50] and it is possible that this effort altered the shape of the minefield and was therefore not shown on the charts the convoy was using when the incident happened. It is also possible that Cubison was unaware of the presence of magnetic mines in the minefield, and had not, therefore, taken the appropriate countermeasures. However, given the convoy's premature change of bearing to 270 degrees, it is unlikely that a narrowing of the minefield gap *per se* would have had any material effect on the final outcome.

On the subject of the lack of D/F beacons to assist navigation in the Denmark Strait ACIC commented that the issue was already being addressed. Dalrymple-Hamilton had also picked up on some implied criticism voiced by Admiral Tovey, C-in-C HF, that he had not done something about the outgoing and incoming convoys that got into ice and other trouble. These were, of course, QP13 and PQ17. In justification of his actions, or lack thereof, Dalrymple-Hamilton wrote to Tovey on 19 July[51].

Having explained the difficulties in obtaining timely information on ice conditions in the Denmark Strait at that time of year, particularly those in the minefield gap, he suggested routing convoys south about especially after a northerly blow. The questions surrounding the fate of QP13, however, rested on two issues: In view of the conditions that made it difficult to locate the minefield gap, should the convoy have been ordered to turn round? And/or should a trawler have been despatched to guide the convoy in? The first course of action ACIC turned down, because the precise position of QP13 was unknown, as were the prevailing weather conditions at that time. He also deferred to the commanders on the spot, Cubison and Hiss, who should have been sufficiently qualified and experienced 'to know what to do when making a dangerous area in thick weather if they were not sure of their position'. He acknowledged that it was his responsibility to render every assistance, but suggested that an order to turn round would not necessarily have helped in the circumstances; indeed it might well be quite the reverse, and so he decided not to give it. The trawler beacon idea had been discussed many times before, but ACIC had rejected it on the basis that trawlers, equipped with magnetic compasses, had to navigate coastal waters by frequently taking land fixes. Keeping in with the land was not easy in rough weather, and he maintained that if the trawler lost the land she would not be justified in transmitting beacon signals 'as in that event she might be more of a menace than an aid'. And 'If the convoy were relying on her signals they might come nearer the danger point than was desirable before turning round.' These were therefore the reasons for not sending a trawler to guide the convoy through the minefield gap, but Dalrymple-Hamilton then went on: 'Perhaps they were insufficient, and it is undoubtedly true that even if the beaconing trawler had misled the convoy the situation could not have been much worse than it was.' He concluded by stating his intention to send one next time to anchor in Adalvik Bay, as it was much nearer the scene of required action than Isafjiord. Reading between the lines, it would appear that Tovey expected a more proactive stance from ACIC and following the tragedy of QP13 he was beginning to get it. The added circumstance of mistaking an iceberg for the coast and prematurely altering the course of the convoy was an exacerbating factor that, all too often in war, tips the scales of success or disaster one way or the other. Perhaps the last word should go to

Woodman, who cautioned against making comparative judgements whilst pointing to those who unwittingly initiated these tragic chains of events: 'Yet tragedy cannot be evaluated in comparative forms; its magnitude is a constant. Perhaps more pertinent, the root cause of QP 13's losses was almost identical to what was now happening to PQ 17.'[52]

The remnants of QP13 dropped anchor in the early hours of Tuesday 7 July 1942. They remained at anchor for most of that day, making good any damage sustained during the passage from Murmansk to Iceland. In addition to the badly damaged *Exterminator*, that remained in Reykjavik, the *Richard H Lee* and *Capira* were also reported as having sustained damage. However, this must have been slight because both ships were operational later that day, the *Richard H Lee* supplying US Army bases around Iceland and the *Capira* joining Convoy ONSJ110 for the next stage of the passage to the States[53]. ONSJ110 formed up and proceeded to sea at 2130 hours. There were 13 ships in company from Iceland escorted by the destroyer USS *Babbitt* and US Coast Guard cutter *Bibb*. These two escorts returned to Iceland on 10 July as soon as they had safely delivered their charges into the hands of convoy ON110 which had departed Liverpool on 6 July. Apart from the usual precautionary depth charging around the perimeter of the convoy, little else happened on the way back to New York. Walter Hesse in the *Mormacrey,* with measured understatement, remarked that the leg to New York seemed easy compared with the terror they had experienced before. However, he did complain of the poor food situation, having run out of fresh fruit and vegetables, with meat and staples in short supply. Fresh water was also rationed and restricted to drinking and cooking in order to keep the boilers fed and steam up for the journey home. Five days out of Iceland, the *Mormacrey* blew a boiler tube and had to stop and effect repairs in vulnerable isolation before re-joining ON110 the following day. ON110 arrived safely on 26 July. Walter Hesse's memoir ends:

How does it feel to return to the safe normal world? We had been accustomed to a high stress environment and each man reacted to the circumstances in his own way. As we entered the safety of Long Island Sound we felt the tension slowly ebb. Men who hadn't spoken to each other in months, laughed and joked together. Strangers became friends.

By chance, I met the Second Mate on deck at 5.30 A. M. while at anchor in the Sound. He apologised for his behaviour, explaining he thought he would never see his wife and two daughters again. That thought was more than he could handle. The ship docked the next day. As soon as the relief crew arrived we quit the ship without a backward glance. Each man went his separate way.

Not so for that British merchant seaman who had joined the *Capira* way back in November. He had signed on her again and was due to re-run the Atlantic gauntlet in a little over two weeks' time.

# 9 THE SINKING OF THE *CAPIRA*

## (22 AUGUST TO 6 SEPTEMBER 1942)

On a seaman's grave
No roses bloom
On a seaman's grave
No flowers bloom
The only greeting is the white seagulls
And a tear which a small maiden weeps.

Translated from the *U-boat Sailor's Song*

On 16 July 1942, *U609*[1], a Type VIIC commanded by 26-year-old Klaus
Rudloff, a Kapitänleutnant hailing from the north German port of
Willemshafen, slipped unnoticed out of Keil harbour bound for the North
Atlantic[2]. This was Rudloff's first operational command with *U609,* a brand-
new vessel commissioned in February 1942. He had been sent to patrol
an area in the Iceland/Faroes gap. This covered the sea lanes between
Loch Ewe and Reykjavik, the staging post for convoys going further north
to Russia. Unbeknown to the *Kreigsmarine,* convoys to Russia had been
suspended by the Admiralty following the destruction of PQ 17, so it is not
surprising that during the five weeks *U609* patrolled this patch of the ocean,
including the convoy staging posts along the west coast of Iceland, Rudloff
saw very little by way of major sea traffic. The only excitement occurred
early on the morning of 22 July, when he spotted a small convoy of 8-10
steamers escorted by two Catalina aircraft heading for Reykjavik. With the
assistance of *U254*, manned by Kapitänleutnant Hans Gilardone and his
crew, which also happened to be patrolling this area, Rudloff shadowed the
convoy as it made its way towards Iceland. The presence of allied air cover
from Iceland made shadowing the convoy difficult, and *U609* was forced to
submerge the following day to avoid being bombed. In spite of remaining
in contact throughout the 23 July, both *U254* and *U609* could not get into a
satisfactory firing position to attack the convoy. As a consequence the action

was eventually abandoned the following morning after both boats had lost contact. The failure to attack was in large measure due to the close air cover enjoyed by the convoy, however the inexperience of both captains on their first operational patrol in command may have also been a factor in spite of their having an excellent weapons platform at their disposal.

The Type VII was a remarkably successful submarine, arguably the most successful man-made underwater predator conceived thus far. The Type VII design[3] evolved from the UB III Class submarine deployed with great success by Germany during the First World War. Fifty three of these boats had been commissioned during that war, and had accounted for the sinking of 500 allied ships. Eventually, there were seven variants of the Type VII, the most prolific being the Type VIIC. 568 were built between 1940 and 1945, and accounted for the bulk of allied shipping sunk during the Second World War. It had a displacement of 871 tonnes when submerged and could sail 8,500 nautical miles [15,750km] without refuelling. With a surface speed of 17.7kts [33km/hr] it could outpace and overhaul most convoys, especially at night when, before the advent of centimetric radar, its low profile made it difficult to detect. Whilst submerged it could still muster 7.1kts [13km/hr], sufficient to keep pace with the slowest convoys, but likely to lose them as commodores made frequent course changes to throw U-boats off the scent. When threatened, the Type VIIC could dive safely to 230m although it was capable of another 20m beyond that depth before the pressure vessel became vulnerable to crushing. Its destructive power was provided via one stern and four bow tubes firing up to 14 torpedoes or laying 26 mines per mission. To conserve torpedoes for covert attacks, the Type VIIC mounted an 8.8 cm deck gun for engaging softer targets such as lone merchantmen on the surface. There were also various mountings on the boat for anti-aircraft machine guns. The Type VIIC was fitted with sonar for target detection, range and bearing. This comprised a number of microphones arranged in various patterns either side of the U-boat's bow. This was a passive device and was not sufficiently accurate to calculate a firing solution. For this, a visual fix on the target was necessary. Although active sonar devices for use in submarines were available, they were not fitted in *U609;* however, she was equipped with the *Bold* sonar decoy. The Metox device for early warning of attack from aircraft was also available to be mounted on the bridge once the U-boat had surfaced. As well as both short and long-wave radio communications, the Type VIIC carried the naval version of the Enigma encoding/decoding machine. Whilst on the surface, targeting information was provided by the *Unterwasser-zieloptik* or UZO. This was mounted on the bridge and had binoculars attached to it. The device provided the exact bearing and range to the target, information that was automatically passed to the fire control computer thus providing the firing solution, namely the torpedo gyro angle. When submerged, however, the firing solution information was read off from the dials on the attack periscope. Both the UZO and the attack periscope were unmatched anywhere. The optics were manufactured by Zeiss and were world class for their time. With such an array of offensive/defensive, active/passive equipment the Mk VIIC was a formidable fighting machine. But any weapon system is only as good as its crew.

A typical U-boat crew comprised between 44 and 52 submariners. (Rudloff's crew was 47 strong). The Captain (usually a Kapitänleutnant) and three other officers ran the boat. They were the First Watch Officer, who was also the second in command and shadowed the Captain; the Second Watch Officer who was responsible for the watch on deck as well as the *Flak* (anti-aircraft) & deck guns and oversight of the radio room staff; and finally the Chief Engineer. He was a highly experienced officer responsible for the maintenance of the U-boat's machinery including the engines, motors, batteries, and other mechanical systems. He was also responsible for setting the demolition charges in the event the boat had to be scuttled. This meant that many Chiefs went down with the boat, no doubt some of them deliberately. Whilst at sea the Captain held the highest responsibility at all times, as he routinely made life or death decisions affecting the fate of the entire crew. It was not surprising therefore that the crew identified closely with him, and were especially proud if he had been officially recognised in some way, usually by being awarded a medal following a successful patrol.

Four Chief Petty Officers worked under the commissioned officers carrying out navigation, quarter mastering, engineering and disciplinary functions. Subordinate to these were others responsible for the boat's stability & steering, weapon systems, engines, machinery, communications, sonar, control room and catering. Sometimes, especially on the longer patrols, a doctor was present together with meteorologist and intelligence personnel. Like on most ships at sea, the day was divided up into watches. The watch rotation on a U-boat normally consisted of four-hour shifts with engine room personnel and radio operators working six hours at a stretch. Time throughout the German submarine arm was set two hours in advance of GMT and did not vary wherever the boat happened to be.

Like the *Capira,* no-one on a U-boat was underemployed, and each man was highly trained in his particular area of expertise, as well as having to master other tasks subsidiary to his own. One attribute essential to every member of the crew of a submarine, however, was the ability to live cheek-by-jowl with one's comrades, in conditions that redefined the meaning of cramped. There was no privacy whatsoever, except perhaps for the Captain, who had a thick green curtain that stood in for the door to the cubicle he called his cabin. For the majority of the crew, they bedded down where they could. There were less than half the number of bunks for the crew and a system of 'hot bedding' was the norm. Those who could not find a bunk would make themselves as comfortable as they could in any space available. Torpedoes took up a considerable amount of space, and a board placed across two of them would suffice for a table. Of course, more space became available as the patrol progressed and torpedoes were expended. There were only two toilets, one of which was adjacent to the galley and doubled up as a ration store. Plenty of fresh rations were always stowed aboard and the crew ate well for the first week or so, until they ran out, but after that it was a case of living off canned food for the rest of the patrol. And so, after six weeks of fruitless patrolling off Iceland, Rudloff's crew were no doubt heartened by the news received on 26 August that *U609* was to proceed south west to join one of Dönitz' wolf packs codenamed 'Vorwärts[4]' whose purpose was to intercept eastbound convoys making for England.

Convoy SC97 sailed from Halifax NS on the afternoon of Saturday 22 August 1942. It was a relatively large assembly of freighters some 58 in number,[5] flying the flags of ten nations ( as shown in Appendix V). In overall command was Commodore Roy Gill RNR, in SS *Dramatist.* Gill was a convoy veteran, with considerable experience fighting his charges through the hostile waters of the North Atlantic. The previous year he had fought his way across the Atlantic in convoy HX133, steaming from Halifax to Liverpool. During that passage the convoy was attacked three times, resulting in 7 ships being torpedoed, 5 of which sank. Escorts accompanying HX133, however, accounted for 2 U-boats. More recently, (23/31 July 1942) Gill had been commodore of the westbound ON113 which lost 4 merchantmen, 3 sunk and one damaged, again for the loss of 2 U-boats. Whether or not Commodore Gill counted the score more or less even is not recorded. However, he must have faced the prospect of this crossing with a mixture of trepidation seasoned with optimism.

Leaving Bedford Basin at 13.21 hrs and led by SS *Texas,* SC97 began to deploy onto a broad front of 13 columns and 5 rows. Gill in SS *Dramatist* was in the front row at the centre in the seventh column. The rest followed slowly, with the rescue ship RS *Perth* on her 16th voyage in that role, clearing the harbour entrance at 1855 hours. The last ship to leave was the Norwegian SS *Ravnefjell.* Sailing at the centre of SC97 (sixth column, third row – hence #63) with a cargo of trucks, tractors, steel, steel mats, bull dozers, small arms ammunition, foodstuffs (including 203 cases of evaporated milk) and 503 bags of U.S. Mail, was the SS *Capira. Capira* had joined SC97 at Halifax on 22 August, having sailed from New York on 15 August. Most of the crew that had sailed her from Russia were still with her, including the young seaman who had signed on in the Merchant Marine office at London's Victoria Dock over nine months previously.

As usual, she carried a detachment of 13 US Navy Armed Guard, commanded this time by Lieutenant James A. Ravella. The bulk of the convoy, including *Capira,* was destined for the UK but 12 ships were scheduled to proceed to Iceland and thence to Russia in PQ18, which was due to sail north in mid-September.

As they left Halifax the merchantmen of SC97 were joined by the warships[6] that would escort the convoy for the first part of its passage across the Atlantic. HMS *Witherington* and HMNS *Lincoln* were two First World War vintage destroyers of US origin that were transferred to the UK in return for the establishment of US bases on British Crown territory. *Lincoln* had a chequered career that amply demonstrates the paucity of assets across the allied navies during the early years of the war. After transfer to the Royal Navy in October 1940, she was variously operated by Norwegian, Canadian and Soviet Union crews before eventually transferring back to the Royal Navy in 1945. During the passage of SC97, she sailed under the Norwegian flag.

In addition to these 'Four Stackers' there was a Bangor class minesweeper, HMCS *Goderich*. Three Royal Canadian Navy Flower class corvettes, *Matapedia*, *Moosejaw* and *Agassiz* completed the close escort force.

In contrast to the obsolete destroyers, the Flower class corvette was a modern ship, but not particularly comfortable or easier for the crew to operate. Displacing 940 tons, with a maximum speed of 16kts [30km/hr] and armed with a 102 mm gun and an array of depth charge chutes and throwers, a Flower class required a complement of 47 sailors to operate her. The first of the class was laid down in 1939, and was built to the requirements for a convoy escort vessel. These included rapid construction, mounting anti-submarine equipment, surviving the heavy seas around the British Isles and matching U-boat speeds. The design eventually adopted was based on that of the whale-catchers laid down in Middlesbrough.

One hundred and forty five were eventually built in the UK and they, plus a number of destroyers, formed the bulk of the escorting warships which fought the battle of the Atlantic. They were, in effect, the first and last line of defence against U-boat attack. Their short length and shallow draught made them uncomfortable ships to live in. A fortnight of constant rolling and pitching on transatlantic convoy duty tended to exhaust all who sailed in them. The ratings in the crews were mostly reservists with only a few key positions, such as Cox'n, Chief Bos'n's Mate, Gun layer, Chief Engineer etc., being filled by regular or recalled personnel. The officers were reservists, almost without exception, with the Captain usually ex-merchant navy. Service aboard these warships was monotonous and debilitating for long periods, either because of the need for constant vigilance in the face of those twin dangers, the sea and the enemy, or because of, in the North Atlantic at least, the cold. When off duty there was little if any comfort to be had in such cramped and unpleasant conditions. Sleeping conditions on board for officers and petty officers were relatively reasonable, but for the seamen in a crowded, stuffy and water laden forecastle, induced great hardship. In company with U-boats, the inability to store perishable food for more than a week at most led to a boring repetition of corned-beef and powdered potato for breakfast, lunch and dinner. Since most of the crewmen were young conscripts, persistent sea-sickness with its debilitating nature was an ever-present problem.

The protection provided by these vessels was complemented by thick fog that had set in before SC97 assembled, and had lasted for three days, providing ships in the convoy with cover from submarines, aircraft and surface raiders alike. However, this proved to be a double-edged sword. In the days before surveillance radar was commonplace on merchant ships, fog was a formidable problem; especially for those steaming in relatively close formation in convoy. Station-keeping was difficult, and collisions were not uncommon. Sometimes ships found themselves alone, having straggled from the convoy in fog. One such in SC97 was the SS *Bridgepool*. AB Hawkins[7] noted in his diary: 'Sunday 23rd – Lost convoy during night through fog. Pick up with six other ships 3pm. Fog lifting slightly have not yet found convoy. Monday 24th – Still very foggy. Sighted oil tanker afternoon. By ourselves at nightfall. Tuesday 25th – Found by a destroyer today and have been taken back to convoy. Weather improving. Fog gone.'

Commodore Gill, in his post-convoy report, commented that radio had 'proved invaluable for assisting the scattered convoy to form up.'[8] This seems somewhat at odds with the policy of radio silence then in force, the contravention of which would have signalled the convoy's departure to any attentive enemy. Maybe it was this breech of security combined with the fact that the Germans had to some extent succeeded in deciphering British signal traffic that alerted Dönitz to the departure of SC97 and in turn was instrumental in deploying *Vorwärts* on 25 and strengthening it with *U609* on 26 August.

Assistance for those now straggling in the fog was forthcoming in the shape of the rescue ship *Perth*. Her master A. Williamson had steamed her cautiously out of Halifax at 5 kts [9km/hr] after the pilot had disembarked in thick fog. After sighting the East Halifax Light Vessel, he increased speed to 6.5 kts [12km/hr] until the morning of 23 August, when he was ordered by the escort commander to act as commodore for 14 merchantmen that had straggled from the main body of the convoy. Williamson later reported that 'thick fog continued until 1100 hours on the 25 August when Escort informed me we were ahead of Commodore's section.'[9] This goes to prove how difficult convoy handling could be in such conditions.

At midday on 26 August, as SC97 was steaming through 48.20 N, 51.13 W, the close escort handed over protection of the convoy to the taskforce that would see it through to the UK. HMSs *Burnham* and *Broadway* formed the destroyer element with accompanying corvettes HMCSs *Drumheller, Dauphin, Brandon, Morden* and HMS *Polyanthus. Burnham* and *Broadway,* like *Witherington* and *Lincoln,* had been laid down just after the First World War and were, at best, obsolescent.[10] With the new escort in place, there came an improvement in the weather sufficient enough for effective air cover to be deployed. Some time later, the first alarm was raised. At 1900 hours, one of the escorting aircraft reported a submarine 20 miles to the north of the convoy. HMCS *Burnham* and HMS *Broadway* proceeded to hunt. A little over an hour and a half later they signalled to re-join the convoy, the sighting having been a whale. Such false alarms were commonplace and only served to heighten the tension felt by all those in the know. Merchantmen and their crews sailed on, however, oblivious to the frequent hive of activity going on around them.

SC97, like many eastbound convoys at this time, crossed the ocean more or less within the narrow band known as the Great Circle, the shortest route across the Atlantic. This was in contrast to westbound convoys nine months earlier (See Chapter 2). These sailed closer to Iceland to take advantage of air cover and refuelling opportunities for the escorts that only accompanied merchantmen part way across the Atlantic before convoy dispersal. Westbound convoys, however, were accompanied by escorts during their entire passage, but escort duties were handed over mid-way at the ICOMP (See Chapter 4). This was not the case with air cover, however. Allied aircraft at this stage in the war could only partially cover convoys either side of the Atlantic. This left a zone in mid-ocean, where submarines could operate without fear of observation or attack from the air. Following the Great Circle route also had the disadvantage of predictability. Dönitz would therefore place his wolf packs across the most likely convoy paths. Perhaps some deviation from the Great Circle route would have saved more ships for as Dönitz pointed out in his log for 9 September:

It is astonishing with what persistence the English have plied the routes immediately north and south of the Great Circle during the last few months in spite of several large-scale attacks by U-boats. For several weeks boats have been disposed in the same area each time to pick up west-bound convoys. Nevertheless, the English have stayed on their old route ...[11]

Wolf packs had their share of problems too. Getting into likely intercept areas, coordinating movements within the pack and locating their prey, all presented formidable challenges. Therefore, they relied to a great extent on intelligence forwarded from the *Kriegsmarine*, other boats within the pack and when available air reconnaissance. Intercepted U-boat broadcasts would give an indication of the boat's whereabouts, but it should be recalled that at this point in the war their Enigma-encrypted signals could not be decoded. So, within certain tolerances and timeframes, convoys could be notified of likely enemy whereabouts but had no clear understanding of their intentions. In such circumstances, convoys would periodically take evasive action by zig-zagging or even changing course completely in another direction for several hours in an attempt to throw the enemy of the scent.[12]

The fog having lifted, air cover was provided from North America from the afternoon of 25 August. For the next few days, SC97 enjoyed fine weather and made good progress. About midday on 28 August, the convoy entered the air cover gap and for the next 3–4 days was at its most vulnerable until mid-morning on 1 September, when air cover would resume from the UK. Early on Friday 29 August, the convoy received added protection in the shape of USCGs *Ingham* and *Bibb*[13]. These were modern US Coast Guard cutters out of Reykjavík in Iceland. Their task, together with USS *Shenck* another First World War vintage destroyer that joined convoy on the evening of 31 August, was to escort 12 of the convoy's merchantmen to Iceland and thence to Russia. By this time, the weather had deteriorated again and Ensign Joseph Matte III the Assistant Gunnery Officer on the USCG *Ingham* recorded in his journal:

> Saturday, 29 August -- (0745) Rain and fog. Visibility 1/2 to 1 mile. We have just picked up radar interference ahead, indication of an approaching convoy. (0815) An escort vessel is sighted. (0830) *Ingham* and *Bibb* join the escort group under Commander Task Unit 24.1.12, bound to the eastward with 54 ships in convoy. We take station on starboard half of van, zigzagging at 114 1/2 knots. Convoy speed 7.5 knots." [14]

The following day, Ensign Matte is lamenting the fact that the ASDIC, or as he put it, 'Our QC underwater sound machine has been out of order all day, robbing us of at least 80% of our effectiveness as an anti-submarine unit.' Thankfully it was fixed later that evening, for little did Matte or the convoy and its escorts realise what U-boat strength and formation awaited them in mid-ocean.

The *Kriegstagebücher* (KTB), the War Diary of the Commander in Chief Submarines[15] captured at the end of WW2, records that on 1 January 1942 Dönitz' U-boat fleet comprised 249 vessels. Of these only 91 were designated for combat operations, the others either being on trials or used for training purposes. Of the 91 no less than 54 were in dock for one reason or another, leaving 37 at sea. Allowing for passages to and from the operational areas, this left an average daily number of about 14 U-boats at sea on operations. By 1 August 1942, the fleet had increased to 342 vessels, 152 of which were operational. This dramatically raised the average daily number at sea and on operations to about 70. Bearing in mind that only a proportion of this number were deployed in the North Atlantic, such an increase, nevertheless, allowed Dönitz to establish two patrol lines at the eastern and western edges of the mid-ocean air gap from August onwards. And so it was that from midnight on 29 August, *Vorwärts* was ordered to begin its reconnaissance, set on a course of 250 degrees with the ten U-boats spread out on a broad front, carefully searching 120 miles [220km] of ocean that day.

*U609,* at the northern edge of the patrol line, was the first to spot Convoy 49, the designation given to it by the BdU. The time was 0555 hours on 31 August. SC97 was making steady progress in a light northwesterly wind and had reached **57.13N/33.40W**. The sea was slight and the sky clear; even so, the convoy was not zig-zagging at the time, which suggests that neither the commodore nor the escort commander had any inkling of the danger they were in. Rudloff, having taken *U609* to periscope depth, reported the convoy's position and direction, selected his targets and calculated the firing solution. At 0605 hours, and to the complete surprise of the accompanying escorts, the SS *Bronxville*[16] (in convoy position #81), a Norwegian freighter carrying 800 tons of general stores and 531 tons of explosives, was torpedoed. She was struck on the starboard side near number one hatch, resulting in a fire breaking out in number one hold, with the flames leaping high in between the hatches. A few minutes later she was burning furiously forward, and within 7 minutes she had gone to the bottom, mercifully before the explosives could detonate. All 39 members of her crew were picked up from the boats in calm seas within 20 minutes by RS *Perth,* steaming at the rear of the convoy.

The *Bronxville* had been located about 4 points off the starboard bow of the *Capira,* which was in convoy position #63, and as she was torpedoed the alarm bell on *Capira* sounded. All hands were ordered on deck and the 4-inch gun was manned by the Armed Guard. Five minutes later, a second salvo fired by *U609* struck the *Capira* in number four hold on the starboard side, near the after end of the engine room. Flooding of those spaces occurred at once. The Chief Engineer Thomas Kinnear, his number two Thomas Michison and a Maltese Oiler, Carmelo Cutegar, did not make it onto the deck and were never seen again. Benjamin Reid, a member of the US Armed Guard on board the *Capira* that morning, also recalled the horror of that moment, seeing his best friend William Larry Freeman, an S2c from Florida, mortally wounded as a boom came loose from the explosion, hitting him in the head. Another crew member also witnessed this incident, and later recalled that there was little to be done for him because the immediate priority was ensuring those that remained alive got safely away from the sinking ship; his body was not recovered. Ensign Matte also noted the attack in his journal: 'Monday, 31 August -- The week started off with a bang, for two ships in our convoy were torpedoed this morning about 0815. Several of our lookouts sighted a torpedo track between Ingham and another escort just before the explosions. Within 15 or 20 minutes both ships had gone to the bottom.'

Within a matter of minutes of the attack Jensen, the *Capira*'s master, saw that the situation was hopeless. As he gathered up the various code books and other classified documents into a weighted bag prior to dumping it over the side, he gave the order to abandon ship. The crew, already at their action stations, managed in the general confusion to lower three boats and two rafts into the water but there were problems as the *Capira*'s signaller, Stafford Ricks, recalled some fifty years later:

> … it was an uneventful voyage until the morning of August 31st, at which time we were torpedoed. The time of that event was at first light and a few days short of our destination which I believe was Scotland. The ship

sank very quickly as I recall, and the launching of the life boats did not go smoothly resulting in most of the hands swimming away. [17]

In fact, it was only one of the lifeboats that capsized and those on it had to swim for the other boats and rafts[18]. As the crew began to haul or swim away from the sinking vessel, one of the ship's Chinese cooks, Young Foo Ching, remained on deck; in spite of many entreaties to jump, he refused to do so and went down with the ship, bringing the number of fatalities that morning to five. The master of the *Perth* later reported the rescue operation as follows:

> During the time we were going to her (*Bronxville*'s) assistance the S.S *Capira* was also torpedoed which looked to me as if she were struck abaft of the engine room. At 6.25 we picked up the 39 survivors of the M/V *Bronxville* from their own boats without any difficulty and then proceeded to render assistance to the crew of the S.S *Capira* which had sunk at 6.30. On arrival at this position we saw some of the crew in two boats and one raft. One of the corvettes were (sic) rescuing some of the crew. The only difficulty was that boats were scattered and I think it ought to be impressed upon the Masters at the Conference to inform their crews whenever a rescue ship is in the convoy, because quite a number of the persons we picked up from the S.S *Capira* of whom we rescued 33 did not know about the rescue ship. After picking up all persons from boats and raft we circled and searched amongst wreckage but could see no other members of crew. At 7.10 we proceeded at full speed to re-join convoy. At 9.30 took up station again in convoy.[19]

The corvette that Williamson, master of the *Perth*, referred to in his report was HMCS *Morden*. *Morden* was skippered by Lieutenant John J. Hodgkinson RCNR. He was an experienced merchant seaman, described as a hard-bitten type who was nevertheless very popular with his crew. Under his command, the corvette had received intensive anti-submarine training at HMS *Western Isles* in Tobermory, Scotland in February 1942 and had received passing grades from the assessor, Commodore G.O. Stephenson, RN, who remarked that she '...has the makings of a first-class ship. She is lucky in having a Commanding Officer and First Lieutenant who realize that they have got to keep on with the working-up'. It appears therefore that this was a ship with a well-trained crew and a highly experienced and effective captain, as later events bore out. Her captain's account of the rescue makes interesting reading:

> At 0803[20] Aug. 31st, Ships 83[21] and 63 were observed to be torpedoed. The former caught fire, was seen to blaze from foc'sle to bridge and (cant?) almost immediately by the stern. The latter was torpedoed within a few minutes – a puff of smoke was observed, following which she fell out of station and sank within ten minutes. "*Perth*", #75 in the convoy, and *Morden*, detailed as rescue ships stood by to pick up survivors. *BRANDON* was ordered to screen the rescue operation. While "*Perth*" was picking up survivors from #83, *Morden* observed a boat from #63 (*Capira*) swamped and in danger of sinking. *Morden* therefore proceeded to rescue the occupants of this boat. Unfortunately due to inexperience of personnel in the boat, it was overturned while coming alongside. *Morden* therefore put over starboard sea boat to pick up these men. Meanwhile a raft drifted alongside to port, and survivors on the raft were taken aboard over our scrambling mat. A/B Jos. Breckon then dived overboard and rescued one man clinging to a spar. 16 survivors were rescued by *Morden* and landed in Londonderry.[22]

In hastening to the rescue, *Morden*'s screws came perilously close to the other lifeboat from the *Capira*, and those in it feared that they too might be pitched into the waves; in the event, they managed to remain upright in the wash, and were eventually rescued by *Perth*. This may account for Williamson's comment about the survivors being scattered.

Benjamin Reid, who had witnessed his friend William Freeman killed so tragically on the deck of the *Capira*, was rescued by *Morden* and taken to Northern Ireland where he remained for nine months before being moved to Liverpool and assigned to another ship. However, those from boats rescued by RS *Perth* were eventually landed in Gourock, Scotland. Unlike those Armed Guard personnel left waiting in Ireland for a ship back to the States, those fortunate enough to be landed in Scotland were soon repatriated. Merchant seamen keen to pick up another ship, out of economic necessity rather than any desire to be put in harm's way, were soon looking for work again. Several managed to obtain a passage in the liner the Queen Mary, and were swiftly taken back to the USA; within 4 weeks of the torpedoing of the *Capira,* the sailor who had been on her since walking into the Merchant Marine office at London's Victoria Dock nine months previously was plying the Caribbean in a freighter. In later life, he recalled that his most anxious moment on SC97 was not the attack and sinking itself but the fear of being turned over by the screws of HMCS *Morden* as she went about her rescue tasks.

The initial signal notifying the Admiralty of the attack was sent by the task force commander at 0830 hours. It only reported the sinking of both *Bronxville* and *Capira.* The follow-up signal sent at 1243 hours reported the rescue of the entire crew of the *Bronxville* by *RS Perth* and 16 members of *Capira*'s crew by the *Morden.* Somehow the fact that *Perth* had also rescued 33 of *Capira*'s crew was not passed at the time and the signal reported 38 men missing. The true figure was 5.

In the immediate aftermath of U609's[23] attack, the escort went through a well-rehearsed drill referred to as Operation Banana. Banana was designed to deter further attacks from the starboard side of the convoy i.e. the direction from which the first attack was thought to have originated. No less than five further contacts (some of which would have undoubtedly been shoals of fish) were made that day, and attacked without apparent success. The result was that the escort gained the impression that the convoy was gradually becoming surrounded by the wolf pack and further attacks were imminent. However, we can now build a picture, albeit incomplete, of subsequent U-boat movements against SC97 from the German *Kriegstagebücher.*

Following Rudloff's successful attack on *Bronxville* and *Capira,* other U-boats in the pack began to gather. At 1034 hours, *U92* spotted SC97 and reported 18 smoke clouds on a course of 70 degrees proceeding at 9 kts [17km/hr]. It continued to shadow SC97 as it changed course at 1300 hours to 20 degrees, returning to its original bearing an hour later at 1400 hours. At 1555 hours the convoy was observed to be on a main course of 50 degrees. At 1528 hours, *U756* spotted smoke rising from the convoy and ten minutes later *U91* also made contact. *U756* managed to get into position and made an attack at 1904 hours. However, at 2008 hours *U91* was driven off, probably by *Broadway* and with *U756* subsequently lost contact with the convoy. KTB records[24] indicate that two submarines maintained contact after sunset. *U604* trailed the last ship in the middle column while reloading after a failed attack and *U756* shadowed the starboard side of SC97. *U609* also regained contact in the course of the night. She fired 2 single shots at the convoy at 0400 hours and reported one probable hit. However, this turned out to be wishful thinking on Rudloff's part. Thereafter *U609*, having fired all her torpedoes, continued to act as the shadower in an attempt to vector other U-boats on to SC97. According to the KTB *U407, U411, U409, U92, U659* and *U91* reported sighting the convoy, but apparently few of them were in a position to mount a successful attack, especially as it became light on 1 September and the convoy hauled even closer to air cover. The KTB recorded subsequent events as follows:

> The following attacked:  U604 at 0733/1[25]... She scored a probable hit at a 5,000 tonner. U659's attack was frustrated by the convoy's making a leg just beforehand. Shortly before that U409 was picked up by an escort vessel for a short time and depth-charged. Both periscopes out of order. U407 tried a night attack... We could not fire as the enemy again made a sharp leg. U91 fired a quadruple miss at dawn.

Kapitänleutnant Horst Höltring[26], the captain of *U604* was also wrong about the results of his attack. The KTB account continued:

> In the morning U211 was also ordered to operate against the convoy. She is outward-bound from home... At 0850 U407 reported a Sunderland... and another one at 1153... From then on the convoy had continuous air escort, and boats were constantly forced to submerge. U91 reported that she was forced to dive once or twice every hour by a/c. This made hauling ahead very difficult and practically impossible for boats which were astern of the convoy. Ops. Control recommended the boats try a night attack and, if this proved impossible, to haul ahead so that a day attack could be made after first light.  At 0123 the first shore-based a/c was reported... As experience had shown that further operation in the area under constant

air patrol was useless, Ops. Control decided to break off the operation after first light. Boats which were in a position make an underwater attack at this time were to take their chance and then move away to the west. No successes were scored during the night.

In fact quite the reverse happened as far as the escort were concerned, although the results of their actions that night were not recognised until forty years or so after the event[27]. Towards midnight on 1 September, the moon rose, increasing visibility to 10 miles [18.5km] silhouetting the merchant ships to the darker, starboard side. The wind was force 3 from the north and the sea was moderate with a long, low swell. At 0050 hours, whilst on the port leg of a zig-zag two miles astern of SC97, HMCS *Morden* picked up a contact 1,500 yards [1,400m] on the starboard quarter on its SW2C radar and Hodgkinson altered course to investigate. *U756* was spotted on the surface at close range steaming in the direction of the convoy. *Morden* immediately increased speed and opened up with her Oerlikon whilst manoeuvring to ram, but Harney, *U756*'s captain, foiled the attempt by crash diving. *Morden* dropped two depth charges set to fifty feet by eye on the swirl. Hodgkinson thought it difficult to imagine that the U-boat could have avoided being hit by the depth charges. The corvette made ASDIC contact afterwards, and at 0128 hours ran in for a second attack. *Morden* lost the contact at 300 yards [275m] and fired a pattern of five depth charges set to 150 feet [46m]. Hodgkinson opened out the range and re-established contact with *U756*. The contact was lost at 300 yards [275m] again and *Morden* fired a pattern of ten depth charges set to 150 and 300 feet [46 and 92m]. In the darkness the crew sighted no debris, oil, or other evidence of damage on the surface to mark the destruction of *U756*.

Ensign Matte on the *Ingham* noted the encounter and recorded it in his journal:

About 0100 Tuesday a corvette in the rear of the convoy sighted a sub and attempted to ram it, then depth charged it. This was listed as a probable kill. On the theory that other subs might be around, all the other escorts and some of the merchantmen opened up with star shell fire. This was a fantastic, dream-like scene, with star shell bursts now in one sector, then in another, some of the shells whining by the ship, apparently close by.

AB Hawkins on the *Bridgepool* also witnessed the scene and, like many others, was convinced that they were being attacked by a number of U-boats and that they had been beaten off by gunfire from ships in the convoy. Below the surface, however, *U604* had gone deep to 150m where Höltring had heard ASDIC sounds and released a *Bold* submarine decoy. He heard the last depth charge attack, further off and therefore of little immediate concern for the safety of his boat and crew. During a brief search the corvette failed to regain contact with its prey. In the meantime, Commander Thomas Taylor, RN, the Senior Officer in HMS *Burnham*, had ordered Operation Raspberry, another set piece manoeuvre designed to deter an attack, in case other U-boats were present and instructed *Morden* to return immediately to the convoy, on the assumption that hostile units were still in its vicinity.

Although the Admiralty initially assessed *Morden*'s attack as insufficient evidence of damage, there is no doubt, more than sixty years after the event, that it destroyed *U756*. *U756* made no further signals and the logs of the other submarines present reveal that none of them had been the U-boat sighted and attacked by *Morden*. A Catalina B from VP-73 Squadron attacked a U-boat on 1 September, in position 58⁰08n/27⁰33w. Initially this was assessed as being *U756,* and the Catalina was formally credited with its destruction. However, it later transpired that the Catalina's target submarine was *U91,* which suffered some slight damage as a result[28]. The targets of all other counter-attacks by the surface and air escorts of SC97 have since been identified. Thus, *Morden*'s attack must have accounted for *U756*. This success was all the more surprising, as it was the first time that a U-boat detected by SW2C radar had led to a kill. Conditions must have been exceptionally good because, as already noted, the SW2C was not designed to detect smaller, low profile vessels such as submarines. Interestingly *Morden*'s rather stark report of events mentions that the radar broke down after detecting *U756* and recommended that: 'temporary failure of RDF apparatus suggests the importance of carrying RDF 1 ratings, if they are available, for care and maintenance of Type SW2C sets.' However, the evidence suggests that the corvette's detection systems, especially its primitive radar and type 123A ASDIC, were capably handled and the training received during the vessel's work up was put to good effect in the heat of the battle. But above all the commitment and determination of Lt. Hodgkinson, the *Morden*'s captain, combined with his well-motivated crew were decisive in achieving the kill.

*Vorwärts* eventually gave up the pursuit of SC97 the following day, as the convoy began to enjoy continuous air cover. The KTB concluded:

> The following boats are returning:  U609 because of fuel, U409 because both her periscopes are out of order, and U604 because her electric and Junkers compressors are out of order... Except for U756, all boats reported their position and fuel as ordered and moved away to the S.W. ...U756 was ordered to report her position. Operation against this convoy is now concluded.

The BdU's post operational analysis of the attack on SC97 bears a strong resemblance to the Admiralty's grave concerns over the lack of air cover, especially for Russian convoys. On 3 September Dönitz wrote:

> The early appearance of enemy aircraft to protect their convoys has had a restricting effect on convoy operations and this fact forced me again to demand an effective aircraft to combat the enemy air force protecting convoys.... The use of enemy aircraft to escort convoys has again severely restricted convoy operations and caused the total failure of the operation against Convoy No. 49. (i.e. SC97)... the English have succeeded in gaining air control of a large sector of the North Atlantic by increasing the ranges of their shore based aircraft and have thus narrowed down very much the area in which U-boats can operate without danger from the air... Apart from the serious effects enemy aircraft have so far had on U-boat warfare... B.d.U. is gravely concerned at the prospect of the same unfavourable air situation over the convoys extending to almost all parts of the North Atlantic, the main battleground of U-boats; this will undoubtedly be the case if things develop at their present rate. Unless suitable counter-measures can be taken U-boats will be reduced to an unjustifiable extent... The urgent need of counteracting enemy aircraft protecting convoys must therefore be emphasized once more... B.d.U. therefore requests that every emphasis be laid on the development of an

effective aircraft with long range, in the interests of a continued effective U-boat warfare.

Dönitz was a thoroughly professional sailor not given to overstatement. The above can therefore be interpreted as genuine concern, albeit at a time when the outcome of the Battle of the Atlantic was still perceived to be in the balance by the allies and, in spite of further reverses, would not be turned in their favour until well into the following year. Dönitz also had another concern too at this time, which he set out in his memoirs; that of U-boat construction. His conviction grew that: '...irretrievable time had been lost. We had already been at war with Britain for two and a half years, and still only a small fraction of the numbers of U-boats were available, which were essential if we were to achieve the requisite high rate of sinking and which I myself had demanded in 1939.'

On 14 May 1942, in a meeting with Hitler, Dönitz, emphasising this and the fact that US ship construction would soon outstrip Germany's ability to stem the tide of supplies to Britain, sought a change in policy. However, this and his plea for effective maritime air cover would be to no avail. The Führer's fixation on defeating Russia, and Göring's domination of the Luftwaffe and aircraft production prevailed (thankfully) over professional opinion.

In his final report on SC97, the Commander Task Force 24 concluded that: 'SC97 was fortunate only to lose 2 ships to such a concentration of U-boats. On the other hand, the escorts never gave the enemy a rest, and by their constant activity <u>foiled</u> several attempted attacks.'[29] With hindsight, this is an accurate assessment given the lack of Enigma intelligence on the U-boats in contact, and the opportunity for them to attack SC97 before air cover became available. The fact, unknown at the time, that one U-boat had been sunk and another damaged by the actions of the escort was again remarkable given the lack of centimetric radar and the unreliability of the SW2C Radar on *Morden*. Towards the end of the engagement the presence of air cover and the Metox early warning system were enough to keep U-boats submerged during daylight hours and throw them off the scent. This was no doubt an added factor in no further ships falling to the wolf pack following Rudloff's initial attack. However, even after the pack had withdrawn from the convoy there were still many contact reports of U-boats in the vicinity. Ensign Matte's words again: 'During the day on Tuesday we received air coverage by patrol bombers from Iceland. These planes reported submarines on the surface at various times through the day; as many as four having been reported at times. The destroyers spent most of the day chasing these contact reports.' Later that same day, Matte commented on *Ingham's* passage through the convoy: 'we went to general quarters twice as contact was reported astern. In the course of our prowls at this time we went down the center of the convoy on our way astern. It was interesting to see the strange deck loads of ambulances, jeeps, trucks, landing barges, etc., and the gun crews on every ship waving to us as we passed.' Later that evening, at 1800 hours convoy time, *Ingham*, *Bibb* and *Shenck* broke away from the convoy with the 12 ships bound for Reykjavík.

For those in the *Bronxville* and *Capira,* the attack and subsequent rescue plus the events of the following day had been sufficient excitement for a lifetime. It is somewhat ironic, therefore, to read in Ensign Matte's journal the following: 'Wednesday, 2 September -- Monday and yesterday were the kind of days that keep us from going batty from monotony. Monday afternoon we sighted a mine and sank it with about 2,100 rounds of 30 caliber rifle and machine gun fire. It looked like an old British mine and probably was unrelated to the attack in the morning.'

Commodore Gill had the highest praise for the escort, for in his words: '...either sinking, damaging or putting down Submarines, thereby saving the convoy from further attack and suffering more casualties. They did a grand job of work.' However, he did recommend that at least one escorting ship be fitted with HF/DF, for spotting U-boats making sighting reports or homing signals. In spite of the major danger from U-boats having passed, the ordeal was not yet over for the remaining ships in the convoy, and especially for some of those who had been rescued. The report for 31 August from RS *Perth* continues: 'The Lieut. (USNR) of the gun crew of the S.S. *Capira* was put into hospital suffering from severe sea-sickness.' And on 3 September: 'Doctor reported to me that W. Owens, fireman of S.S. *Capira*, was in hospital with suspected influenza.' For those who had run and survived the U-boat gauntlet, there was one more trial to face. In the understated prose of Commodore Gill's report: 'On the afternoon of 3rd September a south westerly gale sprang up and kept company with the convoy until arrival in the North Channel when it subsided somewhat.' His log also records that at various times and various locations on 3 September SS *Blairdevon*, SS *Star* and SS *Flowergate* lost the convoy in the gale. AB Hawkins aboard the *Bridgepool* was not so restrained in his description of the prevailing weather conditions. On 3 September he wrote: 'Weather worse, terrific breakers breaking over decks, water in cabin, starboard lifeboat carried away during night.' RS *Perth* was also labouring and straining heavily and at 1645 hours she hove-to because the vessel would not steer at the slow speed of the convoy. *Perth* re-joined the convoy early the following morning.

As she approached the Scottish coast at 0245 on 6 September, *Perth* sent the following signal to Navy Charge Gourock: 'Important. 72 survivors US line ship *Capira* and (Norwegian?) ship (*Bronxville?*) torpedoed. Nationality 14 British, 26 Norwegians, 7 Canadians, 11 Americans, 3 Chinese, 2 Latvians, 2 Dutch, 2 Estonians, 1 Belgian, 1 Maltese, 1 South African. 2 cot cases. Arrive boom (0900?) GMT 6th September. 300 tons coal required.' She eventually anchored off Gourock at 1045 hours on 6 September. The two cot cases were immediately sent ashore and at 1130 hours the remaining survivors transferred to the tender *Greeting*.

It was a Sunday morning, and the pubs were shut.

# 10 ON REFLECTION

"There's a divinity that shapes our ends,
Rough-hew them how we will."

*Hamlet*

The young seaman who walked into the Merchant Marine office at London's Victoria Dock, on that cold November day ten months previously, was my father. Although his ten months on *Capira* spanned but a fraction of the time he spent at sea, it was undoubtedly one of the more eventful highlights of his seafaring career. Once he signed on the *Capira,* he remained with her until she was torpedoed by *U609* at the end of August 1942. Sadly, he left no written record of his wartime experiences, and spoke but fleetingly of them. It was only after his death that his discharge papers were examined and his seagoing record pieced together. Apart from a few incidents on what he referred to as 'The Russian Run', he never related the full story of his time on the *Capira*. Hopefully this narrative has to some extent filled in the gaps and redressed the balance.

In the euphemistic prose of the Royal Navy, convoys PQ15 and QP13 were more remarkable for their unfortunate occurrences rather than any knavish tricks of the enemy. The casualties in human lives, shipping and materiel that were accidentally self-inflicted during *Capira*'s various passages far outweighed any damage wrought by German planes or U-boats. As for the enemy's knavish tricks, they accounted for the loss of 4 merchantmen going to and from Russia, one of which was sunk whilst at anchor in the Kola Inlet and one damaged. Two more were lost on the return passage across the Atlantic 77 merchant seamen were killed as a direct result. All this was achieved at the loss of just three German planes plus one U boat and their crews. Our own self-inflicted unfortunate occurrences resulted in 5 merchantmen going to the bottom and one damaged. In addition, one destroyer, one minesweeper and one submarine were sunk and one battleship damaged and put out of action for two months. As a result, over 360 RN, Merchant Navy and civilian lives were lost. Nearly all of these singular tragedies were shaped by decisions taken by commanders on the spot, trained and required to act under the enormous pressure accompanying operations of war. Decisions taken with insufficient information, especially under severe time constraints, inevitably lead to misjudgements and wrong decisions taken for seemingly the right reasons.

The pilot of the seaplane that attacked the *Gray Ranger* en route to refuel the destroyers escorting PQ15 was convinced that he had spotted and legitimately engaged the enemy. It was the overarching need for secrecy and a false assumption that the convoy had left the pilot's operational area that precipitated a near tragedy. Similarly, the officer on watch on the *Punjabi* who, in poor visibility made an immediate change of course to avoid a mine, thereby inadvertently placing his ship directly in the path of *King George* V, was also acting in good faith. A mis-appreciation of the position of the leading ships in the task force provided by *Punjabi*'s echo sounder undoubtedly contributed to the root cause of this particular disaster. Also, the captain of the *St Albans* who, on forcing the *Jastrzab* to the surface, was sure that his ship was being threatened as the submarine turned its bows towards him, and lost no time in opening fire. This was in spite of seeing a yellow flare indicating a friendly submarine under the surface. An observation that was either ascribed to something else, as he reported, or overridden in his mind by his concern for the protection of his own ship and the need for an instantaneous decision. A change of convoy course, coupled with the fear of U-boat attack, plus *Jastrzab* being out of its operational area inevitably contributed to that disaster. Decisions taken by those in command in these instances were taken in good faith, based on scant information and the situation as they saw it at the time. Moreover, their tactical imperatives and concomitant choices centred on the greater good of the convoy, to the possible detriment of individual ships, and serves to hammer home the truth of the observation that a great part of the information obtained in war is contradictory, a still greater part is false, and by far the greatest part is of doubtful (if not deadly) character[1]. But regardless of the importance or level of decision to be taken, the executive order invariably rests on a single pair of shoulders; shoulders bearing not only responsibility and authority but also accountability, especially when things go wrong. That is why command at any level is a lonely business, and becomes lonelier still the more onerous the responsibility.

The disaster that overtook QP13, whilst exhibiting the same features of misjudgement and decisions taken on the basis of doubtful information, had many other exacerbating factors. Chief among them was the fact that neither the newly-appointed commodore nor the escort commander had recently navigated the narrow channel between Iceland and the British minefield in the Denmark Strait. Added to this was the unscheduled change of plan that left the commodore with a complex convoy reorganisation to carry out before negotiating the minefield, that up to that point he had not been told about; and what's more in a ship with no functioning echo sounder. Other factors included inaccurate charts, a lack of up-to-date information on the extent and nature of mines in the minefield, compounded by poor visibility, malfunctioning radar and navigational uncertainty[2]. In some respects, it is surprising that there were not more disasters of this nature given the rapid expansion of both the RN and RCN at this time and the need to train both officers and ratings in the rudiments of seamanship and war fighting in a short space of time. It should also be borne in mind that such friction in war affected friend and foe alike. German misinterpretation of signals intelligence falsely led them to the view that, co-incidental with the passage of PQ15, the Allies were about to mount an amphibious attack on north Norway; an operation that they were manifestly in no fit state to carry out at that time.

Decisions taken at a politico-strategic level far from the operational theatre also had a direct bearing on the tactical options of convoy and battle fleet commanders at sea; their effect should not be underestimated. Churchill's insistence on supplying the Soviet Union via the North Russian ports made little tactical sense, especially when air support for naval operations was so sparse. The use of some of Harris' long-range bombers for German airfield interdiction in Northern Norway to coincide with the passage of convoys at critical times may have gone some way to blunting German air attacks. However, Harris' career had largely focused on the development of the bomber for its strategic use. Following his appointment as Commander-in-Chief Bomber Command, there was little that could be done to divert assets from the strategic bombing campaign for uses, that from other perspectives, were even more strategic. No doubt relying on their experiences during the last war, sailors such as Tovey and Pound appreciated fully the threat to

Britain's strategic lifelines across the Atlantic, and through the Suez Canal to far flung parts of the Empire, that was posed by U-boats and German capital ships. In attempting to balance these strategic imperatives, there were bound to be losers at certain points in time. The futile battle waged by the Navy in 1942 for air assets amply demonstrates where the strategic emphasis lay at that juncture and, as the then Director Naval Intelligence observed of the RAF, how difficult it was to change the habits and thoughts of years in a few weeks. Neither was such intransigence the preserve of officials on this side of the Atlantic. Admiral King was equally adamant in his delay over the marshalling of merchant ships into convoys when proceeding along the US Eastern Seaboard. The extent to which this was due to his prejudice against the Royal Navy, who were ahead of the game early in 1942, remains a matter of debate; as does the adverse effect British inter-service rivalry had on the strategic conduct of the war at that time.

Whilst reflecting on the conflicting strategic approaches taken by Allied politicians and leaders, one must not neglect the role played by the Russian people; a large majority of whom had suffered much under the Soviet system before the German invasion. It has to be said that the criticisms voiced by senior British naval officers on the behaviour of ordinary Russians and their political masters in and around Murmansk that have been documented here were very much coloured by what they had come to believe about Russia since the revolution. Their observations must also be seen in the context of a nation still reeling from the sudden shock of the Nazi assault before it had had time to regroup and gear up to repulse the German Wehrmacht. Indeed, many individual criticisms of the Soviet system would have also been the product of personal experience following participation in the Allied intervention in the Russian civil war between 1918 and 1921.

For the population of Murmansk, this would have been of little immediate concern, however, as their aim in the spring and summer of 1942 was to survive the daily bombing attacks and prepare to defend their city from a direct assault by the combined German and Finnish forces. Their stoicism and fortitude in the face of such an existential threat exemplified by Vladimir Loktev's diary entries can only be admired. They had no option but to stand and fight, and they can be justifiably proud of their role, and that of hastily assembled units such as the Polar division in countering the direct threat from Dietl's mountain troops and their Finnish allies. Such resilience was not appreciated at a time when there was a real fear of Russia suing for peace. Neither was there any inkling of the enormous sacrifice that the Russian Motherland would make in the eventual defeat of Nazi Germany. Estimates vary, but the butcher's bill alone came to over 20 million Russian dead (by far the greatest pro rata and total casualty figure for any of the belligerent nations), not to mention the destruction of Russian cities, towns and villages and the laying waste of vast areas of the Russian countryside. It would be irresponsible not to assimilate these and other incontrovertible facts into our collective psyche before those who experienced them fade from living memory. We ignore them at our peril.

As we have seen, decisions taken by commanders and acted upon by their subordinates set in train a chain of events; events that impinged directly upon the wellbeing and survival of all. The chain of command worked best, therefore, when it was accompanied by a bond of trust between commander and commanded, thus ensuring a confidence that all would act in the interests of the common good. How that translated to the DEMS gunner circling his gun pit to keep warm in an Arctic twilight, or the lowly greaser servicing the machinery deep in the bowels of a tramp steamer ploughing its way through an Atlantic storm, or the sonar operator in his cramped shack listening intently for the enemy's echo was, nevertheless, a matter for the individual. For Austin Byrne, fresh from the woollen mills of Bradford, there was little respect for those in authority immersed in their own self-regard who manned the training establishments he attended following conscription into the Royal Navy as a DEMS gunner. However, the captain of the first merchant ship he was assigned to, the *Induna*, he held in the highest regard not only for his professionalism, civility and quiet authority, but above all for the way in which he calmly gave the order to abandon ship after it was torpedoed en route to Russia, ensuring that all who could get off did so in good order, and in the process remained in command on the bridge until he eventually went down with his ship[3]. For Tom Chilvers, veteran of the Spanish Civil War, there was an undoubted ideological backdrop to his service in the Merchant Navy that compelled him to volunteer in spite of being recently wed. Through his diary we perceive a mature, independently-minded character not averse to speaking out against what he saw as injustice but ever conscious of the need to work as a team. For my father, a professional merchant seaman before, during and after the war, there were good ships and bad ships, good skippers and bad skippers. Be that as it may, he was always clear that in a small, tight-knit crew you could never contemplate letting your shipmates down irrespective of their country of origin, colour or politics. They relied on each other and could not afford personal considerations to hinder the task in hand, especially in the heightened circumstances they now found themselves.

The bottom line was that merchant seamen who continued to pursue their civilian calling in wartime, be that through choice or circumstance, existed in an environment where the inherent hazards of their employment were multiplied many times over. Their tasks remained much the same, and the only adjustments to the ship's routine were designed to ensure the corporate safety and security of the convoy, its individual components and, above all, themselves. Their battle, the Battle of the Atlantic, remained at its height from the outset until well into 1943, after which its intensity diminished but never completely disappeared until the end of hostilities. It was certainly not apparent in 1939, but may have slowly dawned upon some as time went by that their pro rata attrition rate would place them at the top of the league when set against their compatriots in uniform. Their contribution to ultimate victory should never be underestimated. In maintaining that vital transatlantic bridge, not forgetting those other routes to far flung outposts of empire, they ensured not only the survival of the United Kingdom, but also the build-up of men and materiel essential for the eventual liberation of continental Europe. In addition, the Arctic convoys contributed in a very practical way to the Soviet Union's fight back against Nazi Germany. It also nurtured a bond between the inhabitants of those north Russian ports, the Allied seamen and their descendants that exists to this day.

The contribution of the *Capira* and her crew in that endeavour during her final ten months may seem relatively insignificant when set against the wider context of the losses incurred during her final voyage. Nevertheless, we should not lose sight of the vital part they and many others like them played in sustaining the United Kingdom and the Soviet Union. In the wider context of the men who crewed and protected merchant ships at this time, we must draw a distinction between those who sailed as hostilities-only volunteers keen to do their bit, like Tom Chilvers; or as conscripts, like Austin Byrne; against those who had chosen the sea as a means of earning a living, as a way of life. It was the Merchant Seaman, men like my father, for whom the war was an unwelcome interference, as opposed to an interruption, in their professional seagoing lives that they learnt to bear with stoicism. Given that their employment during peacetime was precarious; their conditions primitive and their occupation not without considerable inherent danger; they were, in all probability, initially better equipped, psychologically if not physically, to deal with the added rigours occasioned by war. To appreciate, even in some small degree, their reactions and later reflections, especially in moments of extreme danger, requires us to occupy their sea boots, tread their decks and think their thoughts. Were that possible, then we might have an entirely different perspective on the events narrated here. The past is indeed a foreign country where things are done differently, and those who occupy it are also manifestly apart from us in the experiences that shaped their view of the world. Those caught up in these events were raised in the shadow of the First World War in a society still suffering the psychological impact of that conflict, a conflict subsequently followed by the Great Depression, mass unemployment and the threat from the rise of the European dictators. A seafaring life was a means of escape for some, my father included. Although still in his early 20s, he was well-travelled and had no doubt about the dangers and imminent threat of fascism. Austin Byrne, having secured a job in the woollen mills of Bradford and intent on earning a living, understandably did not pay a great deal of interest to what was happening on the Continent. Others, like Tom Chilvers, motivated by an ideology fundamentally opposed to fascism, chose another route and were proactive in their stance against it. Such experiences, coupled with that unpredictable balance between nature and nurture, shaped their perceptions, hard-wired their view of the world, and determined their reaction to it.

Failing the discovery of new evidence, the major events recorded here are not in dispute, even though some details are still open to debate depending on the way they were perceived and reported at the time. Nevertheless, the facts remain open to reinterpretation by future historians, raised and educated in a time and culture far removed from that narrated here. How they will view this particular episode of the past remains to be seen. May we never lose sight of the fact that those who manned the merchant ships, escorted the convoys and fought the enemy were ordinary men, called upon to do extraordinary things, and we owe them a debt of gratitude.

Sunset and evening star
And one clear call for me!
And may there be no moaning of the bar
When I put out to sea,
But such a tide as moving seems asleep,
Too full for sound and foam,
When that which drew from out the boundless deep
Turns again home.
Twilight and evening bell,
And after that the dark!
And may there be no sadness of farewell,
When I embark;
For tho' from out our bourne of Time and Place
The flood may bear me far
I hope to see my Pilot face to face
When I have cross'd the bar.

*Crossing the Bar* by Alfred Lord Tennyson

# Appendix I

## SS *Mormacsul* – PQ15 Cargo Manifest

| | |
|---:|---|
| 27208 | Rounds 75 mm Shells and |
| 12788 | Detonating fuses |
| 6000 | Cases TNT |
| 1200000 | Rounds 45 Cal cartridges |
| 150 | Boxes 45 Cal Thompson Sub-machine Guns |
| 4 | Boxes Ailing Gun Webbing |
| 15 | Boxes Accessories |
| 30 | Magazines |
| 10 | M3 Medium Tanks American with guns mounted |
| 64 | Boxes American tank parts |
| 100 | Fargo 1½ Ton W.F. 32 Trucks |
| 32 | Studebaker 2½ Ton 6x4 Trucks |
| 22 | Universal Gun Carriers |
| 1020 | Drums Lubricating Aviation Oil |
| 9 | Drums Alcohol |
| 8 | Carboys Battery Electrolyte |
| 6 | Drums SAE 10 Motor Oil |
| 5 | Drums SAE 80 Gear Lubricant |
| 8 | Pails No 2 Cup Grease |
| 1 | Pail No 4 Water Pump Grease |
| 1 | Case Hydraulic Break Fluid |
| 12 | Boxes Milling Machines |
| 1 | Case Hydraulic Universal Grinders and Equipment |
| 1 | No 2/24 Plain Automatic Milling Machine and Equipment |
| 1237 | Bundles Tin Plate |
| 10370 | Reels Barbed Wire |
| 1045 | Cases Cartridge Brass Sheets |
| 240 | Packages Sheet Steel |
| 420 | Containers Coke Tinplate |
| 425 | Barrels Ferro Silicon |
| 900 | Packages Special American Standard Elexite Coke Tinplate |

| | |
|---:|:---|
| 8361 | Bars Electrolytic Copper |
| 1071 | Drums Crude Linseed Oil |
| 32532 | Yards Woollen Cloth Drab No 33 |
| 280 | Cases Anaconda Yellow Brass Wire |
| 6200 | Shoulders and |
| 146 | Bales Innersole Leather |
| 118 | Drums Unfiltered Yellow Phosphorous |
| 9360 | Pairs Service Shoes |
| 70 | Cases Aluminium Tubing |
| 2536 | Hide Bends |
| 25459 | Cases Lunch Meat |
| 1125 | Boxes Lard |
| 10 | Infantry Tanks |
| 10 | Cases Radio |
| 20 | Packages Oil |
| 1 | Case Aerials |
| 4 | Cases Gun and Parts |
| 4480 | Rounds Two Pounder Armour Piercing Shells |
| 74880 | Rounds 303 Ball Cartridges |
| 112480 | Rounds 303 Tracer Cartridges |
| 45000 | Rounds 300 Ball Cartridges |
| 22500 | Rounds 300 Cal Tracer Cartridges |
| 22500 | Rounds 300 Cal Armour Piercing Cartridges |
| 1596 | Rounds 45 Automatic Ball Cartridges |
| 1494 | Rounds 2 inch Bombs |
| 11396 | Ingots Aluminium |
| 200 | Barrels 80/85% Ferro Silicon |
| 13000 | Bags Wheat Flour |

# Appendix II

## Merchant Ships in Convoy PQ15

| Ship | | GRT | Speed | Destination | Remarks |
|------|------|------|------|------|------|
| *Krassin* | Russia | 4902 | 11 | Archangel | HX178 |
| *Montcalm* | Canada | 1432 | 7½ | Archangel | SC72 |
| *Deer Lodge* | USA | 6187 | 9½ | Archangel | SC74 |
| *Lancaster* | USA | 7516 | 9½ | Murmansk | SC74 |
| *Alcoa Rambler* | USA | 5500 | 10 | Murmansk | HX180 |
| *Expositor* | USA | 4959 | 10 | White Sea | HX180 |
| *Paul Luckenbach* | USA | 6606 | 13 | Murmansk | HX180 |
| *Empire Morn* | UK | 7092 | 10½ | Murmansk | Clyde (CAM Ship) |
| *Southgate* | UK | 4862 | | Murmansk | Clyde |
| *Cape Race* | UK | 3807 | 9 | White Sea | Sunderland |
| *Botavon* | UK | 5848 | 9 | White Sea | Tyne (Ex PQ14) |
| *Cape Corso* | UK | 3807 | 11½ | White Sea | Hull |
| *Jutland* | UK | 6153 | 9 | Murmansk | Dundee |
| *Empire Bard* | UK | 3114 | 10 | Murmansk | Dundee (Ex PQ14) |
| *Topa Topa* | USA | 5356 | 10 | Murmansk | SC77 |
| *Mormacrey* | USA | 5946 | 10 | Murmansk | SC77 |
| *Hegira* | USA | 7588 | 10 | White Sea | HX178 (Ex PQ14) |
| *Mormacrio* | USA | 5940 | 11 | White Sea | HX177 (Ex PQ14) |
| *Capira* | Panama | 5625 | 10 | White Sea | SC77 |
| *Zebulon B Vance* | USA | 5001 | 11 | Murmansk | SC77 |
| *Texas* | USA | 5638 | 9 | White Sea | SC77 |
| *Alcoa Cadet* | USA | 5035 | 10½ | Murmansk | SC77 |
| *Bayou Chico* | USA | 5401 | 10 | Murmansk | SC77 |
| *Seattle Spirit* | USA | 5627 | 8½ | White Sea | SC72 (Ex PQ14) |
| *Francis Scott Key* | USA | 7000 | 10 | White Sea | H178 (Ex PQ14) |

Information taken from ADM 237/166. No record of convoy positions is currently available. Most ships were unloaded in Murmansk because of the adverse ice conditions in the White Sea but the two ice breakers, *Krassin* and *Montcalm*, were escorted there later. This was the first convoy to deploy a Catapult Armed Merchantman (CAM) ship, the *Empire Morn*.

The *Cape Corso, Botavon* and *Jutland* were torpedoed and sunk at sea, whilst the *Alcoa Cadet* was bombed and sunk in Murmansk and the *Deer Lodge* bombed and damaged but subsequently repaired.

# Appendix III

## Convoy QP13 Cruising Order on Leaving Russia

The ships denoted * are listed on a document which has been given the convoy designation QP13U and sailed directly to the Clyde. The remainder staged via Iceland before their passage across the Atlantic.

Br=British, Pa=Panamanian, Am=American, Ru=Russian, Du=Dutch,

| 1 | 2 | 3 | 4 | 5 | 6 | 7 | 8 | 9 |
|---|---|---|---|---|---|---|---|---|
| 11 Mormacrey (Am) | 21 Nemaha (Am) | 31 Empire Baffin* (Br) | 41 Michigan (Pa) | 51 Empire Selwyn* (Br) | 61 American Robin (Am) | 71 Lancaster (Am) | 81 Atlantic (Br) | 91 Mauna Kea (Am) |
| 12 Pieter de Hoogh* (Du) | 22 Hegira* (Am) | 32 Richard Henry Lee (Am) | 42 Heffron (Am) **Sunk** | 52 Stary Bolshevik (Ru) | 62 American Press (Am) | 72 City of Omaha (Am) | 82 Massmar (Am) **Sunk** | 92 Hybert (Am) **Sunk** |
| 13 John Randolph (Am) **Severely Damaged** | 23 Exterminator (Pa) **Damaged** | 33 St. Clears* (Br) | 43 Budenni* (Ru) | 53 Komiles* (Ru) | 63 HMS Alynbank | 73 Rodina (Ru) **Sunk** | 83 Yaka (Am) | 93 Capira (Pa) |
| 14 Empire Stevenson* (Br) | 24 Empire Meteor* (Br) | 34 Kuzbass* (Ru) | 44 Petrovki* (Ru) | 54 Alma Ata* (Ru) | 64 Archangelsk* (Ru) | 74 Mount Evans* (Pa) | 84 Empire Mavis* (Br) | 94 Chulmleigh* (Br) |

# Appendix IV
## Convoy QP13 Order of Battle

**Close Escort – Sailed from Archangel:**

| | |
|---|---|
| ORP *Garland* | Destroyer (Polish crew) |
| HMS *Intrepid* | Destroyer (With Iceland section of QP13 until 7 July) |
| HMS *Alynbank* | Aux AA Ship |
| HMS *Honeysuckle* | Corvette |
| HMS *Starwort* | Corvette |

**Close Escort – Sailed from Murmansk:**

| | |
|---|---|
| HMS *Achates* | Destroyer |
| USSR *Gremyaschi* | Destroyer (As far as 30 degrees E) |
| USSR *Grozni* | Destroyer (As far as 30 degrees E) |
| HMS *Inglefield* | Destroyer (With Iceland section of QP13 until 7 July) |
| USSR *Kuibyshev* | Destroyer (As far as 30 degrees E) |
| HMS *Volunteer* | Destroyer |
| HMS *Hyderabad* | Corvette |
| FFL *Roselys* | Corvette (Free French crew) |
| HMS *Hussar* | Minesweeper (Accompanied Iceland section of QP13) |
| HMS *Niger* | Minesweeper (Accompanied Iceland section of QP13. |
| | **Mined off Iceland 5 July 1942** |
| HMT *Lady Madeleine* | ASW Trawler (Accompanied Iceland section of QP13) |
| HMT *St Elstan* | ASW Trawler (Accompanied Iceland section of QP13) |
| HMS *Trident* | Submarine (As far as 23 degrees E) |

**Covering Force:**

| | | |
|---|---|---|
| HMS *Duke of York* | Battleship | (C-in-C Home Fleet) |
| HMS *Victorious* | Aircraft Carrier | (Second in Command Home Fleet) |
| USS *Washington* | Battleship | (Commander Task Force 99) |
| HMS *Cumberland* | Heavy Cruiser | |
| HMS *Nigeria* | Light Cruiser | (Commander 10th Cruiser Sqn) |
| HMS *Blankney* | Destroyer | |
| HMS *Douglas* | Destroyer | (Force Q – escort to the fleet oiler *Gray Ranger* joined QP13 2 July) |
| HMS *Faulknor* | Destroyer | (Captain (D) 8th Destroyer Flotilla) |
| HMS *Marne* | Destroyer | |
| HMS *Martin* | Destroyer | |
| USS *Mayrant* | Destroyer | |
| HMS *Middleton* | Destroyer | |
| HMS *Onslaught* | Destroyer | |
| HMS *Onslow* | Destroyer | |
| USS *Rhind* | Destroyer | |
| HMS *Wheatland* | Destroyer | |
| HMS *Ashanti* | Destroyer | |
| HMS *Bramble* | Minesweeper | |
| HMS *Hazard* | Minesweeper | |
| HMS *Leda* | Minesweeper | |
| HMS *Seagull* | Minesweeper | |

# Appendix V

## Convoy SC97 Cruising Order

Departed Halifax on 22 August1942 and arrived Liverpool on 7 September (Arnold Hague gives 59 ships)

Br=British, Du=Dutch, Nor=Norwegian, Est=Estonian, Ice=Icelandic, Am=American, Yug=Yugoslavian, Pol=Polish, Bel=Belgian, Fr=French, Da=Danish, Gr=Greek, Pa=Panamanian. RV=Rescue Vessel.

| 1 | 2 | 3 | 4 | 5 | 6 | 7 | 8 | 9 | 10 | 11 | 12 | 13 |
|---|---|---|---|---|---|---|---|---|----|----|----|----|
| 11 USS Aquila | 21 | 31 Empire Nightingale (Br) | 41 Llandaff (Br) | 51 Lord Byron (Br) | 61 Empire Cormorant (Br) | 71 Dramatist (Br) | 81 Bronxville (Nor) **Sunk** | 91 Egba (Br) | 101 Bonneville? (Nor) | 111 Empire Steelhead (Br) | 121 Empire Moon (Br) | 131 Stornest (Br) |
| 12 Richard Basset (Am) | 22 Medina (Am) | 32 Kathariotsa (Gr) | 42 Jurko Topic (Yug) | 52 Dunsley (Br) | 62 Shirvan (Br) | 72 Ravnefjell (Nor) | 82 Dunav (Yug) | 92 Radport (Br) | 102 Barrwhin (Br) | 112 Zogloba (Pol) | 122 Empire Norse (Br) | 132 Hjalmar Wessel (Nor) |
| 13 Oliver Ellsworth (Am) | 23 Malantic (Am) | 33 Star (Nor) | 43 Berto (Nor) | 53 Beacon (Am) | 63 Capira (Pa) **Sunk** | 73 H. H. Rogers (Pa/Am?) | 83 E. G. Seubert (Am) | 93 Texas (Am) | 103 Bridgepool (Br) | 113 British Dominion (Br) | 123 Ampetco (Bel) | 133 Rizpa (Am) |
| 14 Wichita Falls (Am) | 24 Katia (Ice) | 34 Peter Helms (Am) | 44 Moscha D. Kydoniefs (Gr) | 54 Aghios Vlasios (Gr) | 64 President de Vogue (Nor) | 74 West Maximus (Am) | 84 Uranienborg (Da) | 94 Aquarius (Am) | 104 Flowergate (Br) | 114 Albert Le Borgne (Fr) | 124 Zouave (Br) | 134 Keila (Br/Est?) |
| 15 El Almirante (Pa) | 25 City of Fort Worth (Am) | 35 | 45 Blairdevon (Br) | 55 Evviva (Nor) | 65 Blairnevis (Br) | 75 Perth (Br) RV | 85 Empire Toiler (Br) | 95 Henrik Ibsen (Nor) | 105 Berkel (Du) | 115 Empire Flame (Br) | 125 Loke (Nor) | 135 Akababra (Nor) |

Source: https://warsailors.com/convoys/sc97.html

# Notes on Sources

**The US National Archives & Records Administration:** (8601 Adelphi Road, College Park, Maryland, 20740 6001) has custody of reports from US Navy Armed Guard detachments aboard non-navy ships during the Second World War. These reports, among the Records of the Office of the Chief of Naval Operations (Record Group 38), usually include Armed Guard crew lists, voyage reports, data relating to armaments and supplies provided by the US Navy, correspondence relating to recommendations for medals for members of the Armed Guard crew, orders and miscellaneous correspondence.

**The Guildhall Library:** (Gresham St, London EC2V 7HH) retains archives of Lloyds Lists and Voyage Record Cards. The latter give details of a ship's sailing and docking dates and a few other details such as any damage sustained. They are, however, written in shorthand and require some interpretation.

**The National Archives Kew:** (51 Leyborne Park Kew, Richmond Upon Thames TW9 3HB) is the main source for convoy, naval, war office and cabinet office papers, as well as Enigma intercepts, Second World War technology and survivors' reports. They appear under the ADM, BT, CAB, HW and TNA series in the endnotes.

**The National Maritime Museum Caird Library:** (Romney Road, Greenwich SE10 9NF) has a treasure trove of personal papers, letters, etc from senior officers down through the ranks to the lower deck. These appear under the HTN, MSS and WDG series in the endnotes.

**Websites:** All websites consulted are contained in the notes, however those covering a wide variety of relevant material for the researcher are:

War Sailors at: http://www.warsailors.com

U Boat Net at: http://www.uboatarchive.net

However, the researcher is well advised to crosscheck material from all sources as errors are frequently encountered.

# Select Bibliography

| | | | |
|---|---|---|---|
| Arthur. M, | *Lost Voices of the Royal Navy* | Hodder | 2005 |
| Bennett. GH & R, | *Survivors* | Hambledon | 1999 |
| Carruthers. B, | *The U-Boat War in the Atlantic Volumes 1, 2 & 3* | Pen & Sword | 2013 |
| Coulter. JLS, | *The Royal Naval Medical Service, Volume 2* | HMSO | 1956 |
| Dönitz. K, | *Memoirs – Ten Years, Twenty Days,* | Weidenfeld & Nicolson | 1959 |
| Edwards. B, | *The Road to Russia* | Leo Cooper | 2002 |
| Edwards. B, | *Dönitz and the Wolf Packs* | Cassell | 2002 |
| Edwards. B, | *War of the U-Boats* | Pen & Sword | 2006 |
| Edwards. B, | *The Quiet Heroes* | Pen & Sword | 2010 |
| Edwards. B, | *The Wolf Packs Gather* | Pen & Sword | 2011 |
| Elphick. M, | *Life Line* | Chatham | 1999 |
| Hague. A, | *The Allied Convoy System 1939–1945* | Chatham | 2000 |
| Hastings. M, | *Bomber Command* | Dial Press | 1979 |
| Hewitt. N, | *Coastal Convoys 1939–1945* | Pen & Sword | 2008 |
| HMSO | *Merchantmen at War* | HMSO | 1944 |
| Jordan. D, | *Wolfpack* | Spellmount | 2002 |
| Kahn. D, | *Seizing the Enigma* | Frontline | 2012 |
| Keegan. J, | *The Price of Admiralty* | Century Hutchinson | 1988 |
| Kemp. P, | *Convoy – Drama in Arctic Waters* | Arms & Armour | 1993 |
| Krzyształowicz, M. | *Type VII* | Seaforth | 2012 |
| Lambert. J, & Brown. L, | *Flower Class Corvettes* | Seaforth | 2014 |
| Mann. C, & Jörgensen. C, | *Hitler's Arctic War* | Brown Partworks | 2002 |
| Milner. M, | *North Atlantic Run* | Naval Institute | 1985 |

| | | | |
|---|---|---|---|
| Niestlé. A, | *German U-Boat Losses During World War ll* | Frontline Books | 2014 |
| Ogden. G, | *My Sea Lady* | Hutchinson | 1963 |
| Patterson. L, | *U-Boat War Patrol* | Chatham | 2006 |
| Peterson. J, | *Darkest Before Dawn* | Spellmount | 2011 |
| Prysor. G, | *Citizen Sailors* | Viking | 2011 |
| Ruegg. B, & Hague. A, | *Convoys to Russia 1941–1945* | World Ship Society | 1992 |
| Skates. John Ray, | *The Invasion of Japan: Alternative to the Bomb* | University of South Carolina Press | 2000 |
| Seabag-Montefiore. H, | *Enigma – The Battle for the Code* | Phoenix | 2011 |
| Smith. A, | *U-108 at War* | Pen & Sword | 2012 |
| Smith. K, Watts. C.T, & M.J, | *Records of Merchant Shipping & Seamen* | PRO | 2001 |
| Ed. Syrett. D, | *The Battle of the Atlantic & Signals Intelligence, U-Boat Tracking Papers* | Ashgate | 2002 |
| Walling. M.G, | *Forgotten Sacrifice* | Osprey | 2012 |
| Werner. A H, | *Iron Coffins* | Cassell | 2004 |
| Whinney. B, | *The U-Boat Peril* | Cassell | 1999 |
| Williams. A, | *The Battle of the Atlantic* | BBC Publishing | 2003 |
| Woodman. R, | *Arctic Convoys 1941–1945* | Murray | 2004 |
| Woodman. R, | *The Real Cruel Sea* | Murray | 2005 |
| Ziemke. E.F, | *The German Northern Theatre Of Operations 1940–45* | Naval & Military Press | |

# Endnotes

## CHAPTER 1

1  Information regarding the crew presented in this chapter is taken from the US National Archives and Records Administration copy of *Capira's* crew manifest when she docked in New York on 27 July 1942. This is accurate only for the period 22 March to 27 July 1942 but serves as an example of a typical crew profile at that time.

2  Life on board SS *Empire Baffin* during the passage of convoy PQ16 is taken from Tom Chilvers' diary MSS-87-090

3  See p. 107 Hague. Arnold, *The Allied Convoy System 1939-1945*, Chatham Publishing, 2000

4  www.usmm.org/ww2.html

5  MSS-88-009

6  BT64/1944

7  *Ibid*

## CHAPTER 2

1  The reason for *Capira's* rather circuitous route before a trans-Atlantic crossing was to avoid the more dangerous passage through the English Channel.

2  Full convoy details taken from the *Norwegian War Sailors* website at http://www.warsailors.com/convoys/onconvoys.html

3  *Befehlshaber der Unterseeboote* (**BdU**) was the title of the supreme commander of the *Kriegsmarines* U-boat Arm (*Ubootwaffe*) during the Second World War. The term also referred to the Command HQ of the U-boat arm itself. The title was established on 17 October 1939, when Karl Dönitz was promoted to Rear Admiral (*Konteradmiral*). His previous title had been U-boat Leader (*Führer der Unterseeboote*), a position he had held from January 1936.

4  ASDIC was the acronym for Anti-Submarine Detection Investigation Committee though no committee bearing this name has been found in the Admiralty archives. Sonar, the more modern term stood for Sound Navigation And Ranging.

5  In spite of remaining distant from the Nazi Party Dönitz took over from Raeder in January 1943 and eventually took over from Hitler as Chancellor following the latter's suicide at the end of the war. He was arraigned at Nuremburg and imprisoned for 10 years. Following his release he wrote his memoires *Ten Years, Twenty Days* from which his biographical details and career have been taken.

6  The detail is based on the The *Kriegstagebücher* (KTB), the War Diary of the Commander in Chief Submarines captured at the end of WW2 given at http://www.uboatarchive.net/BDUKTB30301B.htm

7  http://www.uboatarchive.net/BDUKTB30301B.htm

8  This was due to the BdU adding a fourth rotor to naval Enigma machines thus greatly increasing their effectiveness.

9  For a useful synopsis see Arnold Hague *The Allied Convoy System 1939–1945* Chatham Publishing, p. 156.

10  See Lloyds List Casualty Sections for 7, 14 Jan and 24 Mar 1942.

11  All information on *Capira*'s Armed Guard Detachment, armament and protective measures is taken from US National Archives & Records Administration RG 38 370/12/23/03 Box 103.

12  This later became a Butlins holiday camp.

13  *Induna* was sunk during its passage to Russia and Austin Byrne spent four days in an open boat before being rescued by a Russian destroyer and taken to Murmansk.

14  It should be remembered that merchant seamen had to provide their own clothing and in general the DEMS gunners were better equipped.

15  Austin Byrne's experiences were recorded in conversation with the author on 23 August 2016

16  C/JX313519 AB J Hawkins RN – diary in the author's possession.

17  The 'First Happy Time' (*'Die Glückliche Zeit'*), occurred earlier and refers to the phase of the Battle of the Atlantic between July and October 1940 during which German U-boats enjoyed significant success against the Royal Navy and its allies. It started almost immediately after the Fall of France, which brought the German U-boat fleet closer to the British shipping lanes in the Atlantic. From July 1940 to the end of October, 282 Allied ships were sunk off the north-west approaches to Ireland incurring a loss of 1,489,795 tons of merchant shipping. Such success was largely due to a lack of Allied radar and HF/DF equipped ships to detect and counter U-boat surface attacks at night.

18  As late as 13 April 1942 *U123* was reporting 'From "Canaveral" to "Hatteras" all lights as in peace-time.' http://www.uboatarchive.net/BDUKTB30306A.htm

19  Although Hardegen never saw the Manhattan skyline, only its aura, fabricated stills were added to Tolle's footage from the patrol, purporting to show that he did. The resultant films were shown in German cinemas and are still available on U Tube.

20  Taken from an interview on U Tube to be found at: https://www.bing.com/videos searchsearch? q=u+tube+hardegen&view=detail&mid= C816924EE41B66CBFEB5C816924EE41B66CB FEB 5&FORM=VIRE

21  Hardegen sank or crippled 9 merchant ships during this patrol and a further 10 during *U123*'s second visit to the Eastern Seaboard. He was awarded the Knights Cross with Oak Leaves and the rare U-boat War badge with Diamonds, receiving both personally from Hitler. He died, aged 105, on 9 June 2018.

22  Skates. John Ray, *The Invasion of Japan: Alternative to the Bomb*, University of South Carolina Press, 2000

23  ADM 178/323

24  *Ibid*

25  *Ibid*

26  Similarly there were a few tense and nervous moments in the BdU on the following day as British Commando forces raided St Nazaire. An emergency order was put out for boats ready for departure to put to sea. immediately for battle in coastal waters. Later, when it was recognised that the raid was a limited operation to deny German capital ships the use of the dry dock, Dönitz reflected on the dangers of having his headquarters so close to the coast and hastened its relocation to Paris at the end of March.

## CHAPTER 3

1 See p. 11, Hague. Arnold, *The Allied Convoy System 1939-1945*, Chatham House Publishing, 2000.

2 See p. 225, Keegan. John, *The Price of Admiralty*, Century Hutchinson Ltd, 1988.

3 Cit op, Kemp. Paul, *Convoy! – Drama in Arctic Waters*, Arms and Armour, 1993

4 See p. 27, Hague. Arnold, *The Allied Convoy System 1939-1945*, Chatham House Publishing, 2000.

5 See Milner. Mark, *North Atlantic Run*, University of Toronto Press, 1985, for an account of the difficulties this presented to the RCN and how they were eventually overcome. Milner also documents SC97 and the sinking of *Capira* and *Bronxville* but beware of some inaccuracies in the account on p. 151.

6 BT64/1944

7 Statistics taken from: http://www.battleships-cruisers.co.uk/merchant_navy_losses.htm and agree closely with those given by Hague p. 107. It should be noted that, for various reasons, figures vary from source to source. Hague has used the figures kept by the Trade Division of the Admiralty and these are slightly different from those provided by the Register General.

8 Statistics taken from: http://uboat.net/technical/shipyards/

9 Quoted from: *A Difficult Time. 'Westward, Look, the Land is Bright'*, BBC London, 27 April 1941

10 This was, of course, before the introduction of the Plan Position Indicator (PPI) later in 1943 that gave a far better visual indication of the air and sea picture surrounding the transmitter.

11 *HMS Nigeria* was later to form part of the escort for PQ15.

12 Information taken from Tom Heley's Record of Service and other papers kindly lent to the author by Jill Britton.

13 The key to this was the development in the UK of the cavity magnetron now an essential component of microwave ovens.

14 Surface Warning 1st Canadian.

15 For a discussion on these aspects see Jerry Proc's article at: http://jproc.ca/sari/sarrad1.html and Hague p. 63. An interesting personal account of radar development is also to be found at: http://www.vectorsite.net/ttwiz_02.html.

16 ASV (Air-Surface Vessel)

17 http://www.naval-history.net/xGM-Tech-HFDF.htm HF/DF had its first trials in a destroyer in March 1941 and by January 1942 it was fitted into 25 escorts and rescue ships. Early on in the war due to electromagnetic compatibility issues HF/DF could not be fitted in same ship as radar.

18 For a comprehensive account of the signals' intelligence war see Sebag-Montefiore. Hugh, *Enigma – The Battle for the Code*, Phoenix, 2011.

19 The crew of the *München* had time to throw the Enigma machine and its current settings overboard but the June settings were still in the ship's safe.

20 Ironically *U110* was captained by Lieutenant Commander Fritz-Julius Lemp who, when in command of *U30*, had sunk the *Athenia*. Lemp and 13 of his crew were killed during the fight to capture *U110*.

21 Quoted p. 409 Woodman. Richard, *The Real Cruel Sea*, John Murray, 2005.

22 Quoted in Jürgen Rohwer's introduction to Dönitz' *Memoirs*, Stuttgart, 1990.

23  Taken from: http://jproc.ca/sari/asd_et1.html

24  Typically in the range 14-22 KHz.

25  Short for *Kobold* i.e. Goblin.

26  Description of the convoy conference is largely taken from *Merchantmen at War* an HMSO publication from 1944 which at that time could be purchased for the princely sum of 1/9<sup>d</sup>.

27  ADM 116/4313

28  *Ibid*

29  ADM 237/166

## CHAPTER 4

1  Part of a note appended to the SC77 cruising order cited on the *Norwegian War Sailors* website.

2  Armed Guard – Gun Crew No 189 Report – May 6 1942. US National Archives – RG 38: (370/12/23/03: Box 103)

3  HMS *Walker* and HMCSs *Columbia, Halifax, Calgary* and *Midland.*

4  HMCSs *Dianthus, Orillia, Fennel, Amshurst* and *Brandon.*

5  Commodore Taylor in his post convoy report described the passage as '… quiet, except for a gale on 9/10 April.' In fact the gale was strong enough to force three ships to part company, with two of them eventually managing to catch the Iceland group after it had left the main convoy.

6  It is little wonder that SC77 had such an uneventful passage when Dönitz was having a field day with his U-boats off the US coast. The German U-boat war diary records: 'On 15.4 3 months have elapsed since U-boats made their first appearance on the east coast of America and since the weight of all U-boat activity was transferred to that area. During this time 229 ships of 1,521,000 BRT have been reported sunk and 23 ships of 82,506 BRT damaged in the North Atlantic alone, … U-boat warfare must continue to be concentrated on the east coast of America as long as conditions of anti-S/M activity and possibilities of successes remain at all the same as they are at present.' http://www.uboatarchive.net/BDUKTB30306A.htm

7  http://www.warsailors.com/convoys/pq14memoirs.html

8  PM's letter to Stalin 9 March 1942.

## CHAPTER 5

1  Prime Minister Winston Churchill to Sir Charles Portal, October 7, 1941, quoted in Hastings. Max, *Bomber Command,* NY: Dial Press, 1979, p. 121.

2  Prime Minister Winston Churchill to Air Minister Sir Archibald Sinclair, December 30, 1940, quoted in Hastings. Max, *Bomber Command*, NY: Dial Press, 1979, p. 117.

3  CAB 66/18/37

4  TNA Air 14/1218

5  ADM 178/323

6  CAB 79/20/14

7  The 'Cherwell Memorandum', reproduced in Hastings. Max, *Bomber Command,* NY: The Dial Press, 1979, pp. 127–128.

8  ADM 199/604 SBNO Report

9  HTN-251

10  ADM 199/660

11  It is a matter of conjecture but it is suggested that the basis for Tovey's arguments were as much about his moral distaste for strategic bombing of civilians borne of his strong Christian faith.

## CHAPTER 6

1  Excerpt – Letter from Lieutenant T.B. Johnston RNVR in HMS *Niger.*

2  ADM 237/166

3  PQ15's departure was coordinated with that of QP11 leaving Murmansk ADM 237/165.

4  ADM 237/166

5  He remarked that one commodity not listed on the cargo manifest was also present – fear

6  Quoted from: *Convoy to Murmansk – PQ15*, which may be found at: http://www.sunymaritime. edu/stephenblucelibrary/pdfs/Convoy%20to%20Murmansk%20-%20PQ%2015.pdf

7  A personal account of PQ14 by Olly Lindsay a 16 year-old apprentice on *Botavon* may be found at http://www.warsailors.com/convoys/pq14memoirs.html

8  Extracted from: http://www.convoyweb.org.uk/russian/index.html Russian Convoys Website

9  This was corroborated by Captain J. Barnetson, the master of the *Cape Race* but it is somewhat at odds with the master of the SS *Empire Bard*, Captain Saalmans, who recalled in his post convoy report that ships were formed up in eight columns. The passage of time coupled with unreliable recall may account for the discrepancy as Austin's report was dated 4 June 1942 and Barnetson's 26 August 1942. Both confined their reports to the passage of PQ15 while Saalmans' report covered several convoys and was dated a year later on 23 June 1943.

10  Now preserved as a museum in St Petersburg, Russia.

11  ADM 237/166

12  MSS-87-090

13  On *Empire Morn*'s return to the UK in QP12 the Hurricane was launched during an air attack and shot down an enemy aircraft. The pilot subsequently bailed out but his parachute failed to open and he was killed. However his body was recovered and later buried at sea.

14  HMSs *Badsworth, Boadicea, Venomous, Matchless, Somali* and H Nor MS *St Albans.*

15  See Woodman. Richard, *Arctic Convoys*, John Murray, 2004 p. 118.

16  ADM 199/1837 and ADM 199/721

17  ADM 237/166

18  ADM 199/721

19  Unfortunately no record can be found of the fate of the Captain and those on the raft.

20  HW1/535 & 536

21  HW1/537

22  These were: *U88, U251, U378, U405, U436, U589* and *U703.*

23  Between September and October 1981 all but 34 ingots were salvaged from *Edinburgh*'s war grave.

24  HW1/540 and HW1/544

25  HW1/537

26  HW1/540

27  HW1/548

28  MSS-88-009

29  ADM 199/721 – Commanding Officer *Ulster Queen*'s Report which is highly critical of the AA ship's place in the convoy.

30 ADM 237/166

31 *ibid*

32 *ibid*

33 *ibid*

34 Quoted from: *Convoy to Murmansk – PQ 15*, which may be found at: http://www.sunymaritime. edu/stephenblucelibrary/pdfs/Convoy%20to%20Murmansk%20-%20PQ%2015.pdf

35 HW1/541 Although *Kreigsmarine* Enigma transmissions to and from U-boats in the Atlantic could not be read at this time, *Lufwaffe* transmissions and those U-boats detached under command in northern waters continued to use a three-rotor system and were therefore decipherable by Bletchley Park personnel.

36 In addition there were 4 Hunt class destroyers, HMS *Inglefield* and 3 more US warships, USS*s Wainwright*, *Madison* and *Plunkett*. ADM 237/166

37 HW1/540

38 http://www.mikekemble.com/ww2/punjabi.html

39 ADM 199/427

40 ADM 156/227

41 MSS-81-004

42 WDG-201-2

43 ADM 199/721

44 Storheill's assertion about the duplicity of German U-boat commanders may have been widely held but is not entirely borne out by the facts. There are well documented accounts of U-boat captains assisting torpedoed survivors with rations and a bearing to the nearest land.

45 ADM 267/114

46 Some six months later the Director Signal Department commented that this unfortunate incident again emphasised the need for a new type of submerged grenade, the Patt. 65, that was now in the course of production. ADM 199/721

47 ADM 178/279

48 It would appear that navigation, especially if one was relying on dead reckoning was a precarious business even for surface ships in these high latitudes. As an example PQ15's Commodore recommended in his report that his ship be equipped with a gyro compass and an echo sounding machine because the magnetic compass is unsteady and means of obtaining observations for finding the compass error are few.

49 ADM 199/721

50 Except where indicated all quotations regarding this attack are taken from reports gathered in ADM 199/721.

51 According to the Master of the *Botavon* she did not go down until *Badsworth*, having already fired two shells into her, eventually dropped a depth charge under her whereupon she sank quickly.

52 Lloyds War Losses – WW2 Vol 1 1939-45 P414

53 ADM 199/2140

54 http://www.pwsts.org.uk/jackwhyte.htm

55 Armed Guard – Gun Crew No 189 Report – May 6 1942. US National Archives – RG 38: (370/12/23/03: Box 103)

56 http://www.wartimememories.co.uk/mb/board1/2245.shtml

57 ADM 199/2140

58  Given the short survival time in Arctic waters half an hour seems to be an exaggeration.

59  ADM 199/721

60  *ibid*

61  See account at http://uboat.net/men/timm.htm

62  HW1/546 and HW1/548

63  Source: http://www.mercantilemarine.org/archive/index.php?t-434.html

## CHAPTER 7

1  In addition to referenced archive material this Chapter has also drawn on eye witness accounts recorded in an unpublished account of Convoy PQ 13 by Alan Blyth.

2  Information taken from *The Front Album* by Colonel S Kolomiets. ("Фронтовой альбом". Сборник документов и воспоминаний", Мурманск, 2015 г., 302 стр.

3  MSS-90-020

4  NARA 370/12/23/03: Box 103

5  See MSS-87-090, Chilvers' Diary entry for 27 May. Running out of ammunition was also mentioned by crew members of the *Capira* during the passage of PQ15 to Murmansk.

6  Quoted from: *Convoy to Murmansk – PQ 15*, which may be found at: http://www.sunymaritime. edu/stephenblucelibrary/pdfs/Convoy%20to%20Murmansk%20-%20PQ%2015.pdf

7  https://uboat.net/allies/merchants/ships/2657.html

8  ADM 199/1104

9  His diary was kept by his sister and finally published in 2011.

10  MSS-87-090 Chilvers' Diary entry for 31 May onwards.

11  Extracts drawn from the published Russian text.

12  MSS-90-020 Boucher's account.

13  MSS-88-009 Saunders, HMS *Trinidad.*

14  ADM 199/2140

15  Bill Short, Fourth Engineer, SS *Induna.*

16  *Coxswain in the Northern Convoys*, S A Kerslake http://www.naval-history.net/WW2Memoir-RussianConvoyCoxswain06.htm

17  Jim Campbell, Steward's Boy, SS *Induna.*

18  SBNO 7th Monthly Report, February 1942. ADM 199/1104

19  ADM 199/604 SBNO Report

20  http://www.halcyon-class.co.uk/stress.htm

21  *The Royal Naval Medical Service*, Vol ll, JLS Coulter P328.

22  *Royal Naval Psychiatry. Organisation, Methods and Outcomes 1900-1945*, Jones & Greenberg.

23  MSS-87-090 Chilvers' Diary entry for 28 May.

24  *Coxswain in the Northern Convoys*, S A Kerslake http://www.naval-history.net/WW2Memoir-RussianConvoyCoxswain06.htm

25  Story related in a conversation with a *Capira* crew member.

26  ADM 199/604 SBNO Report

27  ADM 1/12039

28  *Coxswain in the Northern Convoys*, S A Kerslake http://www.naval-history.net/WW2Memoir-RussianConvoyCoxswain06.htm

29  *ibid*

30  Apparently he was known as 'Bonham the Bad' as opposed to his brother 'Bonham the Good'!

## CHAPTER 8

1   Twelve ships sailed from Archangel and joined QP13 further out in the Barents Sea.

2   ADM 199/1104 SBNO North Russia Report for June 1942.

3   Unfortunately Commodore Gale perished in the tanker MV *Athelsultan* when it was torpedoed by *U617* in the Atlantic on 23 September 1942 whilst leading convoy SC100.

4   It would appear that the lesson learnt on the deployment of anti-aircraft ships during the second attack on PQ15 had not been fully assimilated.

5   This narrative is taken from Combs report, but Commander A.G. West on HMS *Inglefield* insists the plane in question was a JU 88.

6   ADM 237/176

7   Excerpt – Letter from Lieutenant T.B. Johnston RNVR in HMS *Niger.*

8   HW1/689

9   MSS-81-004 (Excerpt from Tovey's despatches quoted in the London Gazette of 13 Oct 1950).

10  HW1/689

11  HW1/699

12  *My Sea Lady* p147

13  War Diary 73 Ptl Sqn, US Atlantic Fleet.

14  ADM 237/176

15  HMS *Intrepid,* HMS *Inglefield,* FFL *Roselys,* HMS *Niger,* HMS *Hussar,* HMT *Lady Madeleine* and HMT *St Elstan.*

16  ADM 199/1104 SBNO North Russia Report for March 1942.

17  ADM 1/11063 T 271 Trials Report.

18  These were known as Plan Position Indicators (PPI) displays.

19  ADM 237/165

20  http://www.naval-history.net/xGM-Ops-Minelaying.htm

21  HTN-225-6

22  *My Sea Lady* p150

23  ADM 237/176 ACIC's Report

24  ADM 267/115 Report of an interview with CO HMT *Lady Madeleine* at Grimsby on 30 July 1942.

25  *My Sea Lady* p149

26  *Ibid* p150

27  From correspondence with Patricia Hartley daughter of Lieutenant T.B. Johnston RNVR in HMS *Niger.* Her Mother and Grandfather met Wishaw in London before he returned to Australia where he died not long after the disaster.

28  ADM 237/176 ACIC's Report

29  ADM 237/176

30  It is not clear if *Negafel* was in company with the two RN trawlers at the time or what she was doing when *Kent* came across her. It is possible that she was fishing in the area and enlisted by HMS *Kent* at the time or she may have been requested earlier to assist in the rescue.

31 The 15 inch gunned heavy cruiser HMS *Renown* was anchored near Reykjavik in Hvalfjord at the time.

32 Home Commands War Diary.

33 Bergeret and Ogdens' courageous rescue attempts in the minefield were later recognised in a letter from Tovey. ADM 237/176

34 Library of Congress – *Veterans' History Project* – http://memory.loc.gov/diglib/vhp/story/loc. natlib.afc2001001.02320/pageturner?ID=pm0002001&page=1

35 Home Commands War Diary

36 These were according to the US Iceland War Diaries US 305421-A1 535: *American Robin, Mormacrey, City of Omaha, Richard H Lee, Lancaster, Nemeha, Michigan, Mauna Kea, Yaka, Capira, Stary Bolshevik* and *Exterminator.*

37 http://skerray.com/information/john-randolph

38 In September 1952 the hulk was towed to the Firth of Forth to be scrapped. However, she broke loose about 150 miles NW of the Hebrides and finally went ashore at Torrisdale where she remained until broken up some time later.

39 Home Commands War Diary

40 ADM 237/176

41 http://www.worldwideinvention.com/articles/details/312/Naval-mine-contained-explosive-device-placed-in-water-to-destroy-ships-or-submarines.html

42 See Chapter 2

43 http://www.halcyon-class.co.uk/niger/hms_niger.htm

44 http://www.shipsnostalgia.com/guides/Soviet_Merchant_Marine_Losses_in_WW2

45 Correspondence Chuter/Fridthor Eydal 8 March 2013

46 ADM 237/176

47 There is a suggestion in Woodman's book *Arctic Convoys* (P 197) that *Niger*'s primitive radar confused Cubison in the matter of a landfall but this seems unlikely, most probably it was out of action. This is supported by an earlier report on QP11 by the CO of HMS *Bulldog* who, under the heading of 'Gadgets' stated that the RDF was out of action almost continuously in three of the escorting vessels and that it did not appear that the apparatus was sufficiently robust for use under sea-going conditions. (ADM 237/165). Relegating the radar to the category of 'Gadget' may also indicate a complete loss of faith by this particular CO, and maybe others, in radar as a useful adjunct for navigation.

48 ADM 237/176

49 Walling, Michael, *Forgotten Sacrifice – The Arctic Convoys of WW2*, Osprey, 2012.

50 http://www.naval-history.net/xGM-Ops-Minelaying.htm

51 MSS-81-004

52 Woodman, R. *Arctic Convoys*, John Murray, 2004 p. 197

53 *US Iceland War Diaries* US 305421-A1 535

## CHAPTER 9

1 *U609* was part of the 6th *Frontflottille* (Combat Flotilla) based at St Nazaire.

2 Information on the movements of *U609* have been taken from.
http://www.uboatarchive.net/BDU/BDUKTB30311.htm

3 Type VIIC technical data has been taken from *Type VII – Germany's Most Successful U-boats* by Marek KrzysztaŁowicz, published by Seaforth.

4 *Vorwärts* (Let's go!) comprised *U91, U92, U211, U407, U409, U411, U604, U609, U659* and *U756.*

5 http://www.warsailors.com/convoys/sc97.html

6 ADM 199/2100 *Convoy SC97 Report*

7 All references to SS *Bridgepool* are taken from C/JX313519 AB J Hawkins RN – diary in the author's possession.

8 ADM 237/196 Commodore's Report.

9 ADM 237/196 Captain's Report RS *Perth.*

10 However, and in spite of her advanced years, *Broadway* had earlier taken part in the successful attack on *U110.*

11 http://www.uboatarchive.net/BDU/BDUKTB30311.htm

12 The previously mentioned ON113 spent several hours retracing its steps steaming east in an attempt to throw a wolf pack off its scent.

13 USCG *Bibb* was deliberately sunk in 1987 off the Florida Keys and has since become a marine wildlife park and divers' paradise.

14 http://www.uscg.mil/hq/g-cp/history/Matte%20on%20Ingham.html

15 Statistics taken from http://www.uboatarchive.net/BDUKTB.htm

16 Her master at this time was Bjarne Bolt

17 Author's correspondence with Stafford Ricks

18 From the Armed Guard Report

19 ADM 237/196

20 Naval reports use GMT which in this case was 2 hours ahead of convoy time.

21 Probably a mistake as *Bronxville* was in convoy position #81 at the outset but may have changed position during the passage.

22 ADM 237/196 Captain's report HMCS *Morden.* There are also accounts on the web that indicate HMCS *Drumheller* rescued survivors from the *Capira*. These may be discounted as *Morden* had been designated as a rescue ship and documents in ADM 237/196 are clear that *Drumheller* was engaged in an anti-submarine sweep astern of the convoy. Moreover there is documentary evidence of her docking in Liverpool and not disembarking survivors in Londonderry.

23 *U609* under the command of Klaus Rudloff went on to complete another three patrols but without sinking any further ships. She was sunk with the loss of all hands on her fourth patrol in position 55.17N/36.33W by the Free French corvette *Lobelia* on 7 February 1943.

24 Quoted in article at: http://www.familyheritage.ca/Articles/summer1942.html

25 This would have been 0533 GMT as the U-boat command used MESZ – *Mitteleuropäische Sommerzeit* at this time of year. This was the same time as in the German capital city of Berlin and was known as German Central Time or Berlin Time and was 2 hours ahead of GMT.

26 Kapitänleutnant Höltring, the commanding officer of *U604*, was something of a madcap. He was ambitious and daring. Drink and firearms seem to have been his weaknesses. Survivors said he carried a revolver at all times. When *U604* was lost to air attack on 11 August 1943 the crew transferred to *U185* which was standing by. Eleven days later *U185* was sunk also. According to survivors, Höltring was in his bunk in the officers' quarters, with his pistol, as always, close at hand when the attack on *U185* began. In the bow compartment lay a member of *U185*'s crew

with a bullet wound in his leg, sustained in a previous action. Unable to walk, he was trapped as chlorine gas began to spread. Seeing Höltring rush into the bow compartment with his pistol in hand, the youth cried to Höltring to shoot him. According to survivors' accounts, Höltring shot and killed the boy, then shot himself through the head.

27  Much of this account has been taken from *Tactics, Training, Technology and the RCN's Summer of Success, July-September 1942* © Robert C. Fisher 1997.

28  *German U-boat Losses During WW2* p 226

29  ADM 237/196 Comd TF 24 Report

## CHAPTER 10

1  From Clausewitz *On War.*

2  It is, perhaps, also an irony of history that about 25 years later and in some considerable ignorance of the events surrounding QP13 that the sons of Lt Ogden, Captain of the *Lady Madeline* and John Chuter, a sailor aboard the *Capira*, were serving together as cadets at the Royal Military Academy Sandhurst. Sadly neither had any idea of their respective father's connection with the convoy or the unfortunate occurrence in the minefield. Had they had known and got their fathers together what a fascinating conversation might have ensued.

3  In spite of being conscripted as a navy gunner Austin Byrne's allegiance remains with the Merchant Navy. On special occasions he raises the Red Ensign on a flagpole in his back garden in honour of those who did not survive.

# Index